THE
FULL
CATASTROPHE

THE
FULL
CATASTROPHE

Travels Among the New Greek Ruins

James Angelos

CROWN PUBLISHERS
NEW YORK

Copyright © 2015 by James Angelos

Published in the United States by Crown Publishers, an imprint of
the Crown Publishing Group, a division of Penguin Random House
LLC, New York.

www.crownpublishing.com

CROWN is a registered trademark and the Crown colophon is a
trademark of Random House LLC.

Library of Congress Cataloging-in-Publication Data is available
upon request.

ISBN 978-0-385-34648-1
eBook ISBN 978-0-385-34649-8

Printed in the United States of America

Map by Mapping Specialists
Jacket design: Na Kim
Jacket photographs: Henrik Sorensen/Getty Images; Zoran
Kolundzija/Getty Images

10 9 8 7 6 5 4 3 2 1

First Edition

For my parents and grandfather, who have known xeniteia

Contents

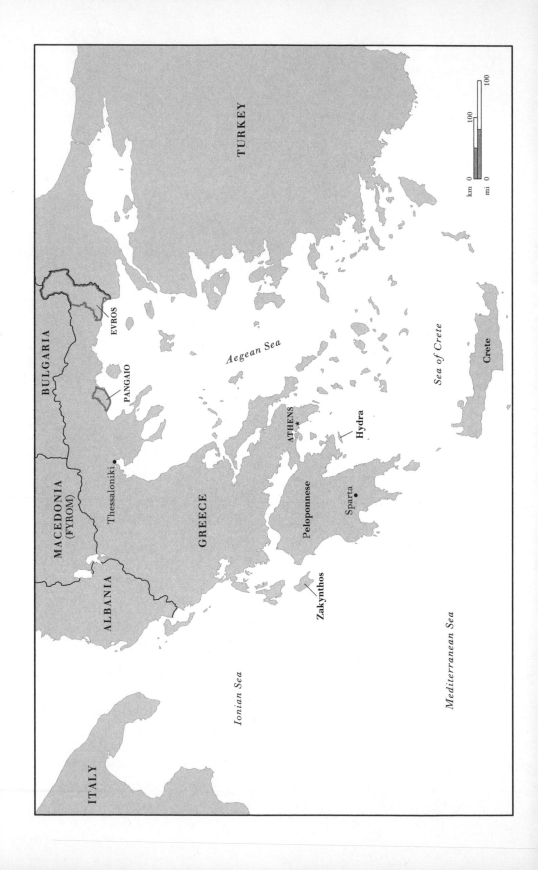

ITALY

BULGARIA

MACEDONIA
(FYROM)

ALBANIA

EVROS

PANGAIO

TURKEY

Thessaloniki

GREECE

Aegean Sea

ATHENS

Hydra

Peloponnese

Sparta

Zakynthos

Ionian Sea

Sea of Crete

Crete

Mediterranean Sea

km 0   100
mi 0   100

Introduction

We are all Greeks.

—Percy Bysshe Shelley, 1821

On March 25, 2014, Greeks marked the 193rd anniversary of the start of their war of independence against the Ottoman Empire. Young boys across the country dressed like klephts, the rebel highland bandits who fought the revolution, in white, pleated skirts called *fustanellas*, white stockings, red fezzes, and clogs topped with pom-poms. Girls wore traditional garb, tasseled headscarves and long colorful dresses embroidered with angular patterns distinctive to their region of Greece. In school auditoriums on the eve of the holiday, children performed plays about centuries of suffering under Ottoman rule. In a small valley town in the region of Messenia, the southwestern tip of the Peloponnese, a teenage boy dressed like a revolutionary bandit entered stage right and professed a yearning to fight for freedom: "What can I do? I can't go on! My chest is heavy. The slavery of the Turk." His mother, played by a girl in a yellow headscarf, urged him to stick to shepherding and to raising a family instead, but the young man was defiant. "Mother, bring the sword and the heavy rifle." In a preschool on the Aegean island of Santorini, children young enough to still be wobbly on their feet tentatively circle-danced in front of their parents to "Dance of Zalongo," a folk song about a mass suicide on a mountain in Greece's rugged northwestern region of Epirus, where local women are said to have thrown their infants and themselves off a precipice rather than fall under the yoke of an Ottoman pasha. The preschool children in Santorini nearly fell over one another as the mournful song played over the speakers: "Farewell poor world, farewell sweet life, and you, my poor country, farewell forever."

Such Independence Day rites are repeated annually with little variance, and though this was the first time I experienced the commemoration in Greece, I recognized a lot of these customs from my childhood on Long Island, where my Greek immigrant parents obligated me to attend Greek language and Sunday school classes at the local Greek Orthodox church. The church served as an outpost of cultural programming from the old country, and so the pom-pom shoes, the circle dances, and the indoctrination regarding Turkish tyranny were therefore already familiar to me. Still, this year in Greece, it was clear the usual rituals had taken on far greater significance. About four years earlier, Greece had begun hurtling toward bankruptcy, a situation that, owing to the nation's eurozone membership, presented a potentially catastrophic threat to the global financial system. In order to prevent immediate ruin, a trifecta of institutions known as "the Troika"—the European Commission, the International Monetary Fund, and the European Central Bank—agreed, despite deep reservations in Germany and other northern European countries, that it would be a good idea to sustain Greece, in particular its ability to keep servicing its vast debts, by pledging it tens of billions of euros in loans to be paid out in dribbles over a few years. The European leaders and IMF officials who committed the funds considered their intervention a "rescue," though it didn't seem that way to a lot of Greeks. The financial assistance was contingent upon wage and pension cuts, among many other profoundly unpopular conditions outlined in a memorandum of understanding—the *mnimonio,* as the Greeks called it. Control of the domestic policy was ceded almost entirely to the Troika, which used the threat of imminent bankruptcy as leverage to get Greece to obey its recipe for improving the country's finances. But the recipe did not work out very well, and Greece's economic collapse would begin to deepen to Great Depression–like levels, necessitating, less than two years after the first bailout, a second one. In total, Greece received 245 billion euros in loan pledges and the largest debt restructuring in history, which reduced its outstanding debt by 107 billion euros at the expense of private holders of its bonds. Moreover, the European Central Bank sustained damaged Greek banks with a constant flow of cheap short-term loans. In exchange for the bailout, Greek politicians promised profound changes to nearly every aspect of their governance, from the country's deficient tax-collection practices to its regulations on the shelf life of pasteurized milk. The specificity of the required measures—the simplification of customs procedures for feta cheese exports, or the creation of a nationwide system of cadastral offices—underscored the Troika's lack of faith that Greece could reform itself without strict oversight. In order to ensure compliance, Troika experts visited quarterly to check up on Greece's progress. Failure to comply resulted in the withholding of scheduled payments. The Greeks, in short, would be forced to change under sustained duress. To a lot of Greek citizens, therefore, the rescue seemed more like a new foreign occupation. Independence Day seemed as good a time as any to reflect on this.

Much of the national musing on this day took place in church. Greek Independence Day falls, not entirely by coincidence, on the Feast of the Annunciation, the day Christians believe the Archangel Gabriel announced to the Virgin Mary that the Son of God would arrive in the world through her womb. The country's founders saw it as fitting that the advent of the modern Hellenes' struggle to conceive a national heir to Ancient Greece should fall

on the day the Savior was also conceived. The Christian symbolism woven into the country's founding did not end there. Greece's
identity since its inception has been closely tied to Orthodox Christianity. The Greek word for revolution, *epanastasis,* closely resembles the word for resurrection, *anastasis,* and the independence
struggle was also couched in resurrectional language—Classical
Greece had arisen. And so on Independence Day, formally dressed
Greeks, among them solemn-faced politicians and military officers festooned with medals, filed into churches around the country to hear the nation's full-bearded clerics deliver sermons on the
dual incarnations—of Christ and nation. In a small church in the
town of Spata, east of Athens, a portly priest stood before the altar
in a blue and white vestment that matched the colors of the Greek
flag that congregants held stretched out before him. The priest
brought the congregation to tears with stories of Greeks' slaughter at the hands of the Turks, and then read out the names of the
revolutionary heroes. Theodoros Kolokotronis, the most esteemed
bandit warrior of the revolution. "Present!" yelled a male con-
gregant. Markos Botsaris, another heroic fighter, killed in battle.
"Present!" Laskarina Bouboulina, a widow from a wealthy maritime family who financed a fleet of ships for the fight, shot dead,
not in battle but in an argument with a neighbor. "Present!" a
woman replied. The revolutionary martyrs had painted the soil
red with their sacrifice so that Greece, a nation of true and holy
faith, should be free, the priest said. And now, he added, what had
today's Greeks made of this sacred inheritance? "We received a
free nation and we subjected it to another slavery," he said, his
voice quivering as if he might begin sobbing. "We speak of freedom? What freedom, my brothers. When you can't claim what
you're entitled to. When they snatch your life. When they snatch
what you've worked for. We're talking about the kind of freedom
that enslaves nations," he said. "And because we have reached this
point, the soil of Greece moans."

The sentiment was similar at the day's main ceremony in Athens, where Greece's president, Karolos Papoulias—an octogenarian who as a teenager had fought in the World War II resistance—sat under a small canopy in front of the country's spare, neoclassical parliamentary building watching a procession of rows and rows of soldiers, tanks, mobile missile systems, and artillery guns. It was the kind of militaristic display one might think of as more fitting for Pyongyang than a European capital, but Greece, long an avid weapons buyer in comparison to its European peers, had a tradition of parading its military procurements on patriotic holidays. The purchases were justified on the grounds of enduring hostilities with Turkey, but they also contributed significantly to the nation's fiscal problems. The peculiarity of the scene was amplified by the fact that there were very few people around to watch it. The government had largely closed off the city center to spectators, citing security reasons, though most people saw it as an effort to prevent the large anti-austerity protests that had tarnished such events in previous years. When the procession was over, Papoulias, his thin, gray hairs fluttering in the breeze, approached a cluster of microphones and spoke to the nation watching on television. "One hundred and ninety-three years ago, a small people with big hearts, with great souls and extraordinary bravery, unfolded their virtues and clashed with an empire, the Ottoman, for their freedom and won. Today, our people are battling and struggling to break the stranglehold of the creditors. Our history guarantees that we will also be victorious in this fight."

Papoulias's comments did not reflect the kind of gratitude Greece's European and IMF creditors may have expected in return for their assistance. Nor was this sentiment indicative of the brotherly affinity between European nations the euro was supposed to engender when it was conceived, little more than two decades earlier, in the treaty that officially created the European Union. The euro was thought of as the capstone of the decades-long project of forging an ever-closer political and economic union in order to forestall the habitual bouts of tremendous continental bloodletting that had characterized Europe's past. For a while, it seemed to be working out well for everybody, particularly for the Greeks. Greece officially adopted the euro on New Year's Day 2001, two years after the currency's birth, though it didn't start using euro notes and coins until a year later. To accommodate the Greek alphabet, euro bills were printed with the Greek for "euro"—*EYPΩ*; and a Greek version of the two-euro coin depicted the mythological scene of Zeus, in bull form, abducting the bare-breasted maiden Europa. For years after Greece joined the currency, investors deemed lending money to its government to be only marginally more risky than lending to Germany, a far wealthier and more fiscally prudent nation considered one of the safer places in the world to put your money. With the new ease with which it could borrow, Greece's government doled out big raises to its workforce, raised pension benefits, and spent several billion euros on the 2004 Olympic Games in Athens. Greeks freely spent their newly acquired money, which benefited other eurozone economies (they bought nice German cars, for instance) and Greece, too (spending at local restaurants and shops, and a construction boom). From the time of its euro entry until the crisis began to take its toll at the end of 2008, Greece's GDP grew by an average of nearly 4 percent a year, faster than all other eurozone countries with the exception of Ireland.

To some degree, I had witnessed some of this rise in fortune. When I was a boy growing up in the 1980s, I often visited my grandmother in Greece during the summers. She lived across the road from the ruins of Ancient Corinth, and from the front yard, you could see the seven remaining columns of an Apollo temple standing against the deep blue backdrop of the Corinthian Gulf. The village, which surrounded the ruins of the ancient city, was humble and largely agrarian and quite different from what I was used to on suburban Long Island. The latest technology in my grandmother's house was an electric water heater for the shower, so you did not have to boil water on the propane stove to take a warm bath. A very poor old lady lived near us in a crumbling stone house, which seemed to have no running water at all. I used to go swimming in the gulf, and I remember sometimes seeing her in the water with a shower cap and a bar of soap, using the sea as her bathtub. The old woman's situation was rather exceptional, but still, her presence seemed to attest that even as Greece was becoming more prosperous, times of hardship belonged not to some very distant past. Over the course of a decade of intermittent visits, I observed a change. Greece, which had long benefited from remittances sent by Greeks living abroad, found a new funding source when it joined the European Community—the precursor to the European Union—in 1981. Admitted despite its relative underdevelopment and economic backwardness, Greece began benefiting from a flow of European agricultural subsidies and infrastructure funds. Additionally, the new government at the time—led by Andreas Papandreou, a messianic, free-spending socialist and former Berkeley economist who had founded the center-left PASOK party in the previous decade—began borrowing a lot of money and finding ways to dispense it to the population, raising wages but also stoking inflation and the national debt. Families started buying nicer cars and renovating their homes, often buying real estate to protect themselves from the drachma's steep devaluation. Living standards continued to rise and after one summer visit, I remember thinking that lifestyles in Greece were no longer utterly incomparable with those of American suburbia. "It must not be that hard to become a modern country," I thought at the time. After my grandmother died, I stopped visiting the village as often, but the trend seemed only to accelerate. By the time I returned for a visit several years after Greece joined the eurozone, the village had a few villas, sleek cafés, and more Mercedes and BMWs on its roads.

The cheap, post-euro-entry borrowing that fueled part of this boom was not so much a reflection of the country's economic fundamentals as a display of faith: investors' faith that eurozone membership would act as a guarantee of the nation's fiscal stability. This faith began to unravel after the failure of Lehman Brothers, which caused investors to rethink the safety of their worldwide investments. When that happened—a worrying divergence began to appear in the eurozone. Borrowing costs in Greece, and in other eurozone countries perceived to be vulnerable, began to rise, while Germany's began to fall as investors looked for a safe place to keep their money, even if that meant not making any more of it.

The event that sparked much bigger problems in Greece, however, came in October 2009, when it announced a big accounting revision. The government's projected budget deficit for that year would not be 3.7 percent of gross domestic product, as initially forecast, but 12.5 percent. The deficit was revised again, repeatedly, ultimately reaching beyond 15 percent. On one hand, the 2009 revision was partly understandable based on the fact the global financial crisis had set in, causing hits to government budgets everywhere. Yet the magnitude of Greece's revision, and the fact that it had made often-sizable upward revisions every year since it had joined the eurozone, confirmed for Eurostat, the statistical office of the European Union, that the Greek government had engaged in "widespread misreporting" of its deficit and debt figures. Big accounting revisions had become a custom in Greece, particularly following elections. In 2004, the new party in power, the center-right New Democracy, said that the previous ruling party, center-left PASOK, had badly messed up the statistics, revealing that Greece's eurozone entry—which was based on meeting "convergence criteria" like keeping an annual deficit no greater than 3 percent of GDP—had been based on false numbers. Then, in 2009, when PASOK regained power, it said the big revision at the time was due to New Democracy's massive concealment of its true spending. To the rest of the world, which didn't particularly care about Greek political wrangling, the essence of the matter was that Greek statistical practice was more art than science, and that the country's finances seemed to be dangling from a rapidly deflating helium balloon. Two days after Greece announced the initial revision, it received its first credit-rating downgrade. Further downgrades quickly followed. Greece soon wouldn't be able to borrow any more money on the market at all, at least without paying loan-shark rates.

By itself, the fiscal demise of Greece, a small nation of some 11 million people until then regarded more for its nice island beaches, marble ruins, and ancient philosophers than for its economic significance, wouldn't have presented a colossal threat to the global financial system. Yet the country's euro membership uniquely positioned it to wreak outsized havoc. German and French banks were the biggest foreign owners of Greek debt, and a sudden default could further destabilize the already hobbled European banking system. It also quickly became clear that Europe's monetary union had some profound design flaws. No one, it seemed, had seriously considered what would happen if a eurozone nation went bankrupt and was forced to return to its own currency. Ireland and Spain were also having a great deal of financial trouble after their housing bubbles burst, forcing their governments to step in and bail out their banks. Italian and Portuguese finances weren't looking good either. If Greece were to go, who else might follow? The "single and stable currency" initially conceived by European leaders was under grave threat, and it had begun in Greece.

The Hellenic Republic, as Greece is officially called, had been included in Europe's endeavor to form a closer union in no small part because of its symbolic importance to the continent. The beautiful Europa is a figure of Greek mythology, after all, and where would Europe be it if weren't for the ancient Hellenes, the fountainhead of Europe's common heritage, the originators of democracy and Western civilization? At the time Greece applied for European Community membership in the 1970s, French president Valéry Giscard d'Estaing, one of the architects of the European Union, believed Greece was "the mother of all democracies" and therefore could not be excluded. Yet, later on, Greece's immense troubles seemed to expose the dreaminess of this thinking. Greece's creditors, given a license to pull back the veneer of legitimate statehood and take a look at the Greek government's internal organs, found big problems almost everywhere they looked. A deeply entrenched tradition of political patronage meant politicians handed out social benefits to select groups in exchange for votes, while often leaving the most vulnerable to fend for themselves. Tax evasion was pervasive, and Greek tax collectors frequently cooperated with tax evaders. Public workers were hired for life, often not because of their qualifications, but because an aunt or a cousin knew a mayor or a parliamentarian, leading to profoundly ineffective public administration. An incomprehensible, opaque bureaucracy and lax enforcement of the law allowed politicians to engage in brazen corruption with little fear of getting caught. Greece's pension system was underfunded and byzantine. Its building codes were frequently ignored, resulting in a million illegally constructed buildings and houses. Its courts were often futilely slow. Its public schools were poor, necessitating parents who wanted their kids to go to college to pay for private tutoring.

This wasn't the twenty-first-century European state the EU's founders had envisioned for their club. In a 2012 interview with the German magazine *Der Spiegel*, Giscard d'Estaing seemed to have had a change of heart. "To be perfectly frank, it was a mistake to accept Greece," he said, speaking alongside his old partner, former German chancellor Helmut Schmidt. "Greece simply wasn't ready. Greece is basically an Oriental country." When Europeans use the term "Oriental," in this context, it's not meant as a compliment. The Greeks in other words, were other, Middle Eastern, backward when compared to loftier Europeans. Addressing Schmidt, Giscard d'Estaing added: "Helmut, I recall that you expressed skepticism before Greece was accepted into the European Community in 1981. You were wiser than me."

Such bipolar feelings about Greece's "Europeanness" have been evident since the nation won its independence. During the revolution, well-educated Europeans, driven to revive the Ancient Greece they so revered, provided the Greek rebels with financial assistance, and pushed their governments to give the military support that made victory possible. (One should therefore not only ask where Europe would be without Greece, but where Greece would be without Europe.) Britain, France, and Russia eventually backed the independence cause, and provided a guaranteeed loan to the fledgling Greek state (which it later defaulted on). English romantic poets lent ideological reinforcement. In 1821, the year the Greek revolution began, Shelley wrote in *Hellas*:

> Another Athens shall arise,
> And to remoter time
> Bequeath, like sunset to the skies,
> The splendour of its prime;
> And leave, if nought so bright may live,
> All earth can take or Heaven can give.

Yet at the same time Europeans often expressed disappointment that the modern Hellenes didn't match the splendor of their classical predecessors. Even Shelley was apparently not free from doubt about the prospects for the rising of another Athens of the sort he had in mind. While visiting an Italian port during the time of the Greek revolution, Shelley and a friend, Edward John Trelawny, boarded a Greek trading ship in order to meet the crew. The pair was not impressed, according to Trelawny's later written account of the encounter. "They squatted about the decks in small knots, shrieking, gesticulating, smoking, eating, and gambling like savages," Trelawny wrote. He also noted that the ship's captain did not support the revolution on account of what it might do to his business.

"Does this realize your idea of Hellenism, Shelley?" Trelawny said.

"No! But it does of Hell," said Shelley, according to Trelawny. "Come away! There is not a drop of the old Hellenic blood here. These are not the men to rekindle the ancient Greek fire." Shelley added: "I had rather not have any more of my hopes and illusions mocked by sad realities."

Greeks, too, have long suffered similar vacillations of self-image. At the time the country achieved independence, agrarian Greeks did not have the same level of consciousness or reverence for the storied Hellenic past as did, say, the English romantic poets. They had never read Plato or Euripides, and were far more faithful to Christian Orthodox conservativism than to the Enlightenment ideals they were said to have inspired. The new Hellenic state would succeed in inculcating its masses with immense pride in their ancient past, but this came with its own unique burden. Doomed to perpetually contrast themselves with the unmatchable splendor of their predecessors, Greeks often confront a nagging sense of inadequacy and strain under the weight of their own historical narrative like few other people on the planet. This sentiment is expressed by a common Greek quip: "We gave light to the world and held on to the darkness." And yet Greeks also often see themselves, on account of their ancient legacy, as a kind of chosen people, superior to others. "We had culture when they were still living in caves!" I have repeatedly heard Greeks say of their northern European counterparts. Greeks consequently often feel that Europeans should be grateful for being shown the way out of the cave and into the light. This sometimes grand self-image has also had the effect of making the country's perceived subjugation at the hands of its creditors all the more bitter. After all, the Europeans owed them.

Introduction

The cave dwellers of old, for their part, openly deliberated whether it would be wiser to sever Greece from the eurozone like a gangrenous limb. Germany, which, as Europe's biggest economy, was Greece's biggest state lender, was particularly hesitant to help the Greeks, which only worsened the market's fear of impending doom for both Greece and the euro. Other eurozone nations—Ireland, Spain, Portugal, Cyprus—also needed bailouts, but German disdain was mostly reserved for Greece. That was not only because Greece needed more money than all those other countries combined, but because most of the other governments got into financial problems after having to bail out their irresponsible banks. In Greece, the banks were doing fine until the government got into financial trouble on account of its own considerable failings. Germans judged the excesses of politicians and citizens more harshly than those of banks and consumers, and saw the Greek government's negligence as a betrayal of the European project itself. In February 2012, Timothy Geithner, then U.S. Treasury secretary, had dinner with some of his European counterparts and, according to an interview transcript obtained by the *Financial Times*, later summed up the feelings they expressed to him about Greece like this: "We're going to teach the Greeks a lesson. They are really terrible. They lied to us. They suck and they were profligate and took advantage of the whole basic thing and we're going to crush them." The attitude, Geithner added, was: "Definitely get out the bats."

The punitive nature of the initial bailout agreement—the bringing out of the bats, in other words—somewhat quieted the German electorate's misgivings about helping the Greeks. German chancellor Angela Merkel made sure to emphasize the toughness of the agreement to her voters, assuring them the Greeks were being adequately chastened, that moral hazard was being avoided. Other eurozone countries would "do all they can to avoid this themselves," Merkel told the German newspaper *Bild am Sonntag* after Greece's first bailout. For their part, many Greeks did everything they could to avoid it too. One might imagine the somber mood around a company office after the management announces employee wage cuts and a downsizing plan. In Greece, that was the mood on a national scale. Just before the Greek parliament was to vote on a big austerity bill it had promised in exchange for the first bailout, Greek unions called a general strike and protestors assembled in front of the parliament building. Many of the parliamentarians inside had spent their careers bestowing benefits, and now they were taking them away. This did not sit well with the people outside. At one point, the protestors tried to storm the building. The chaos and plumes of tear gas released by riot police forced the ceremonial guards, wearing revolutionary brigand garb in front of the Tomb of the Unknown Soldier, to abandon their posts. Nearby, a bank was set on fire, killing three employees, including a pregnant woman. This was just the beginning of the strikes and demonstrations. Over the next four years, more than 20,000 protests and rallies took place across the country.

Many protesting Greeks were well aware that foreign control over their country's affairs represented a historical norm. In 1893, for instance, following a collapse in the global price of currants, the main Greek export, and beset by problems the country still has today—insufficient tax collection, high military expenditure, a wasteful public administration—Greece defaulted. Upset European holders of Greek bonds—particularly in Germany—pushed for international control of Greek finances to ensure repayment of the outstanding debts. For this purpose, an entity called the International Financial Commission was established in Greece a few years later, during a moment of national weakness following the country's defeat in a short war with the Ottoman Empire. The commission presided over Greek finances until the Second World War, taxing Greek stamps and tobacco, establishing customs duties, and absorbing revenues from state-owned manufacturers of match sticks, cigarette paper, and salt. While the commission had some positive effects—under its control, Greece was able to establish creditworthiness that allowed it to take additional public loans—Greeks deeply resented the foreign domination.

Now, Greeks felt, the country's fate was in the hands of creditor overseers once more. In contrast to the Greeks, these new overseers made some rather bright predictions. The structural reforms and wage cuts demanded under the first bailout would correct the excesses of the boom years and rapidly improve economic competitiveness. According to the Troika's initial forecast, the measures would start to bear fruit by 2012, when Greece would begin growing again and be able to resume market borrowing. Unemployment would peak at around 15 percent, and though the national debt would reach hazardous levels, Greece would be able to pay it all back. The country would have to "swim against the tide" in order to meet these objectives, a European Commission report at the time acknowledged, in no small part because the spending cuts would have to take place while the economy was shrinking. This was, it turned out, quite an understatement, and the Troika's forecast proved delusionally optimistic. Cutting government spending and people's incomes in the middle of a recession while also raising taxes, a lot of economists will tell you, is likely to worsen a recession, and the Troika very much underestimated the degree to which this would occur. IMF officials later admitted some errors.

For many Greeks, the worse-than-expected economic free fall and skyrocketing unemployment were evidence that the first *mnimonio* wasn't working. By the time, therefore, that European and IMF leaders struck a second rescue agreement during a late night of negotiations in Brussels in the fall of 2011, Greeks were loath to abide by another *mnimonio*. The PASOK prime minister at the time, George Papandreou, the son of the Andreas who had founded the party, had the idea of trying to legitimize the agreement by giving Greeks a chance to vote on it with a yes-or-no referendum. When he announced the idea, however, European

leaders were outraged that the deal they had painstakingly ne-
gotiated could be subject to the whims of the Greek electorate.
Papandreou, who was born in Minnesota, had gone to Amherst
College, and retained a trace of an American accent (Greeks de-
risively called him the "little American"), was already deeply
unpopular at home for the first bailout, and amid the chorus of
criticism at home and abroad, he abandoned the idea and was compelled to step aside. Lucas Papademos, a former European Central Bank vice president, was ushered into power in order to lead
a short-term provisional government tasked solely with pushing
through the second bailout agreement. On the winter night the
Greek parliament passed a major package of cuts in exchange for
the second rescue, the violent protests made Athens look like a war
zone, as hooded youths set fire to buildings throughout downtown.
So functioned democracy in the mother of all democracies.

By the time Greeks were given a chance to vote in May 2012—
the first parliamentary election since the bailout agreements were
struck—it was evident that the previous political order was disin-
tegrating, and anti-bailout parties were on the rise. An amalgamation of far-left groups, the Coalition of the Radical Left, or Syriza,
won a great deal of support by vowing to cancel the *mnimonio* and
restore social spending. Greece had become a colony of a neoliberal
regime in Germany, its leaders declared, and they vowed to raise
money by making Germany pay reparations for damages inflicted
on Greece during the World War II occupation. Greek right-wing
voters took a far more extreme turn toward Golden Dawn—a neo-
Nazi party that denied being neo-Nazi—which was expanding its
popularity beyond the ragged central Athens neighborhood where
it had unleashed assault squads to hunt dark-skinned immigrants
on the streets. Many Greeks reacted positively to Golden Dawn's
assertions of Hellenic superiority, and its pledge to put the nation
above all else.

In the May election, Syriza came in second just behind the

center-right New Democracy party, and Golden Dawn won its way into parliament. No party, however, had enough votes to form a government, and so a new election was called for the following month. In the interim, the country seemed to be succumbing to ungovernable chaos. Global financial markets convulsed in fear of an impending win for Syriza, whose young, necktie-averse leader, a former communist youth activist, threatened to renege on Greece's debt obligations. German politicians renewed public deliberations over whether it would be best to eject Greece from the eurozone. "Grexit" became a frequently used word. Greeks started removing cash from their bank accounts over fears that ATM machines would soon start spitting out worthless drachmas. The severe bank run that resulted and the deepening cycle of doubt did not create an environment conducive to economic recovery, which of course made Greece's problems even worse.

In the next election, New Democracy, which depicted itself as the safe choice for voters wishing to remain in the euro, eked out a narrow victory, and on account of a parliamentary seat bonus afforded to the party with the plurality of votes, was able to form a coalition government that included its former rival, PASOK. Antonis Samaras, the new prime minister—who, incidentally, had also gone to Amherst College, where he had been roommates with Papandreou—vowed to European leaders that he would honor the second bailout agreement, though he had railed against the first one when still part of the opposition. German chancellor Merkel, wary of who would take power should Samaras falter, silenced Greece's critics in her government and started praising Greece's reform effort.

Greece had been rescued, but by this point, it was perishing by a thousand cuts. A Greek hotel owner once summarized the country's predicament to me like this: "First, Greece has the problem of itself. Second, Greece has the problem of the Troika." This seemed to me like a pretty good way to think about the Greek crisis. Greece had driven itself to fiscal and economic collapse. In response, however, its European and IMF creditors—who, in fairness, faced uniquely vexing challenges in trying to come up with a solution—made big mistakes. Initial European ambivalence over how to deal with the crisis and an overdose of self-defeating fiscal austerity deeply worsened Greece's situation. Despite the spending cuts and tax increases meant to fix Greek finances, the country's debt load in relation to the size of its economy continued to rise. At the same time, Greece's options for restoring growth were severely constrained by the eurozone membership it had earlier so benefited from. Unable to control its monetary policy or boost its export competitiveness through currency devaluation, Greece's only hope was to lift exports through wage cuts intended to make Greek products cheaper. The same cuts, however, had the effect of obliterating consumption at home, and the small rise in exports came nowhere near to offsetting this. At the same time, Greece lagged on healthy reforms contained in the *mnimonio*—those that would have made its economy more open and competitive by doing away with burdensome rules that benefited only powerful interest groups.

By the time of Greece's independence celebration, the economy had contracted by 25 percent over the previous six years. Slight growth, driven by tourism, would soon reappear, but the kind of sustained and robust expansion needed to undo the depression's damage seemed a distant possibility. Unemployment remained not far off its peak of around 28 percent. Greece had become a country where many people found it hard to fathom a future, sparking an exodus of job seekers abroad. Greek newspapers ran stories about children fainting in schools from hunger. Parts of Athens and its suburbs were lined with shuttered stores. Lines at church and municipal food kitchens went around the block. During the winter, a harmful plume of smoke hovered above Athens, as people chose to burn wood rather than pay the high price of heating oil. At the same time, Greek government debt—the source of the country's problems to begin with—was near its crest of around 176 percent of GDP. All along, only a small fraction of the bailout loans Greece received directly financed state operations; the biggest chunk of the money went to service older debts and recapitalize banks. The Greek bailouts had preserved the euro, but Greece, by any measure, was buckling.

In a bid for survival, the conservative-led government tried to emphasize the positive news. In addition to slight economic growth, the country attained a small "primary surplus," meaning that it was covering its expenses, except debt interest. This marked a drastic adjustment from the deep deficits that had led to Greece's troubles. Greece also made a relatively successful cameo appearance on the bond market for the first time since the initial bailout agreement. Greeks, however, did not take much encouragement from abstract notions like a bond sale or "primary surplus." The government may have dramatically improved its budgeting, but Greek families' finances were far worse as a consequence.

At the beginning of 2015, Greek voters, exhausted by economic gloom and rule of the *mnimonio,* completed the razing of the established political order that had begun a few years earlier. After a snap general election, Syriza won decisively, at least by the splintered standards of Greece's crisis-era parliamentary politics. Alexis Tsipras, the new prime minister, immediately vowed to end the subjugation of the Troika, to discard the *mnimonio,* and to halt the "austerity of catastrophe." His government said it would seek a new and more favorable agreement with its official creditors— one that kept Greece in the euro while providing debt relief and financial wiggle room to restore social spending.

What many Greeks proudly saw as their new government's reassertion of sovereignty, however, eurozone leaders interpreted as recalcitrance and carelessness. This was particularly the case in Germany, where ruling politicians demanded Greece honor the existing bailout agreement and questioned how its government could renege on the deal and still ask for money or debt relief, which would come at a cost to German and other European taxpayers. Given the discordant impasse between the two sides, doubts over Greece's future in the eurozone once again intensified. "Grexit" reemerged in the lexicon, and even as many Greeks heralded Syriza's bold stance toward the Troika, concerned Greek depositors began transferring their euros out of the country, stoking fears of another crippling bank run. Meanwhile, the state's income rapidly eroded as many Greek taxpayers, anticipating Syriza would ease their burden, simply stopped paying, leaving the new government, just weeks in office, struggling desperately to make its debt payments and avoid default.

Running out of time and money, Syriza's leaders—like their predecessors—were compelled to yield to the creditors. In exchange for limited concessions, Greece's new government agreed to extend the bailout program for some months—and along with it, the reviled *mnimonio*—though the agreement contained enough ambiguity to allow Greek authorities to deny this was the case. The arrangement gave both sides a bit of time to try to negotiate a much bigger deal—what would essentially be a third bailout. The negotiations over the terms of further financial assistance promised to be fraught and acrimonious. Whatever the outcome, the inevitable economic and political turbulence promised to further punish the fragile Greek economy, keeping Greece scrambling to pay its bills. Five years after the first bailout, Greece's place in the eurozone seemed as imperiled as ever.

Immediately following Syriza's victory, however, many Greeks seemed to set aside these worries and reveled in what felt like a return to national self-determination, however fleeting or illusory the sensation may have been. "Greece is no longer the miserable partner that listens, that listens to instructions to do its homework," Tsipras declared in a speech in parliament shortly after taking power. "Greece has a voice. Her own voice." For the moment, many Greeks approved. Their country, it seemed, was at last breaking the grip of its creditors and regaining its independence.

The first time I went to Greece as a journalist was near the end of 2011, when I traveled to the Ionian island of Zakynthos to write a story for the *Wall Street Journal* about the alleged dispensation of fraudulent blindness benefits to hundreds of locals. In the following years, I returned for reporting assignments as often as I could. Greece was familiar to me but still foreign enough that I often found myself bewildered by it. The stories in this book show the ruins of the deeply flawed, long-established political order I encountered, and a glimpse of what may arise to replace it—some signs of positive change, but also bleak developments that presage still dark times ahead. I borrowed the title, *The Full Catastrophe*, from a line uttered by the character of Alexis Zorba in the 1964 film *Zorba the Greek*, which is based on the Nikos Kazantzakis novel. The famously spirited Zorba—who, to the point of cliché, came to be thought of as a quintessentially Greek character, prompting many foreign tourists to try to find him among the locals—treats catastrophe both as something to be mourned and a beginning to be embraced. Greeks, given their lengthy past, have many historical catastrophes to lament. Even so, the debt crisis and its accompanying economic depression ranked pretty high on many people's lists. At the same time, many Greeks acknowledged one key benefit of the catastrophe: it had laid bare enduring civic failings and made stark the need for profound political change. Whether Greece would be able to transform itself into a more socially just and economically self-sufficient country without falling apart in the interim, however, remained to be seen.

1

Island of the Blind

Wealth I would have, but wealth by wrong procure
I would not; justice, even if slow, is sure.

—Solon

On the island of Zakynthos, in a square by the main harbor, stands a statue of Dionysios Solomos overlooking the cerulean sea. Born on the island at the end of the eighteenth century, Solomos is often referred to as Greece's national poet, having written the *Hymn to Liberty*, the first two stanzas of which are now used in the Greek national anthem. "From the sacred bones of the Hellenes arisen, and valiant again as you once were, hail, o hail, Liberty," goes one verse. The words were written in 1823, during the revolution, when the Greek intelligentsia looked to an over two-millennia-long history for the ideological adhesive needed to pull together a new nation. Solomos is revered for his lyrical role in the effort, and his likeness stands on Zakynthos with an outstretched right arm in the classical orator's pose, though in reality he probably wasn't much of a public speaker. The poet was an endless reviser and perfectionist, and the hymn is among the very few poems he ever completed.

On a December afternoon in 2011, as I stood in front of the

statue of Dionysios Solomos, European leaders and the IMF had recently offered Greece its second bailout, and in return they demanded that Greek politicians change almost every aspect of the way they governed the country. The Greek government, eager to appear like it was obediently embracing a reform agenda, began efforts to root out some of the corruption that pervaded Greek life, and had by this point captivated the international press. During this time, people reading their newspapers in Europe and the United States learned Greek words such as *fakelaki* ("small envelope"), the Greek slang for a bribe handed over in order to, as Greeks often put it, "oil" the government machinery and make it work a bit faster. In Greece, if you twisted your ankle and had to go to a public hospital, you handed over a *fakelaki* to avoid a long wait to see a doctor. If your electricity went out, and the power company workers who arrived said they would have to come back tomorrow to fix it, you handed over a *fakelaki* to inspire a more immediate solution. ("If you don't oil a bit, nothing gets done," a homeowner once told me after I witnessed the latter take place in front of his house.) People abroad also learned about the *rouspheti*, a word that has Turkish origins and means a special, reciprocated favor. A *rouspheti* often involved a politician and a voter, and often an unwarranted government benefit and a vote, one in exchange for the other. The *fakelaki* and the *rouspheti* were mundane facts of Greek life, long before Greece joined the European Union, and long before it joined the eurozone. Now, though, as Greece was being thoroughly scrutinized by its creditors, the rest of the world was learning about them. So was I, for that matter. I'd come to Zakynthos to report about an alleged scandal involving both the *rouspheti* and the *fakelaki* that had drawn particular consternation and fascination in Greece—and in Germany, where I first heard about it.

I was in Berlin at a dinner gathering when the subject of Greece came up and the middle-aged man sitting next to me, who worked for the German justice ministry, asked me whether I had heard about "The Island of the Blind." He then told everyone about an article he had read about a ridiculously high number of Greeks on Zakynthos claiming to be blind in order to collect a government disability check. He and others at the table were clearly amused and perhaps a bit disgusted. This was the kind of news that made Germans question whether they should be the guarantors of the massive bailout loan package Greece was about to receive. As he told the story, I was surprised to find myself, owing to my Greek heritage, quietly stewing. These Germans! Picking on the Greeks even as Athens is burning! Around that time, Greece was making deep cuts in wages, pensions, and social spending, and, despite rising opposition, was about to push through more cuts in order to secure the second bailout. Athens was witnessing massive protests, and Greece, it seemed, was fraying. Perhaps sensing my sensitivity, everyone moved on to other topics, but after I got home, I read Greek and German press reports about Zakynthos. The Greek health ministry, suspecting fraud, was apparently looking into unusually frequent instances of blindness on the island. As they were doing so, the preponderance of fraudulent disability benefits—what the Greek media call "monkey benefits"—had become a big story in Greece.

A few days later, I called the Greek health ministry and spoke to an assistant to the then deputy minister. My original idea was to report a story about how such scandals attract a great deal of attention, but say little about the average, honest Greek. However, the conversation with the aide did not lend support to this angle. The previous year, the aide said, nearly 700 of the island's population of 39,000, about 1.8 percent of the island's residents, had claimed the blindness benefit—a check of up to 724 euros every two months and perks such as discounted utilities. This ostensible prevalence of blindness, I later found, was about nine times the rate estimated for many European countries, according to a 2004 study published in a World Health Organization journal. "We have very extensive instances of fraud," the aide told me, not just on Zakynthos and not just people pretending to be blind, but all kinds of feigned disabilities in every prefecture of Greece. There is evidence of a huge increase in the number of disability benefits handed out just before election periods, he added. I asked if the ministry was planning on pursuing criminal charges against such disability fakers. The priority, he said, was to put an end to the practice rather than punish those who'd engaged in it. "If you start putting people in jail, maybe you'll have to put half of Greece in jail."

After this conversation, I took a flight to Athens and caught a bus to the western coast of the Peloponnese, where I boarded a nighttime ferry to Zakynthos. On the boat, I sat in a movie theater–like seating area with reclining seats and cup holders while the television in front of me broadcast images of the protests I'd seen that morning in front of the Greek parliament building in Athens. A newscaster noted that Greece ranked at the bottom of Europe, and near Peru and Morocco, on Transparency International's Corruption Perception Index. When we reached the port, I took a taxi toward my hotel in the main population center, Zakynthos Town. On the way, I asked the driver if he had heard about the blindness scandal. Yes, he had, and it was a good thing, he added, that they were finally doing something about this kind of corruption. Then he overcharged me by a few euros and gave me an old receipt that was in the ballpark of what he'd asked me to pay. I was too tired to protest.

The next morning, I awoke to the sound of church bells and happy shrieks of playing children and stepped out onto my balcony. It was sunny, and the Ionian Sea, which had been invisible under the moonless darkness when I arrived, was as azure as it appears on postcards. Below, an elementary school next to the hotel was coming into session. Children ran around a courtyard until a school official in faded jeans emerged and stood on the steps. The children formed a series of haphazard lines in front of him and grew quiet. The man then crossed himself, and the children dutifully followed. This was a public school, but separation of church and state remains a somewhat foreign concept in Greece. The island has a significant Albanian migrant worker population, and the Albanian kids, likely Muslims, lingered in the back of the lines and did not participate. The rest of the children uttered a prayer while crossing themselves to its cadence: "Through the prayers of our holy fathers, oh Lord Jesus Christ, our God, have mercy on us and save us. Amen." The children added a "Good day!" before hurrying into their classrooms.

I'd obtained the name and number of a woman working in "welfare," slang for the local office otherwise known as the Directorate General of Public Health and Social Solidarity, which administered the blindness benefits. When I walked into the office, my contact, Maria, greeted me at her desk. She wore knee-high leather boots, and her red-colored hair was pulled back tightly. She, being among the younger employees, was the only one in the office whose computer was turned on. Though someone had made the decision to modernize the island's public administration by purchasing computers, it seemed that no one had digitized most of the procedures or instructed the older employees to make use of them. Either my presence made Maria nervous, or she enjoyed playing up the intrigue. We'd have to keep our voices down, she said, or the other workers in the office would know she was helping me. She lit an ultra-thin cigarette. "So you want to know about the blind," she said quietly. She would take me across the street to the mayor, who would give me more details. I was lucky they were open on this day, she added. Everyone had been on strike the day before to protest salary cuts. She later showed me one of her monthly paychecks. She had cleared about 800 euros, a few hundred euros fewer than what it used to be, she said.

The office of the mayor, Stelios Bozikis, was housed in a large, columned building with arches in Venetian Gothic style. The island had for centuries been under Venetian rule, and though the old buildings were nearly all destroyed in a 1953 earthquake, the town hall had been reconstructed to resemble the original. The mayor saw me right away. Bozikis had a large nose and a thick, graying beard. He'd formerly been associated with the communist party, but won the mayoral race a year earlier with support from center-left PASOK. He sipped from his coffee, lit a cigarette, leaned back in his office chair, and ran through his fingers a *kombolói*, a string of beads that men in Greece often flick around to pass the time. I turned on my voice recorder, and he began speaking before I could ask any questions. He told me that when he became mayor, he ascertained that a suspiciously high number of Zakynthos residents were taking a blindness benefit at an annual cost to the government of a few million euros. The majority of them were fakes, he said. "I will personally take them all to the district attorney and I will ask for all the money that they took back," he said. "I'm not retreating. This corruption in Greece can't continue." Everything will be "brought to light," he added, because the path of justice was an obligation. For a Greek politician, he struck me as suspiciously noble. He singled out the former prefect, a member of the center-right New Democracy party, and the local ophthalmologist as the main players in the scheme. The ophthalmologist, he told me, I could find at the hospital. As for the prefect, he'd "gotten lost."

That turned out not to be true. Later that afternoon I found Dionysios Gasparos, the former prefect, a urologist, in his nearby office on the ground floor of a pink, three-story building with several balconies. Gasparos had been in office for twelve years until 2010, when prefectures were abolished as part of a whittling down of Greece's multilayered system of regional governance. I rang the bell and Gasparos came to the door. He was a short man with a shock of gray hair slicked back. After I introduced myself, Gasparos responded in a raspy voice, "I don't put you down as blind. The ophthalmologist does." He then stopped and looked around to see if any neighbors were listening. A few dogs barked in the street. He invited me inside.

His office was cluttered with papers and various medical certificates hung on the yellowed walls. It looked like not many patients had been visiting of late. He said he had long called for investigations about the number of blind, and blamed the national health ministry for not responding. "Simply, they are playing political games," he said of the health ministry. "That's what you're going to write." I dutifully wrote "political games" in my notebook. Gasparos's signature authorized the benefits, but as he would have me understand it, his signature was only a bureaucratic technicality, one that enabled the money transfers to the beneficiaries, who had already been identified and confirmed as being blind by someone else. "The doctor!" Gasparos said. "Only he has responsibility. The doctor puts you down as blind. Not the prefect."

"They say that you gave out the blindness benefits in order to get votes," I said.

"That's a lie!" Gasparos snapped.

"They also say the doctor took money to write people as blind," I said.

He paused.

"He took money?" the former prefect said in a much calmer voice. "How would I know? I don't even know him." Gasparos reclined in his chair and tossed his *kombolói*. "The others are criticizing him, saying he took money?" he added, as if the possibility of something so devious had not crossed his mind, which would have made him the only person on the island who had not heard about or entertained the accusation.

I had heard by this point that Gasparos had aspirations to run for parliament in the next election. On my way out, I asked him if that was true. "Yes," he told me, with a bit of hesitation, as if he were weighing whether it would be a good idea to reveal this information. "I'm considering it."

The headquarters of the Greek health ministry in Athens is located in a shabby seven-floor concrete building in an area frequented by prostitutes and junkies. When I visited the place around the same time as my trip to Zakynthos, banners and graffiti tags on the wall near the entrance read: OUR MONEY, YOU ALL ATE IT!!!, THIEVES, and FIVE MONTHS UNPAID. Like many government ministries during this time, its workers were very frequently on strike, underscoring one of the great difficulties Greece had in fulfilling its reform promises. European policy makers were increasingly complaining that the Greeks were not implementing the reforms they had agreed to in exchange for the bailouts. But how could a government institute reforms when its own workers struck in rebellion against them, and then graffiti-tagged their workplace?

I had arrived to see Markos Bolaris, the deputy health minister, who had put off our meeting several times during the day. It was late in the evening by the time I entered the building and passed a bust of Hippocrates in the lobby. In the bathroom, there was no toilet paper, hand soap, or paper towels, and the building was empty except for a hive of activity in the deputy minister's office. There, I met the aide I had spoken with over the phone. He was working in front of his laptop in a black T-shirt, jeans, and a pair of Converse sneakers. He took off his thick-rimmed glasses and rubbed his sweaty face. "Do you smoke?" he said in English. We stepped out onto the balcony. "Everything is so fucked," he said as he looked down onto the street below. He'd gone to school in England, and his combination Greek and English accent made him sound Scottish. "Everyone is panicking and each and every day there are strikes," he said. "How are you going to fix anything without working?" He said he had been putting in twelve-to fourteen-hour days, and was making less than 1,000 euros a month. "And then they say we Greeks are lazy!" he said, before adding that health ministry workers planned to occupy the building the following day; to bolt the front entrance shut in order to prevent the minister's staff or anyone else from working.

Bolaris sent word that he was ready to see me. I walked over to his office and found him behind his large wooden desk, a plump, middle-aged man with a thick gray mustache, wearing a broad red tie and a gray suit. A gilt icon of Mary holding Jesus hung on the wall directly behind him.

"How big is the problem of fraudulent disability?" I asked.

"Very big," he said. Bolaris seemed to like to speak in short sentences, as if this added weight to his words. The Greek government at the time spent nearly one billion euros in disability benefits annually, he said. Over the course of the previous years, hundreds of millions of it had gone out to fraudulent claimants. Local politicians with the authority to grant the disability benefits knowingly signed off on the claims in exchange for votes or political favor, he said, and doctors diagnosed them in exchange for payoffs. To illustrate this point, Bolaris removed a folder from his desk and sifted through some papers. The papers showed that an Athens pulmonologist diagnosed thirty people in Elefsina, a waning industrial area close to Athens, with disorders such as neck pain, back problems, and depression—conditions that had nothing to do with their lungs. "A pulmonologist!" Bolaris reiterated, sticking an index finger in the air. When enough ailments were combined, the patient would qualify for heavy disability and a benefit of up to several hundred euros a month. Furthermore, there was no evidence the doctor had ever seen the patients other than to exchange the paperwork and cash. "They had stores!" said Bolaris, referring to doctors that engaged in the "industrial production of disability certificates."

The government would begin attacking the problem, he said,

by starting to keep centralized records of who was receiving disability benefits on a computer system. This would help them see irregularities such as an inordinate number of disability benefits given out in a particular town, or by a particular doctor. To an outsider, it might have seemed self-evident that a contemporary European government would already have had such a computerized system in place. The fact that Greece did not, however, was due not so much to administrative inertia and ineptitude—though these factors certainly played their parts—but to willful neglect. Politicians and government employees on both the federal and local levels had maintained byzantine record-keeping methods, because doing so obscured accountability, enabling the graft and the patronage from which many of them benefited. Now, under pressure from its creditors, the Greek government was being compelled to start keeping better records in order to determine how it was spending its money. In order to build a database, the health ministry was mandating that citizens receiving a disability benefit show up at government offices around the country and register into the new system. Otherwise, their benefit would be cut.

Of course, because the great majority of people in Greece receiving a disability benefit actually qualified for it, this meant that people with disabilities—including the truly blind—would be forced, unless a caretaker appeared for them, to report to a government office and register their condition. This naturally upset rights groups for people with disabilities, which felt like their members were being unfairly and insensitively singled out for having supposedly cheated the government. Greek television coverage of the disability benefits scandal did not help matters. The issue of benefits fraud was debated on one television channel that ran constant footage of a blind man—or an actor pretending to be blind—navigating the streets of Athens with a walking stick. "The portrayal of persons with disability in the mass media has been absolutely unbearable," the president of Greece's National

Confederation of Disabled People told me at the time. From this perspective, the government's reform effort seemed somewhat farcical, which underscored the fact that the Greek government had not, despite the urgency for change, suddenly become a smoothly functioning entity. One therefore had to beware not only of the government's hesitance or incapacity to undertake reforms, but also of what happened once it tried to undertake them.

Ultimately, some 200,000 of the nation's disabled showed up in government offices around the country to register. This was about 36,000 fewer people than had been receiving the benefits. Presumably, according to the health ministry, these people had not shown up because their benefits claims were fraudulent. The difference translated to annual savings of some 100 million euros. This turned out to be less than an initial estimate given to me by Bolaris, who, along with his aide, seemed sometimes swept away by reform gusto. Still, it was a large sum, particularly when compounded over several years. It was also only the beginning of a process to uncover wider fraud. The new digital registry would be emulated by other ministries to track an additional five billion euros in social welfare benefits handed out annually in Greece. When at this time I tried to find out the precise number of the social benefits in Greece, an aide to a labor minister told me no one knew for sure how many exactly, because management of the benefits was spread among several ministries. There was, it seemed, the possibility to discover more fraud.

The social security system was another problematic area. The Greek labor ministry at the time also undertook a "census" to determine how many people in Greece were collecting a pension, and what kind of pension they were receiving. Greece had an array of underfunded social security agencies that handed out pensions to various segments of the population (this included disability pensions, a separate category from disability benefits). At one point, labor ministry officials said a dubiously high 8,500 pensioners in

Greece were over one hundred years old, at least on paper. That figure, were it legitimate, would have meant that Greece was by far the world leader in terms of its per capita number of centenarians. Rather, government officials determined that a great number of retirement checks were being paid to dead people—or "ghost retirees," as the Greek media called them—whose family members had failed to notify the state of their loved ones' passing. About 40,000 pensions were shown to be fraudulent, the Greek labor minister announced on television following the initial census results. The total cost of all social security fraud since Greece entered the eurozone was hard to measure, and Greek government officials threw out some widely disparate figures. In 2014, the labor minister estimated the cost at some five billion euros. To be sure, fraudulent benefit claims—costly as they were—were not the reason Greece found itself in a financial crisis, but the phenomenon did hint at the broader levels of waste and graft that, together with the custom of political patronage, had cleaned out the government's coffers.

On Zakynthos, a preliminary police investigation found that 498 of the 680 people who received or requested a blindness benefit did not qualify for it. Sixty-one of them had driver's licenses. The apparent scheme on the island cost the state some 9 million euros, according to an initial estimate. Bolaris, the deputy health minister, and other government officials vowed to get back wrongfully taken money, though that would be no easy task.

During my conversation with Bolaris, I asked him why it had taken so long for the government to do something about these "thieveries," as he put it at one point. He answered with what seemed like a line he had used before. "Greece passed through an era of the fat cow," he said. "Now we are the skinny cows. If it didn't matter to some people before, for us today, it must matter." He then offered a historical explanation for why these things happened in Greece. Perhaps someone like me could not understand it, he said, because I had never lived in a nation that has experienced foreign occupation.

"We, Demetri," he said, using my Greek middle name, "in Thessaloniki, in Macedonia, in 2012, we'll celebrate one hundred years of freedom." Thessaloniki is Greece's second largest city, located in the north, and the liberation he was referring to was from the Ottoman Empire. "People had above them the sultan. The one who didn't pay taxes to the sultan was smart. He was a *magas*," an untranslatable and complimentary term that can loosely be understood to mean "badass." "He was resisting the sultan. This happened here in Athens for four hundred years. In northern Greece, for five hundred years. These things don't go away easily." Bolaris was making an argument I heard commonly around this time. Greeks, through centuries of foreign domination, had antigovernment feeling imbued in their blood. The government was a foe, and if you could defraud it, you were not only enriching yourself; in a way, you were a patriot. I wasn't sure I bought this argument, though there was something to the notion that, in Greece, disloyalty to the state did not equate to disloyalty to the nation. Greeks don't necessarily synthesize their *ethnos*—a word that means "nation" but has a racial, tribal connotation—with the republic. The *ethnos* is far vaster. The *ethnos* is thousands of years old, and unparalleled in its magnificence and import to humanity. What contemporary state could embody such grandeur? This has long been particularly true of the Greek state, which Greeks know to be dysfunctional anyway. Scamming the state, therefore, was not the same as scamming the nation.

Bolaris then went on to talk about Ioannis Kapodistrias, the first president of Greece, who was born on the Ionian island of Corfu but had long served as the foreign minister of Russia under Tsar Alexander I. Kapodistrias was living in Geneva, Switzerland, when the revolutionary Greek national assembly, judging his international connections and prestige advantageous, elected him to govern the country. When he arrived in 1828, the condition of the budding Hellenic state and the immensity of the task ahead must have come as a shock. He found a largely agrarian, underdeveloped country, tattered by years of fighting and beset by disease and poverty. A government and an infrastructure had to be built from scratch, a task made harder by the fact that the revolutionary factions fighting for independence were often warring with one another. Kapodistrias had plans to modernize the place, but did not have much of a chance to implement them. A few years after he arrived, members of a powerful Peloponnesian clan he had upset shot him dead. *"Bam bam,"* as Bolaris put it. I wasn't sure what moral the deputy minister was trying to impart by mentioning this, other than to point out how ungovernable the nation was, and perhaps remained. "After that, the barbarians came. From Germany. Otto. Otto came." The Otto he was referring to was Greece's first king, a prince from Bavaria who came to rule at age seventeen, a decision of Britain, France, and Russia, who secured Greece's independence by defeating the Ottomans in a decisive naval clash—the Battle of Navarino, off the southwestern tip of the Peloponnese. Otto arrived in Greece with a considerable Bavarian entourage, including his personal confectioner, in order to establish the new nation and capital in Athens, which was then a small, rustic town, and he brought a Bavarian architect to build a palace, the austere, neoclassical building that today serves as the Greek parliament. I was astounded at how casually the minister referred to Germans as barbarians, but I would later find out that this was commonplace. "He brought German soldiers, German judges, and a government started to form," Bolaris added. "But the Greek on the bottom said, 'Good, it's Greece, but the Germans are in control.' It didn't bother us if we didn't pay taxes to the Germans. Do you understand?" he added. "It was resistance to the foreigner."

.   .   .

On Zakynthos, as I was leaving one of the local government offices one morning, an elfin woman who had heard about the reason for my visit approached me. "My grandmother is one of those who took the benefit," she said. "Now she lost it and she is angry about it. Maybe she will talk to you." This was a terrific stroke of fortune, as I had tried to find someone on the island who had taken the benefit and could see, but no one had been willing to single out an offender. It seemed a worse transgression to squeal than to commit fraud. The woman, who was affluent and had a good job, told me her seeing grandmother had paid the doctor 1,500 euros for the necessary diagnosis. She asked that I say nothing to reveal her or her grandmother's identity.

The next morning, I met the woman and her husband at an outdoor café in a square in the middle of town. As we talked over a cup of coffee, it became clear that they were somewhat depressed about the moral condition of the island. The local stories of corruption were apparently not limited to the suspicious number of blindness benefits. The former mayor, a man named Akis Tsagkaropoulos, was accused of soliciting the services of an Albanian immigrant to burn down the municipal building where financial records were stored. (A municipal police officer caught the Albanian with a great deal of gasoline and other flammable liquids before he could set the building ablaze.) Tsagkaropoulos allegedly had an interest in seeing the records destroyed. He had been accused by city council members of using forged documents to take out millions of euros in municipal loans without their prior approval. A fire in the building where records were housed would have erased evidence of the alleged financial irregularities. Tsagkaropoulos, who was an orthopedic surgeon at the local hospital before becoming mayor, was eventually convicted of attempted arson and sentenced to eight years in prison, though he appealed the decision and was released from custody. He later died at age fifty-six of a heart condition, according to Greek media reports, having maintained his innocence in both the arson attempt and alleged improprieties regarding the suspect loans. "The judgment of people stops with their death," a local newspaper wrote of his passing.

After the woman and her husband finished lamenting their island's politicians, she told me she had some bad news. Her grandmother didn't want to speak to me after all. "She is very embarrassed and she's afraid to talk because she knows the doctor," she said. "The great characteristic of Zakynthos is the hypocrisy. They're not willing to talk. They don't want to confront the problems." I asked if she could call her grandmother again and, taking the phone, I introduced myself as Demetri. That was apparently all that was necessary to change the woman's mind. An elderly voice with a local dialect replied: "If someone comes and says, I will give you a retirement pay, will you say no? I'm poor and I'm sick. Now they cut it. And they want us to pay it back. But where will I find it?" When I suggested we talk in person, she said: "My Demetri, my door is always open to you."

The granddaughter and I got in her car and left immediately. We drove out into the hilly countryside, past olive groves and eucalyptus trees, and pulled up in front of a one-story house. A small, plump woman wearing spotless white sneakers, a plaid robe, and an apron decorated with flower patterns emerged to greet us. We entered the house and in the hallway passed an icon of St. Dionysios of Zakynthos, a sixteenth-century archbishop honored for his extraordinary capacities of forgiveness, having forgiven even his brother's murderer. We sat at the kitchen table and the grandmother offered me a Greek coffee. She began to talk without my having to ask any questions.

"If you have a godfather, you get baptized," she said. "If you don't have one, you don't get baptized." It took me a second to fully comprehend what she meant by this. To be baptized is to be rewarded. To have a godfather make this happen, well, you must sometimes pay. "The *rouspheti* does not cease to be," she went on. "You give money to get the matters settled." I should certainly know about these things, being a journalist, she added. "If they gave you money, you would write that I was eighteen."

"I wouldn't lie," I told her, defending my virtue, and then felt foolish for doing so.

"If they said to you, 'Take these millions,' you would put me down as sixteen!" she snapped back. She then made her voice quiet and weary. "Me, my child, I'm an old woman and you are a child. You are educated and I am uneducated. I always understand, though, that the money rules." She raised her voice again and slapped the table. "Even Jesus himself was betrayed by his disciple, all for money!" She watched me scribbling this in my notebook. "Few people are honest, neither your mother, nor your child. But me, there's nobody like me. Because I'm honest. You should know well. I don't like lies."

"But if you're honest," I said, "how . . ."

"I am!" she said, slapping the table again. "One thing I'll tell you. If I say something, my word is a contract. I'm a pure Greek. I'm not a bastard! I'm not PASOK. And I'm not the devil's!"

"Why are you saying this?" I asked, confused about her reference to the political party, which was by then fighting for survival after signing on to the first bailout agreement.

"Because you're writing it down. This is what I know to tell. I'm a real Greek. I'm not going to change. Do you understand?"

I really liked this woman, even though I wasn't sure I understood her. It would have been futile to try to extract logic from everything she said. With the cryptic baptism line, she had more or less told me in her way what she thought I needed to know. She had the mannerisms and patois of a disappearing generation of Greek ladies, despite the fact that she wasn't wearing black, as most elderly widows do. I asked her about this, and she said she had never liked her husband.

At one point, I gathered the courage to ask her if she could see me.

"I see you well," she replied, before going on to complain about her eye troubles and other various ailments, including anxiety and depression, for which she took ten daily medications. Though I am no medical professional, I wondered if that number of medications was too much for her. Some Greek doctors tended to greatly over-prescribe expensive drugs because they were routinely bribed by suppliers to do so. On the year of my visit to Zakynthos, Greece spent more money on pharmaceuticals as a percent of GDP than all other industrialized countries. The finances of the country's largest social security fund, which footed a lot of the bill for this excess, suffered greatly as a result. The grandmother claimed that her anxiety resulted from the trauma of having endured an armed robbery one night. But for someone traumatized by such an incident, she seemed to derive a great deal of pleasure from telling me the story. She was indeed a very skilled storyteller, even employing the use of props. As she began to narrate the story, she got up from the table, walked over to the drawers, and removed a knife with a six-inch curved blade. She walked over to me, bringing the knife within two feet of my neck.

"Um, be careful," I said.

"Is he afraid?" the old lady said to her granddaughter.

"He's afraid."

"You can live, man," said the old woman, backing away slightly. Standing next to me with the knife in her hand, she then told the story of the break-in as if we were gathered around a campfire.

"I was sleeping inside. I saw the door open and I saw a black glove. I saw a child with a black hood. And he came inside with the knife."

"That knife?" I asked.

"It was this knife. My knife." She lowered her voice to a whisper. "He said, 'I will slaughter you.'"

She then raised her voice: "'I say, 'Leave me alone, you can slaughter me tomorrow!'"

Back to a hush: " 'Don't breathe a word,' he says."

In her usual voice: " 'Didn't I see you when you came inside? I didn't say anything, and now you're putting that knife up to me like you're going to slaughter me like a goat!'

" 'Do what I'm telling you. The money. Bring the money,' " she whispered, impersonating the robber. Two more hooded men came inside, she explained. One of them went to cover her head with a hood.

" 'Go to hell!' I said."

At this point in her narration, she started chuckling.

"They pick up the mattress with me on it, and I started laughing. And they say, 'You're laughing, eh?' 'No, my child,' I say, 'I'm not laughing. What, are we going to the theater to see a movie? It's just us here.' "

The thieves took 800 euros and the gold rings she had hidden under the mattress, and also the gold ring on her finger, she said. They went to the refrigerator and took a freshly slaughtered rabbit and a piece of halvah. They warned her, she said, not to call the police.

"I said, 'I don't want to take you to the police. Why? Because I feel sorry for you. I don't want the police hitting you. I'm a mother, too. And I have kids. And I wouldn't want that. I swear to you.' "

The old lady, I thought, had uncanny poise. Not many people try to pacify robbers by befriending them. She went on.

"One takes off his hood and says, 'Auntie, we're leaving now.' I say, 'Go with the blessing of God. God help you to give up this pursuit, because you'll get yourselves killed. My child, I feel sorry for you, you, so young and gallant. And to get to this point?' " According to her, they were drug addicts, worse than toothpicks, trying to score their next dose. The robbers left, and despite her motherly instincts, she called the police. The officer, a tall guy, as she explained it, said, "What should I tell you, Auntie? Me, I'm an officer and a man, and my heart would have stopped."

Ending her story, the old lady added: "God gave me courage. I wasn't scared."

"How did you get the knife back?" I asked, still aware of its proximity to my arteries.

"They left it on the ground outside."

"Put it back in your drawer," said the granddaughter.

"If someone comes, I'll slaughter them," said the old lady as she walked over to the drawer, and dropped it inside with a crash. "My Demetri," she added. "If I had my youth, I would have taken a gun and chased them."

The granddaughter seemed to be getting tired. She had heard the story before. I asked the grandmother a few more questions about the blindness benefit. She would not say overtly if she had paid the doctor a bribe or not to get the benefit, but she did say: "He's written half of Zakynthos blind! Even the cats!" She then lamented that her benefit had been cut. "I was born poor and I'll die poor," the grandmother said. Though retired farmers received low pensions in Greece, and she led a modest lifestyle, I wasn't sure if I believed her. This woman, after all, had feigned motherly concern even for her robbers, and was collecting a blindness benefit though she could see. Her word, you could say, was not ironclad.

We then talked a bit about "the crisis," about which she offered this monologue: "Are we Greeks? We're not Greeks! We're bastards! Do you see the Germans? They don't betray their country like we do. They support their own country. We're the traitors. We'll make our country into a mess. They'll take Greece. There will be a war." We looked at some pictures of family members, many of whom were long dead. We then walked outside, passing the icon of St. Dionysios and into the sunny day. A few chickens wandered through the front yard. We smelled her parsley and mint plants, and said good-bye. As we got in the car to drive away, she said to me, "This is what I am and this is what I offer you."

· · ·

The next morning, I walked to the public hospital, on top of a hill overlooking the red-tiled roofs of Zakynthos, to see the ophthalmologist. According to local officials, this doctor, Nikolaos Vartzelis, was the only ophthalmologist at the only public hospital on the island, and therefore the only one there with the authority to give medical authorization for the blindness benefit. Inside, the corridors were hot, stuffy, and crowded with patients. I knocked on the ophthalmologist's office door. The door was half opened by the doctor, who was sitting in his chair. I told him I was a journalist who wanted to talk about the blind. He let me in, and I sat across from him at his desk. He had a thick gray mustache. His hair was combed over to cover his balding crown, and he wore a white lab coat. He held his glasses in his hands, which trembled with nervousness. I felt a bit sorry for him. He clearly wasn't the only doctor in the country alleged to have done this sort of thing. Why should he become the national poster boy for it?

Of course, that is the essential problem when justice is sorely lacking and laws are rarely enforced. The application of the *rouspheti*, the handing out of a *fakelaki*, and other technically illegal practices were so widespread that the system had attained its own equilibrium, until the crisis started to set things off balance. If you assumed everyone around you had partaken in some sort of hustle, it seemed like an injustice to be singled out for your own. Therefore it was easy to feel, even if you were guilty of wrongdoing, that if you were caught, you were being unfairly victimized. It did not help that accusations of fraud were often interwoven with political rivalries. One had to wonder if perhaps the island's leftist mayor had something other than, in his words, "the path of justice" on his mind when chasing a scandal that implicated a political rival.

I put my voice recorder down on the table.

"Are we on?" the doctor said.

"Yes." He, too, began speaking without prompting, as if making a prepared statement for the television news.

"The matter arises from two causes." The first cause, he explained, was the political rivalry between the ex-prefect and the current mayor, both of whom were "burning" to run for parliament. The second cause, he said, was the Troika. "I know that some years ago a decision had been taken by the government after the Troika's advice to reexamine benefits within the whole of Greece. Not just the blind benefits. Many, many others. It's the mutes, the mentally ill. It's the others who suffer from cancerous tumors. One part of them is the blind."

He finally arrived at the subject of Zakynthos's blind. "In some areas these persons are many because these pathologies are family pathologies. For example, there is a village near us—we won't say the name—where there is a family of five: mother, father, and three children. Of these five, three take the benefit. Because three out of five of them take the benefit, are we going to call it monkey business?" he said. "No," he said. They got the money for blindness, or as he put it, "They can't even see the light."

"But are there seven hundred blind?" I asked.

"No, no, no," he said quickly. "In comparison with other areas in Greece, we don't have the most blind people. The issue that has come to publicity is owed 100 percent to a political clash."

"And you didn't play a role in this?"

"I'm telling you it's like a process. When we give a certificate, we sign it, committees sign it. Even if there are a hundred signatures, if there are a thousand signatures, if the prefect doesn't sign it, no one gets anything."

"But you signed as well?"

"One of the people who put down a signature was me. But after me, they go to the health department, they go down to the committees, and the final reason, the final decision for someone to get money, I repeat, belongs in each case to the prefect. Without the signature of the prefect, a thousand people could have signed it, and the disabled wouldn't get any money."

"Those people who said you took, say a thousand or . . ."

"Not in any case," said the doctor, denying ever having accepted bribes in exchange for false blindness diagnoses. "This is maligning. Not in any case. There are cases of some people who don't have a shoulder to lean on, they didn't have bread to eat, and maybe there we gave them every leniency." This was a curious comment. Since only the legally blind are entitled to the benefit, there's not a lot of room for leniency. "We were lenient, but within the limits of the law," he added. "The other things that they say, this and that, those are slanders. You should know that Zakynthos is a very beautiful island, it has a lot of good things, but it's an island of gossips."

A few months later, as the health ministry's efforts to publicize its crackdown on the island intensified, the Greek media picked up the story in earnest. Greek television-news talk shows, which are often a cross between *Meet the Press* and *The Jerry Springer Show,* invited the deputy health minister, the mayor, the former prefect, the doctor, and various commentators to discuss the scandal. On one popular show, the mayor of Zakynthos said residents of the island, including some who had received a blindness benefit, had thrown yogurt at him—exhibiting good aim—in protest of his reforms. He said he considered the yogurt attack "a medal and an honor," adding, "I don't care about the political cost." The mayor also claimed a priest on the island was one of those fraudulently receiving the blindness benefits.

"That is to say, he was reading the gospel?" commented one guest on the program.

The show's moderator fumed with anger over the scandal.

"The Troika had to come for us to do such investigations?" he said to the television audience. "It's an embarrassment. It makes you want to go crazy. It makes you want to say, 'Good what's happening to us, good what they're doing to us,' those who've come from the outside."

Television pundits and the mayor called for a criminal investigation, with the doctor receiving the most vitriolic criticism. A few months after my visit, the doctor resigned from the hospital. Over the phone, he told me his decision had nothing to do with the "noise" about the blindness scandal. "I was ready to retire," he said.

One afternoon in Zakynthos Town, I went for a walk in the city center, passing jewelry and designer clothing stores and cafés. At the time, there were no boarded up-stores or other signs of economic misery that were increasingly prevalent in Athens. Rather, the town appeared to be pretty well off. The city government may have long been broke, but the people living there seemed to be doing okay. I passed the offices of the island's religious authorities, located near the mayor's office, and decided to stop in and see if I could speak with someone about the spiritual state of the island. At the door, a man in a black robe asked me the purpose of my visit. I told him I was writing a story about "the blindness."

I was introduced to the general vicar, Panagiotis Kapodistrias, who also wore a long black robe and had a graying beard. On his office wall hung a framed image of Jesus lying dead at the foot of the cross, pierced by two spears. I sat down across from the vicar at his desk, and he offered me a piece of baklava from "Constantinople," as Greeks refer to Istanbul, where he'd recently visited the Ecumenical Patriarch, the spiritual head of Orthodox Christianity. As we spoke about the quality of the baklava, a Polish woman entered the office and asked for money. She had three children, she said, and couldn't find work. She had made twenty-three euros a day over the summer unloading trucks, a job, she said, "only a man should have done."

"I don't ever see you in church," the vicar said.

"I do go," she replied.

"I'm not going to give you a lot," the vicar told her. He filled out a little slip of paper for her, noting the size of the donation—fifty euros—which she could exchange for cash in another office.

"That's a lot," said the Polish woman. "I can live on that for two or three days." She left the office, bowing toward the vicar. "Go with Jesus," she said.

I turned on my recorder and he, like the others I interviewed, began unprompted.

"Greece, as we all know, is undergoing a crisis. The crisis appears to be economic and political, but deep down, it's ethical." Then he proceeded to blame the ethical problems on foreigners, in particular tourists. Zakynthos had an increasingly uneasy relationship with package tourism. In 2008, a group of drunken British tourists conducted an oral sex contest on a Zakynthos beach, outraging locals. Also that year, according to press reports, a Greek woman tried to set a drunken British tourist's scrotum on fire after he exposed it to several local women at a nightclub. Tourism was a form of neocolonialism that corrupted local souls, according to the vicar. Zakynthos citizens, in the process of catering to the visitors by building inexpensive hotels, had become "the slave of the tourists," he said. "This is how the crisis has arisen." To exit it, he added, locals must avoid becoming one with the foreigner and return to what they truly are.

By this point, the cause of the country's fiscal problems had become a hotly debated subject in Greece. There were many theories for why Greece was in trouble and who was responsible. For the rapidly rising far left, the Greek people were generally blameless victims of inevitably doomed neoliberal policies that were benefiting the big capitalists at the expense of everyone else. For the rising extreme right, Jewish bankers and job-stealing immigrants were to blame. The two mainstream parties blamed each other until, due to a rapid decline in their popularity, they were forced to band together in a coalition in order to maintain power. For many, the Troika was most culpable. So was German chancellor

Angela Merkel. Greece was the target of an international plan for economic plunder, many believed. This, however, was the first time I'd heard tourism (albeit quite raunchy tourism), an economic lifeblood for Greece, referred to as the source of the nation's problems. All these explanations shared one commonality: they laid the blame elsewhere, often on outsiders. The tendency is partly understandable. Greece is a small country that has long been subject to foreign sway, and at the time, it was under the dominion of its foreign creditors. The vicar's argument and others like it, however, proved alluring to the many Greeks who wished to avoid considering the extent to which they were responsible for their own decline. The vicar's comments made me wonder what chances Greece had of improving its fate if this was the widespread nature of the self-examination taking place. Before I left his office, the vicar signed a book he had written on the theology of environmental protection and gave it to me. I briefly opened it to the introduction, which began: "Whether we want it or not, we are obliged before a common danger to coexist and to cooperate." I thanked him for the present.

The next day was the feast day of St. Nicholas, and that morning I waited for the ferry departing for the Peloponnese. A stiff wind blew, churning the Ionian waters and sweeping cottony cumulus clouds across the crisp blue sky. In the town center, the modal sound of an Orthodox church service piping through speakers on the domed roof of St. Nicholas Church fluttered in the wind gusts. "Both now and ever and unto the ages of ages," sang the vicar and other clerics. A recitation of the Lord's Prayer washed over the city, mingling with the techno beats emanating from the outdoor cafés, where patrons huddled near heat lamps, smoking and sipping coffee. The sermon was about St. Nicholas, and his capacity for "unadulterated" love. On the main square, city workers hung white string lights in the form of a Christmas tree.

. . .

After I departed Zakynthos, I visited a public hospital in Athens where the health ministry had summoned some four hundred blindness benefit recipients from the island to take an eye exam in order to determine whether they were really blind. Athens was a long way from Zakynthos, but the government did not trust nearby doctors to make accurate diagnoses, forcing island residents to make the long trip. In the hospital waiting room, I met Panagiotis Vozaitis, a skinny, bowlegged, retired currant farmer from Zakynthos. Vozaitis had not received the blindness benefit, but had decided to make the trip with his daughter anyway when he heard the exams were taking place. He had eye problems, he said, and had twice tried to get the blindness benefit, but had been unsuccessful. With his small farmer's pension, he could not afford even the bargain rate of eight hundred euros, paid in two installments, he alleged the island ophthalmologist had requested of him for a blindness diagnosis. "If I had it, I would've paid it," Vozaitis told me. Now he was in Athens to see if he could get the benefit in the proper manner—due to blindness. Vozaitis said he could not see out of his right eye, and had some problems with the left. A doctor later told me the old farmer wasn't impaired enough to qualify for the benefit, for which one has to be almost completely blind in both eyes. I had suspected as much. As Vozaitis and I spoke in the hospital, his pale blue left eye focused alertly on me as he talked about the crisis and derided the politicians who "stole it all." Though he did not technically qualify for the benefit, Vozaitis's story showed how Greece's social safety net, while having been abused as if it were a slush fund by many of the country's politicians, was deficient at fulfilling the purpose for which it was intended. Vozaitis, after all, had traveled several hours because he could not trust he would receive a benefit he might have been entitled to without having to pay a fee. When I mentioned Gasparos, the man who had been prefect when many suspect blindness benefits were handed out, Vozaitis laughed.

"Those who eat a lot also give to those who vote for them,"

he told me. "That prefect is going to become bishop one day." This expression, to "eat," is the ubiquitous Greek shorthand for illicit feasting on public money. Those politicians who ate also bequeathed some of the spoils to the voters, Vozaitis was saying. This way of seeing things, while accurate, was also somewhat controversial in Greece. To the extent there was any consensus on the domestic cause of Greece's fiscal problems, it was that "the politicians ate it all," a phrase I very frequently heard when discussing the crisis with Greeks. There was less often acknowledgment of citizens' eating. When one prominent Greek politician offered a more inclusive theory of how Greece's money had been consumed, it was not well received. The politician, Theodoros Pangalos, was deputy prime minister in 2010 when, speaking in parliament, he offered an answer to the question Greeks were asking the politicians: "How did you eat the money?" Pangalos, a hefty man who barely fit into his parliamentary seat, then answered: "We ate it all together in the framework of a relationship of political clientelism, corruption, payouts, and the debasement of the meaning of the politics itself." This statement—reduced to "We ate it together"—quickly became famous and served as a kind of mantra of the debt crisis, though it was usually uttered in irony and outrage, as Greeks felt that politicians and their powerful associates ate it, or at least a lot more of it than everyone else. Yet that anger did not take into account the fact that politicians did not exist in a vacuum, and had found ways to involve their voters in the feasting, thereby securing their electoral place at the head of the table. The manner in which this allegedly transpired on Zakynthos was flagrant, but the vast majority of the time it was much more mundane, and legal: rapid wage and benefit increases for public workers, for example; generous pensions for people working in certain professions; the protection of monopolistic cartels through arbitrary regulations. Since politicians orchestrated this system and greatly benefited from it, it seemed indecent of them—particularly one like Pangalos, long in the PASOK ruling elite—to implicate the electorate, which, broadly speaking, did not believe that it shared in the responsibility.

Vozaitis had a point about the former prefect and the island's voters. In May 2012, Zakynthos elected Gasparos to the Greek parliament as a member of New Democracy. The result seemed to call into question voters' willingness to upend the political status quo they often decried. On the night of his win, Gasparos walked through the streets of Zakynthos Town wearing a suit and tie striped with the blue and white of the Greek flag. His supporters gathered on the streets and applauded, many of them kissing him on both cheeks. The outcome, Gasparos told the crowd, was a victory for ethical and honorable citizens trying to improve life on the island. "Tonight is not my night," he said. "Tonight belongs to the people of Zakynthos. To the youth. It belongs to hope. It belongs to a better tomorrow."

Unfortunately for Gasparos, his success was short-lived. Nationally, the election was inconclusive, resulting in no clear majority and a hung parliament. A new vote took place one month later, and though Gasparos received more votes the second time around, he nevertheless came in second to a candidate from the surging leftist Syriza. The new victor, a middle-aged lawyer, Stavros Kontonis, said his election represented a condemnation of the corruption that had brought infamy to the island. It proved Zakynthos was not inhabited by corrupt people, said Kontonis, but rather had long fallen into bad political hands.

The outcome also meant Gasparos would not benefit from the parliamentary immunity enshrined in the Greek constitution. He was later charged with fraud, as was the ophthalmologist accused of making false diagnoses, Greek newspapers reported at the end of 2014; both maintained their innocence. Locals accused of wrongly taking blindness benefits would also face criminal charges. This degree of accountability was highly unusual in

Greece, and it indicated a growing appetite for transformation. The outcome of the 2012 elections, however, meant that the two main parties that had for decades fostered the system of political patronage remained in parliamentary power for a few more years by forming a coalition. On the night of his defeat, Gasparos, appearing on television, said there was still cause to celebrate. Despite his loss, his party would be leading the national government. And he offered words of assurance for his supporters. "I'll remain in politics," he said.

2

Off the Books

The just is always a loser in comparison with the unjust.

—Thrasymachus, in *The Republic* by Plato

Hydra is a tall, barren rock that juts from the Aegean Sea just off the eastern edge of the Peloponnese. A few thousand people live on the island, mostly in a settlement of white stone homes in "Hydra Town," which rises like a theater on slopes that form a horseshoe over the main harbor. Hydra derives its name not from the eponymous nine-headed serpent of Greek mythology, slain by Hercules, but from the Ancient Greek word for water—at least according to locals, who say the island once contained an abundance of springs. Today, there is virtually no fresh water on Hydra, and the noxious-tasting auxiliary that flows from Hydriot pipes is shipped in on tankers. Given the paucity of fresh water and arable land, locals have traditionally sailed for a living and once thrived off a vibrant merchant marine business. The island now benefits from a lot of tourism, and the boats entering and leaving the harbor in the summer are often ferries and yachts from Athens, which is a short ride to the north. There are no cars on Hydra, a circumstance that also tends to lure foreign tourists. When they get off the ferry, the tourists usually encounter a row of men offering donkey rides, the traditional transportation method for the island's steep stone alleys. Hydra is an altogether calm place. Riot police are not usually needed to keep order.

One night in the summer of 2012, however, a bit of disarray erupted on the island following a visit from undercover financial-crime police officers. The officers had visited a century-old fish *taverna* on the harbor called Psaropoula—or "fishing boat"—and reported to have observed several violations take place. Greek restaurant owners are required by law to leave receipts on their customers' tables with the delivery of each order, not at the end of a meal as one would be accustomed to in other parts of the world. The rule is supposed to compel restaurant owners to keep official records of their sales, and make it easier to spot when they don't. The government, badly in need of cash, had freshly elevated the consumption tax on restaurant meals and other purchases to a steep 23 percent, though Aegean islands benefited from a discounted rate. Businesses often skirted the tax with the justification that this allowed them to offer lower prices at a time when their customers, due to the economic situation, were getting increasingly thrifty. At Psaropoula, the officers said several tables had not been given proper receipts. They introduced themselves to the restaurateur, Sevasti Mavrommatis, a stocky woman in her mid-fifties with a liking for floral-patterned blouses, and told her that because her violation was flagrant, she was under arrest. Mavrommatis said her blood pressure surged and she began to tremble and feel faint. "I didn't kill anyone," she told me as she recalled the events a few weeks later. "Why put me in jail with the criminals?" The police grudgingly allowed Mavrommatis to go to the local hospital, and instead arrested her son Ilias, who worked at the restaurant as a waiter. The police planned to transfer him by ferry to a jail on the mainland to get his fingerprints taken, but some locals had other ideas.

The perception of unjust tax treatment has throughout history spawned insurrections, and on Hydra, a minor one was about to occur. As word of what happened made its way around the island, anger brewed. When a rumor spread that police had managed to successfully transport Ilias onto a ferry, an angry crowd of some sixty to eighty locals rushed to the port to liberate him. A number of the insurgents boarded the boat and got into an altercation with the crew. Ilias, however, was not on board. The police officers, having heard of the presence of a growing mob, had abandoned their plan to transport the captive and remained in the small island precinct. Port authority officials said they managed to remove the angry locals from the boat, and it departed, but the ferry company canceled service from the island due to security reasons until the situation was deemed pacified.

As night fell, the insurgents amassed around the local precinct, a quaint stone building in a narrow alley surrounded by buildings that resembled it. The officers inside locked the doors and windows, barricading themselves in for a long night. Outside, the locals cut electricity to the station and began to hurl firecrackers and flares at it from surrounding buildings. "Free Ilias," they yelled. In the early morning hours, riot police arrived from the mainland by boat—Ilias described it as a "warship"—to escort the captive to the port. The rebels responded, coming into physical and verbal conflict with the riot police, wrote a local blogger. This resulted "in the throwing of tear gas, jeering and generally a very unpleasant tension on the harbor side, events that our island has never experienced before."

Ilias had his fingerprints taken on the mainland and was quickly released and returned home. Riot police also returned to the island to escort the financial-crime investigators, who were checking additional establishments. One has to wonder what they were thinking, given that stealth is a requirement for such controls to bear fruit. Locals, it seemed, were amused the second time around. Teenagers snapped selfies with the riot police, and some Hydriots described a carnival-like atmosphere. The returning investigators found no other violations, locals told me, as if this proved local compliance with tax laws. The following day, the Greek press eagerly reported on the episode, and the news was covered in northern Europe too, where it was taken as further proof of Greece's unruliness. A lot of locals found the unfavorable attention embarrassing. "It's not nice for our little island to have police here," the mayor at the time told me in his office, which was covered with Victorian-like portraits of prominent Hydriots. "You're a Greek," he added. "What you write has to be correct for our country so an ugly picture of Greece doesn't come out abroad."

The controls were part of a broader government campaign to fulfill the central demand of its creditors: that the Greek government collect more taxes. Tax evasion in Greece was a national preoccupation. The pervasiveness of the habit, and the government's enduring unwillingness to do anything about it, was more than any other factor the cause of Greece's financial troubles. Had more Greeks paid their taxes, the country's debt crisis may have been altogether avoided (assuming, perhaps unrealistically, some degree of responsible use of the hypothetical funds on the part of the government). But because the government had long allowed, even enabled, widespread tax evasion, it now faced the challenge of determining where to begin cracking down. One significant area of tax evasion involved the consumption tax on everyday purchases such as restaurant meals. While people deal in cash and off the books in order to avoid sales tax most everywhere, it was a particularly common phenomenon in Greece, where finding an offense of this type was like shooting fish in a barrel. The summer of the Hydra episode, the finance ministry, which, in addition to the police, conducted its own checks of restaurants and businesses in tourist areas, said it found violations at more than half of the some 4,000 establishments it visited, totaling 31,237 offenses. The annual revenue loss from uncollected consumption tax in Greece amounted to 10 billion euros a year, according to a 2014 report by the European Commission, over 5 percent of its gross domestic product.

Despite stepped-up enforcement efforts like the one on Hydra, however, people actually avoided the tax more as Greece's economic collapse deepened. That is because consumers had less money to spend, which meant not only that they did not consume as much, but that when they did, they also made a greater effort to avoid paying taxes. The growing disinclination to pay also had a lot to do with the fact that a slew of other new taxes were being implemented around that time, such as a hefty property tax automatically tacked onto electricity bills as a way of trying to ensure payment; not paying the tax potentially meant getting your electricity cut. Greeks scornfully called the new property tax the *haratsi*, after a hated levy imposed by the Ottomans. The new and hiked taxes meant that many people's overall tax burden was rising just as their incomes were plunging. Compounded with stepped-up enforcement measures, it all seemed unfair and heavy-handed to a lot of Greeks, particularly because many believed that, while the obligation to pay for the crisis was being loaded on them, enforcement measures did not apply to the worst tax evaders—the rich, the powerful, and the politically connected.

The Hydra episode therefore sparked an emotional debate. Why should a humble tavern owner receive stern justice while the rich remained seemingly untouched? Shortly after the Hydra incident, the conservative-led Greek government felt obliged to justify the action. "The huge problem of tax evasion plagues the Greek economy, canceling every effort for recovery and hope," the government spokesman said. "Wherever this tax evasion comes from, whatever its source, it must be controlled and stamped out immediately and exemplarily," he said. "The demise of the state will not be tolerated." In response, the far-left opposition, Syriza, repeatedly accused the government of an unwillingness to go after the moneyed elite to which it was tied. "The restaurateur in Hydra, you took her in handcuffed," Alexis Tsipras, the party leader, said in the Greek parliament. Would the government likewise handcuff and lock up the big tax dodgers who had hidden billions of euros in foreign bank accounts? "We are waiting to see. You won't take them. We will take them, though."

At the heart of the debate over the Hydra episode was a critical question. The government had run up what amounted to a very large and growing credit card bill of over 300 billion euros. Who ought to pay? In Hydra, the battlefront over this question was roughly partitioned between the wealthy people arriving for vacation on yachts and the island residents who catered to them for a living. That was evident one morning when I walked into a bookstore on the island to buy a reporter's notebook and found two men in the middle of an argument.

"Was what happened on Hydra a good thing?" said one of the men, a vacationing fifty-nine-year-old who was buying a newspaper.

"If you kick a dog, it will bite you!" yelled the owner of the shop, who had a comparatively pallid complexion opposite the vacationer and was justifying the local rebellion.

The vacationer, who wore a T-shirt that said ECONOMICS across the front, contended that a small amount of tax evasion from a lot of small businesses added up to generate "a very big problem." He said he had a company that imported spare parts for cars, and bigger businesses such as his could not avoid taxes as easily as shopkeepers and tavern owners could. "I who eat and drink here, no one gave me receipts unless I asked!" he yelled at the shop owner before heading off to enjoy the cloudless day on a rented motorboat.

The shop owner then discussed the issue with me for an additional half hour. It was no coincidence, he said, that the police arrived on the island just before Prime Minister Samaras took a trip to Berlin to see the German chancellor. "He wanted to show, 'I'm a good boy. I'm going to stop tax evasion,'" the store owner said. "They haven't even begun with the tax evasion of the big capital"—a phrase used by Greek leftists to refer to the rich capitalist elite. "There is no justice." I paid for my notebook with some change, and the shop owner dutifully gave me a receipt.

That evening, I stopped by Psaropoula, the restaurant at the center of the debate. It was primely located on the seaside promenade not far from where the ferries docked. Most of the establishments along the harbor were empty, as people were still waking up from their late afternoon siestas. A growing shroud of evening shade encroached on the town, though the rocky cliffs above it were still brightly illuminated, creating a contrast that my eyes worked hard to reconcile. Inside, I found Sevasti Mavrommatis in the kitchen grilling sardines. The waiter, her son Ilias, who was nearly thirty and had a slight goatee, sat at the cash register underneath a row of icons, counting change collected in ziplock bags. As I waited at a table by the door for them to finish their tasks, I examined the large black-and-white family photographs hanging on the wall. In one of the pictures, a young Mavrommatis in an embroidered dress and white shoes stood next to the restaurant entrance looking happily at the camera while her handsome, grinning father embraced her. The restaurant had been in the family for four generations, and despite Greece's economic problems, business still seemed to be going okay. The instability of the previous few months—two parliamentary elections within a month, massive protests, a bank run over fears the country would exit the euro—were developments that tended to discourage foreign visitors, and Greece that year suffered the consequences with regard to tourism. Still, the island received a loyal mix of affluent Athenians and foreign returnees.

When Ilias joined me at the table, he told me he didn't know why the police wrote them up for what he said were eleven violations. The restaurant, he said, had only three tables at the time for which there were open orders, and receipts for those were on the way. "The whole situation is strange." His mother joined us at the table and told me she offered to pay the officers a fine for any accidental offense, but an arrest seemed very excessive. "I ask you for humanity," she said she told the officers. As I jotted this down in my notebook, a passing customer in a pink dress paused at our table. "The only business that doesn't steal is this one!" she told me in reference to its tax obligations, and then proceeded to the toilet.

Ilias put the number of locals who rallied to his defense that evening at one to two hundred. "They were angry," he said. "Three-fourths of homes have had their electricity cut," he said, very much exaggerating the number of people who suffered the consequences of not being able to afford the *haratsi*. He and his mother, he added, worked from morning until night. "The government catches us and leaves the big ones. They can't catch the big ones. Or they don't want to."

"So they come for us," his mother added.

Around the time of Greece's first bailout, a number of news stories about Greeks hiding their swimming pools appeared in the domestic and international press. Pools in Greece are a taxable luxury, and after the Greek government came under increased pressure to stop tax evasion, it announced that it had started using satellite imagery to ascertain the true number of them in the villa-dense suburbs north of Athens. Only a few hundred Greeks had declared their pools in tax forms, and news that authorities were looking from the sky set off an urgent pool-concealment effort and a spike in demand for camouflaging tarp. The government search nevertheless turned up nearly 17,000 pools. Finance ministry officials at the time told reporters stories about doctors and lawyers with posh homes in rich neighborhoods declaring implausibly low incomes, often less than 12,000 euros a year, which was at the time below the taxable threshold. This all had to stop, the politicians said. This represented a change in tone, though. Before the crisis, politicians had often encouraged tax auditors not to work too hard before elections, so as not to dim voters' views of their elected officials. Now the same politicians were publicizing their fledgling efforts to get tough. But their ability to execute substantive change was deeply limited by the Greek bureaucracy's aptitude, which appeared to be more geared toward colluding with tax evaders than busting them. Changing this would not be easy.

One finance ministry employee, a computer science professor hired to develop programs to detect tax evasion—part of the ostensible effort to rein in the practice—resigned from his post in 2011 after determining that his efforts were futile. Senior tax officials displayed no willingness to act on the information he'd been able to collect, the ex-employee said. Tax collectors, he added, often used a "40-40-20 deal" that worked like this: If a collector caught someone who owed 100 euros to the state, the money would be partitioned in a manner that advantaged everyone, though the state less so—40 euros remained with the taxpayer, 40 would go to the tax collector for the service provided, and the state, as a token, received 20. This revelation underscored a major challenge. The government faced a shortage of scrupulous auditors to perform the prodigious task of reining in tax evasion.

This longtime state of affairs was by no means a secret to Greeks. Tax evasion was such an axiom that banks in Greece did not rely on income tax statements as accurate indicators of their customers' true earnings. Therefore, when determining whether to give loans for cars or homes, the banks came up with "adaptation formulas" to approximate true income based on a number of indicators not directly related to their customers' income declarations. Using the formulas and data involving tens of thousands of credit applications provided by one large, anonymous Greek bank, three academics—Nikolaos Artavanis of Virginia Tech, and Adair Morse and Margarita Tsoutsoura, both from the University of Chicago—determined that self-employed people in high-income professions were among Greece's primary tax dodgers. While self-employed workers everywhere tend to underreport their income, the authors found evidence of some particularly audacious underreporting in Greece. For instance, the authors concluded that from 2003 through 2010, doctors, lawyers, accountants, and people working in lodging and restaurants, among other professional groups, made overall monthly debt payments that exceeded total reported monthly income. No bank would lend to someone—let alone whole segments of the workforce—whose debt payments surpass their reported income, but Greek banks did because they knew the reported income was not a reflection of the real thing. This level of apparent tax evasion among the self-employed in Greece was particularly troublesome for state coffers, because some one-third of Greek workers are self-employed, the highest percentage in the European Union and about double the bloc's average. The authors of the study estimated, conservatively, that 28 billion euros of taxable income from self-employed workers went unreported in Greece in 2009—the year the government's finances were revealed to be unsustainably shaky—with lost government revenue amounting to nearly one-third of the deficit that year.

People in Germany, the Netherlands, Finland—eurozone countries that had, with great reservation, participated in Greece's bailouts—read the stories about the swimming pools, or others about an apparently high per capita number of Porsche Cayennes in Greece, or about rich Greek shipping magnates who benefited from constitutionally consecrated tax-exempt status, and were perturbed. One documentary that aired on German public television called *The Greece Lie* encapsulated the common sentiment, posing the question: Why should Germans help finance the Greek government when Greeks didn't seem willing to? In the documentary, a Greek shipowner, introduced by the theatrical, menacing voice of the narrator as a "tycoon," appears on camera looking comfortable and wealthy in a sky-blue sport jacket as he gazes over the bow of his yacht. The tycoon announces that one ought not to pay taxes to a mismanaged, corrupt state. "Would you give your money to Al Capone?"

In addition to *The Greece Lie*, the German magazine *Der Spiegel* once ran the cover story "The Poverty Lie: How Europe's Crisis Countries Are Hiding Their Fortunes." The article was inspired by a European Central Bank survey which found that people in Greece—as well as in Cyprus and Spain, countries that also received bailouts—had higher levels of household wealth than Germans. While Greece's government was broke, this information suggested, its people were not. In Germany, on the other hand, people weren't doing as well as the government, which was relatively well financed. Median household wealth in Greece was double that of Germany, largely due to the fact that Greeks far more often than Germans own their own homes, and often more than one of them. The data used in the survey was in large part collected before the economic consequences of the European debt crisis set in, and many Greek commentators claimed the statistics were misleading or propagandistic. German chancellor Angela Merkel—likely cognizant of the political consequences of her electorate feeling like it was being shortchanged—agreed the survey result was "distorted," telling the newspaper *Bild* that it did not include Germans' high pension entitlements or assets abroad. Indeed, there was some truth to what Merkel was saying. Germans willingly transfer more money to the state with the faith that they will see it returned to them in the form of good benefits and services. What she didn't say, however, was that a lot of Greeks, though less willing to give their money to the state, had been receiving pretty good pension benefits anyway, at least relative to what they had been contributing.

The Troika wanted more affluent Greek families to cough up some of their hidden wealth, and the increased property taxes, in particular, were a way of getting at it. In an interview with *The Guardian* a few months before the Hydra episode, Christine Lagarde, the head of the IMF, one of Greece's creditors, sounded rather unsympathetic to the effects of austerity in Greece, focusing her attention on tax evasion instead. The interviewer asked Lagarde if she was ignoring the possible consequences when demanding cuts that could mean "women won't have access to a midwife when they give birth, and patients won't get life saving drugs, and the elderly will die alone for lack of care." Lagarde replied: "No, I think more of the little kids from a school in a little village in Niger who get teaching two hours a day, sharing one chair for three of them, and who are very keen to get an education. I have them in my mind all the time. Because I think they need even more help than the people in Athens." Lagarde added: "As far as Athens is concerned, I also think about all those people who are trying to escape tax all the time. All these people in Greece who are trying to escape tax." These comments seemed rather insensitive to a lot of Greeks, and Lagarde's Facebook page was inundated with thousands of angry messages. Lagarde then tried to make amends by writing that she was "very sympathetic to the Greek people and the challenges they are facing," but emphasized again that Greeks, especially the most privileged, should pay their taxes. At the time, Greek politicians were running for election, and many publicly denounced Lagarde for the comments, accusing her of stereotyping and humiliating the Greek people. "Greek workers pay their taxes, which are unbearable," Alexis Tsipras said in response, before going on to criticize the government for its failure to go after "big capital."

The widespread perception that the government was exempting the wealthy and the powerful from its tax-collection campaign was confirmed a few months after the Hydra uprising, when a Greek investigative journalist named Kostas Vaxevanis published the names of some two thousand Greeks said to have accounts in a Geneva branch of HSBC. The names—which included a lot of prominent people, such as relatives of former and acting government ministers—constituted the so-called Lagarde List, after Christine Lagarde. A few years earlier, Lagarde had been French finance minister when her government obtained information on thousands of Europeans with undeclared Swiss bank accounts. French authorities used the information to investigate domestic tax evasion and passed on pertinent information to other European nations so they could do the same. In 2010, the French government passed along a CD of information concerning Greeks to Lagarde's colleague Giorgos Papaconstantinou, a boyish-looking PASOK politician who was serving as Greek finance minister at the time. Papaconstantinou, who later said the sum of the account deposits in question amounted to some two billion dollars, was presumably the right person to see to it that an investigation be launched. By the time Vaxevanis published the names, however, two years had passed and no investigation had taken place. Papaconstantinou later said the original CD had been misplaced, though a copy of the data had been made. From that copy, it turned out, information concerning three people on the list was deleted— that of Papaconstantinou's cousin and two other relatives. Papaconstantinou was later accused of tampering with the list, and the Greek parliament voted to revoke the immunity he received as an ex-minister. A special court eventually found Papaconstantinou guilty of a misdemeanor for document tampering and sentenced him to a one-year suspended prison term, while acquitting him on a felony charge of attempted breach of faith. All along, Papaconstantinou maintained his innocence, denied deleting the names, and said he had been framed. In a speech in parliament, he said he was being scapegoated for the country's misfortunes because, as the finance minister in the early days of the debt crisis, he had performed the unpopular duty of signing on to the first bailout.

A swift investigation may not have come for the people actually on the list; however, it did for Vaxevanis, the journalist who published it in his magazine. Right after it hit the stands, Vaxevanis, a persistent thorn in the side of the Greek government, was arrested, charged with violating a personal data protections law, and had his trial fast-tracked so that it would take place just a few days later. Vaxevanis was acquitted, but a prosecutor found the ruling to be mistaken and ordered a retrial. A year later, Vaxevanis was again found innocent. At the same time, investigations of people on the Lagarde List remained extremely spare and slow. "In Ancient Greek mythology, justice is presented as blind," Vaxevanis wrote in *The Guardian* after his arrest. "In modern Greece, it is merely winking and nodding." The Lagarde List, he added, showed how "the entire system of power" transferred money abroad, and this much had been uncovered only by examining accounts at a single Swiss bank branch. "Meanwhile in Greece, people are going through dumpsters for food."

Vaxevanis was right, and while many affluent Greeks were evading both taxes and justice, other people were suffering. A lot of the Greeks I saw picking through dumpsters in Athens were old and decently dressed people who had given their pension money away to their struggling children or grandchildren. After witnessing scenes like this, I struggled to try to understand the central narrative of the Greek crisis. Were Greeks wealthy and hiding their money from the government—in other words, actors in the so-called poverty lie? Or were they suffering the effects of austerity policies and economic ruin?

After a while, I realized I should stop trying to choose between the two narratives, because both were true. Economic collapses have the unfortunate tendency to disproportionately impact the most vulnerable people in any society, and this was certainly the case in Greece, where income inequality had already long been high by European standards, and the welfare system, which often served special-interest groups rather than the most needy, was piecemeal and fractured. Greece was one of only two EU countries—Italy being the other one—with no nationwide minimum income benefit. While family bonds in Greece provided an informal safety net, this too increasingly frayed as the economic downturn endured. By the end of 2013, 36 percent of the Greek population was "at risk of poverty or social exclusion," according to the EU statistics office. Only Bulgaria and Romania fared worse. One out of every five Greeks suffered severe material deprivation—being unable to afford basic household necessities, pay their mortgages, or adequately heat their homes. What had begun as a public debt crisis in Greece was increasingly becoming a private debt crisis as a rising number of Greeks—faced with lower incomes, an increased tax burden, and mass unemployment—were going broke like their government. Most worrying, families with young children constituted a growing proportion of the Greeks falling into poverty. These were the people who didn't have money to hide in offshore accounts, yet they were paying the highest price for the country's problems.

Many of the most desperate people in Greece gave up hope that things would ever change, that economic opportunity would return, that Greek politicians would create a more just system. One encounter in particular drove this point home for me. It took place not in Greece but in Swabia, a hilly, prosperous region of southwest Germany, a place I visited in the spring of 2013. Swabia, known in Germany for its inhabitants' orderliness and parsimony, is home to a thriving auto industry that has long lured laborers from southern Europe, including many Greeks. Most of them initially came in the sixties and seventies. By the time of my visit, however, a new generation of Greeks was arriving as the economic situation back home was creating an annual exodus of tens of thousands of people. In a small Swabian town dotted with half-timbered houses, I took a tour of a fulfillment warehouse. Business was great, the owner, the son of Greek immigrants, told me, a circumstance that was allowing him to hire some of the Greek newcomers. As we walked around, I met one of them, a slender thirty-eight-year-old woman named Maria Saoulidou. She was hanging packages of children's party supplies—red balloons and yellow streamers—onto a rack that was to be shipped, store-ready, to a discount retailer. Saoulidou had recently arrived from a small city in northern Greece. She told me the supermarket she used to work at there had stopped paying her and the other employees. For a while, she kept on working at the supermarket anyway in the hope that a paycheck would be forthcoming, but it wasn't. Things were not going much better for her husband, a truck driver. When they ran out of money, the couple decided to try to start a new life in Germany, where an already established immigrant uncle could help with the transition. The couple left their two young sons behind in Greece with the childrens' grandparents and left for Swabia. They lived in a basement apartment near the warehouse, a gloomy, dank rental that was sparsely furnished with a mattress and a couple of chairs. They would send for the kids once they were able to establish a suitable home, Saoulidou told me. She missed her boys dearly, of course. "It's very hard," she said, nearly in tears with a package of balloons in her gloved hand. I looked down at the floor and noticed that one of her sneakers was badly torn open near the toe. Once the boys arrived in Germany, she said, the family would never return to Greece for more than a visit. "We're not looking after our future," she said. "We're looking after the future of our children, and unfortunately, there is none for them in Greece."

. . .

The case of the politician Apostolos Tsochatzopoulos demonstrates why, in the eyes of many Greeks, the government lacked the moral authority to tax them. Tsochatzopoulos had attained great wealth through great treachery; he had "eaten" public money ravenously and came to personify the misconduct and avarice of the political elite and their oligarchical peers. He was one of the few powerful people to be punished for such wrongdoing, which made him an unwilling representative of the whole class of corrupt big ones. Utter the five syllables of his last name in an Athens taxi—pronounced *Tso-ha-dzo-pou-los*—and you will invariably hear a tirade against him. Tsochatzopoulos, who sat in a prison cell in an Athens suburb during my time in Greece, is probably the most hated man in the country.

In order to understand the story of how he made himself wealthy at great cost to the nation, one must go back to a late December day in 1995, when a Turkish cargo ship ran into an islet—in essence, a large rock—jutting from the sea some miles off the Anatolian coast. The accident triggered a dispute over whether the rock in question—about ten acres of crag inhabited by wild goats but not people—and another outcrop next to it belonged to Greece or Turkey. Greek authorities, certain of the islet's Greek proprietorship, offered to tug the cargo ship, but the Turkish captain initially demurred, arguing the rock was in fact Turkish, and therefore a Turkish boat should detach it instead. The countries, of course, had a long and famous history of antagonism; they sparred incessantly over the fate of the divided island nation of Cyprus, and feuded over Aegean territorial waters and airspace. At first, this dispute seemed somewhat mundane. The Turkish ship eventually accepted a Greek tug, and later, the Greek and Turkish foreign ministries quietly exchanged notes expressing their competing claims over the islet, known as Imia to Greeks and Kardak to Turks. But the matter was by no means finished.

At the time, Tsochatzopoulos was the acting prime minister, serving in place of his ailing mentor, Andreas Papandreou, PASOK's populist founder. Tsochatzopoulos's PASOK roots stretched back to the late 1960s, when he was a student studying civil engineering in Munich, and an American-backed, military dictatorship known as the Regime of the Colonels ruled Greece. In Germany, Tsochatzopoulos joined Papandreou's antidictatorial Panhellenic Liberation Movement, which operated in exile. The organization's aims would later become PASOK's stated agenda: the reduction of American Cold War influence over Greek affairs, and a socialist economic transformation. The dictatorship crumbled in 1974, and the Panhellenic Socialist Movement, or PASOK, was officially born. Seven years later, Papandreou was elected prime minister and set about increasing government spending and socializing indebted private companies, though he backtracked on pledges to withdraw from NATO and close U.S. bases in Greece. The victory ushered in more than two decades of nearly continuous PASOK rule. The party's triumph also commenced a long ministerial career for Tsochatzopoulos, who came to be known by the diminutive "Akis." Tsochatzopoulos was first appointed minister of public works, and over the duration of PASOK's reign, he remained minister of something or other. Tsochatzopoulos, a dapper man with dark, shrewd eyes and an angular face carved with deep lines, was a smooth talker and maintained a somewhat genteel demeanor. Papandreou was said to have referred to him as "Beau Brummel," after the extravagant nineteenth-century English dandy. Tsochatzopoulos's fealty to the party leader was condensed into a joke: "What time is it, Akis?" Papandreou asked Tsochatzopoulos. "Whatever time you want it to be," replied his devotee.

A few weeks after the boat hit the rock, the aging Papandreou resigned from the premiership due to his rapidly deteriorating health. The loyal Tsochatzopoulos, already acting in his place, was considered a likely replacement. The PASOK faction, however, narrowly elected Tsochatzopoulos's rival, Costas Simitis, to take over the premiership instead. Simitis, whose main goal was to lead Greece into the eurozone, was an unassuming, mild-mannered former professor, seen as a pro-European "modernizer." He had none of the bombast of his predecessor—with whom he often clashed—and, for his technocratic disposition, was derided by his detractors as "the accountant." Two days before Simitis's inauguration, a Greek magazine published a story concerning the "sudden uprising" of a severe provocation from Turkey—the month-old Imia territorial dispute. Soon, Greek newspapers devoted themselves to covering the story, writing things like: "The Turks, who are betting on the weakness of the government, want our island." The abrupt emergence of Imia press coverage following Simitis's victory was not entirely accidental. Simitis's political adversaries relished the opportunity to make him look weak, and employed their vassals in the media to do so.

The conflict with Turkey rapidly escalated. At one point, in order to underscore the islet's Greek nature, a boatload of patriotic visitors from a nearby Greek island visited it. The seafarers consisted of a few men, a priest wearing black vestments, two young boys, and a Greek television journalist with his cameraman. By the time they arrived on the rock, tensions between the two nations had escalated. Fighter jets zoomed overhead and naval boats from both countries navigated aggressively close to one another in the surrounding waters. As this went on, the Greek television camera filmed the visitors holding Greek flags and singing the national anthem. "We place the country above all, and our souls are here, always on the Greek islands, and we're up here now at this moment, and we claim what is ours," the priest told the camera. He and his companions were *"Akritai,"* the priest added, a term for the warriors that defended the Byzantine Empire's eastern frontier from Muslim invaders. "Whoever comes here must first pass over my dead body."

At another point, journalists from the major Turkish newspaper *Hürriyet*, demonstrating an acutely excessive vision of advocacy journalism, landed on the rock with a helicopter, removed a Greek flag earlier visitors had put up, and replaced it with a

Turkish one. *Hürriyet* then splashed a large photo of the action on its front page with the headline "Battle Flag." In response to the Turkish journalists' action, the Greek government sent special forces to the rock, and the Greek flag was restored. The Turks responded by sending their own commandos to the adjacent rock. A score of warships raced to the scene. A Greek helicopter at some point crashed into the sea, killing three crew members. This pageant of human folly might have resulted in a full-scale armed conflict had not U.S. diplomats and President Bill Clinton made some last-minute calls and brokered an agreement for both sides to forgo putting flags on the rocks, and back down from the brink of war.

The Imia episode traumatized the many Greeks who considered their nation's sovereignty over the islets irrefutable, and the American-brokered withdrawal a kind of national chickening-out. (Greece in fact had a far better legal claim over Imia, an American diplomat later determined.) When the newly inaugurated Simitis, during a speech in parliament, thanked the United States for its help during the Imia crisis, he was roundly jeered. Simitis was widely criticized for his handling of the dispute, including from the traditionalist, more nationalist wing of PASOK represented by Tsochatzopoulos, who continued over the following months to challenge Simitis for control of the party. In what was seen as an effort to mend the party rift and mollify his rival, Simitis later made Tsochatzopoulos minister of defense. This was an influential post, particularly at the time.

Greece, due to its interminable rivalry with Turkey, had long been an avid weapons buyer, and as a percent of its GDP, it spent far more than most other European Union nations on its military. But the sense of humiliation among Greeks over the Imia incident led to calls for a new and very large weapons purchasing program. This provided Tsochatzopoulos with potentially monumental job perks. Graft was not an uncommon aspect of Greek governance, but the scale of armaments contracts at the defense ministry provided officials with superior, albeit illicit, possibilities for financial gain. A prominent Greek investigate reporter, Tasos Telloglou, once put it to me like this: "Look, you must be very naive to believe that anybody in this country that goes to the ministry of defense and would have a budget would not become rich."

Following the Imia conflict, Greece launched a massive military modernization program, amounting to nearly 17 billion dollars. Over the next decade, Greece bought American fighter jets, German submarines, Russian surface-to-air missiles, Slovak artillery guns, and later on, German panzers, among many other weapons. The splurge meant that between 2002 and 2006, small Greece became the world's fourth largest arms importer, according to the Stockholm International Peace Research Institute. Suspicions that Tsochatzopoulos had seized the opportunity to enrich himself off this excess arose in 2004, a few years after he left the defense ministry. That year, he married his second wife, Vasiliki Stamati, who was later described by her family as a humble, small-town girl, a former employee for the public electric company who would often return to her parents' village in central Greece to help with chores around the house. The wedding with Tsochatzopoulos that year, though, did not seem a humble affair to most Greeks. It took place in Paris, and the former defense minister arrived at the ceremony in a "shimmering blue Jaguar," according to media reports. The party was held at the Four Seasons, where the pair also stayed, while other guests complained of having been put up in less luxurious accommodations. This all seemed rather expensive, and Greeks wondered how Tsochatzopoulos could afford such luxuries on a minister's salary, which alone would make one affluent but not that wealthy. "How did you get rich, Mr. Tsochatzopoulos?" read the headline of an article in the newspaper *Kathimerini* at the time. People were especially bothered by the fact that Tsochatzopoulos was an ostensible socialist who had spoken out against "big capital," and in favor of social justice and solidarity. Now, some reports contended that he and his wife had stayed in the Four Seasons' 2,630-square-foot, antique-furnished Royal Suite, which according to some rankings was among the top ten or fifteen most expensive hotel rooms in the world. Tsochatzopoulos later said the pair did not stay in an expensive room, and that the media reports were part of an effort to defame him. There were "normal rooms for all people" at the hotel, he said.

Shortly after the wedding, a Greek prosecutor sent parliament case files concerning a couple of Tsochatzopoulos-era armaments purchases, citing information that may have implicated the former minister in wrongdoing. The prosecutor was obliged to submit the files to parliament because, under Greek law, he could not investigate the matter himself. The Greek constitution protects ministers, current and former, from prosecution or investigation on matters relating to the exercise of their duties unless parliament votes to allow it. A special parliamentary committee was therefore formed to carry out a preliminary examination of the deals in question—one for American radar systems critics considered useless and unsuitable for the military's needs, and the other for Russian surface-to-air missile systems deemed too expensive and marginally functional. The committee released a report on its findings, though its members arrived at widely disparate conclusions—split along political lines—on their significance. Those committee members belonging to the then ruling New Democracy party raised some seemingly pertinent questions. With regard to the Russian missile systems in particular, why had the defense ministry awarded a direct contract to buy twenty-one of them for some 800 million dollars when a Greek military review panel had determined the weapons did not meet the necessary specifications, whereas missile systems from other manufacturers did? Also, what was the role of three companies—Drumilan International Hellas A.E., based in Athens; Drumilan Offset Programme Ltd., based in Cyprus; and Drumilan International Ltd.,

which owned 99 percent of the shares of the other two companies and was based in the British Virgin Islands—in the transfer of large sums of money related to the deal? The companies, a
Greek court decided years later, were involved in laundering some
25 million dollars in kickbacks related to the deal, money that
ended up in various international bank accounts connected to Tsochatzopoulos.

PASOK members of the parliamentary committee determined
that Tsochatzopoulos had been "unjustly offended and scorned."
One PASOK committee member, a heavy man named Evangelos Venizelos—later to become the party leader—told parliament
that the committee was "an excellent forum for the disclosure of
reality." Reality, according to him, was that New Democracy was
trying to create a baseless scandal in order to damage his party,
and that no wrongdoing had been proven. The matter, Venizelos said, had "evaporated." To a large extent, it seemed that way.
The Greek parliament did not vote to prosecute Tsochatzopoulos,
though questions about the deals persisted. A few months after
the parliamentary committee submitted its findings, a Russian
court sentenced two former executives of the JSC concern Almaz-
Antey, the manufacturer of the surface-to-air missiles, to four-
year jail terms for abuse of power. The Russian court determined
the company had bestowed monetary "benefits to third parties"
in connection with the Greek deal. The bribers had been caught.
The question of who was apparently bribed, however, remained
unresolved.

Tsochatzopoulos came under scrutiny again in 2010 for his
unexplained apparent wealth. The newspaper *Kathimerini* wrote
that his wife had purchased a three-story neoclassical house on
Greece's most prime strip of residential real estate, the street of
Dionysiou Areopagitou, a pedestrian road opposite the Acropolis,
with a clear view of the Parthenon. She had bought it for 1.1 million euros, a lot of it paid in cash, from Nobilis International LLC,
a company based in Cheyenne, Wyoming. Nobilis had earlier

bought the house from another offshore company, Torcaso Investment Ltd., based in Cyprus, which happened, as it turned out, to be held by Tsochatzopoulos's cousin, a man who later admitted to laundering a lot of money for the defense minister. Living in a house owned by an offshore firm appeared to be a way for the former minister and his wife to enjoy the asset while avoiding tax liability. Their decision to buy the house from Nobilis was motivated by the impending passage of a new law on "the restoration of tax justice and the tackling of tax evasion," which was going to quintuple levies on properties in Greece owned by offshore companies, *Kathimerini* reported.

By this time, the political climate in Greece was far different than it had been five years earlier, when the parliamentary committee examined a few Tsochatzopoulos-era armaments deals. The country was on the verge of bankruptcy. The government was cutting wages and pensions. People were angry. Comedians joked bitterly about the many thousands of euros Tsochatzopoulos's wife was said to have spent on curtains for the bedroom. For all this, a big one finally had to be sacrificed. A leading prosecutor ordered a preliminary investigation into whether there were tax violations or other offenses involving Tsochatzopoulos's house. PASOK suspended Tsochatzopoulos from the party pending the results of the inquiry. This time, his colleagues were not going to defend him.

From that point on, things started going very badly for Tsochatzopoulos. Prosecutors in Munich had begun an investigation of the Germany-based company Ferrostaal, an "industrial service provider with industrial expertise and financing competence," in its own words. One particular financing competence prosecutors were interested in involved the suspected payout of bribes, largely pertaining to submarine deals with Greece struck during Tsochatzopoulos's defense ministry tenure. By this point, the submarine deals in question were already infamous in Greece. A decade earlier, the defense ministry had agreed to buy some state-of-the-art German submarines from a consortium of Ferrostaal and Howaldtswerke-Deutsche Werft, or HDW, a shipbuilding company based in the Baltic Sea port city of Kiel. HDW at the time had developed new "Type 214" diesel-electric submarines and was looking for its first international buyer. In order to win over the Greeks, German prosecutors later found, Ferrostaal managers solicited the services of a group of people they called the "prayer circle." The circle had connections in Greece and could convince Greek defense officials of the benefits of choosing the German vessels. The German companies' prayers apparently came true. The Greeks decided to buy four of the new submarines as part of a program dubbed Archimedes, after the ancient mathematician and scientist. In addition, the two sides signed a second deal for the modernization of three old German submarines already in the Greek navy's possession. Greece paid out some two billion euros, most of the initial cost of both programs.

The deals did not work out very well. The first new submarine, built in Kiel, had troubles during trial runs, at least according to Greek naval officers, who said it tilted at a precariously severe angle under certain conditions. HDW representatives said some initial problems were fixed and that the tilt was normal. "No big deal except taking care of your coffee cup," one retired German naval captain told a Greek television program. The two sides fell into a long dispute. The German manufacturer accused the Greek side of failing to honor the contract and of complaining about the sub in order to delay further payments. Whatever the case, the dispute meant that a decade after the Imia incident inspired the urgent purchase of expensive submarines, Greece still didn't have any new or refurbished subs to show for it. In 2010, months after the Greek government agreed to the first bailout, it reached a complex agreement with HDW to supplant the disputed deals with a new one. Greece decided to finally take the "leaning submarine," as it had become known among Greeks, fairly or not, in addition to five more vessels of the same type. One of Greece's old subs would also be refurbished. The agreement came at an additional cost to the Greek government of over one billion euros. By this point, however, bankruptcy posed a far more imminent threat to Greece than did the Turks, and buying subs did not seem like a wise expenditure. Even as its creditors were compelling it to deeply slash social spending, the Greek government was still buying German subs and other weapons. This fact wasn't well received by a lot of Greeks.

The submarines came to symbolize both Greek government fecklessness and German hegemony. I once ran into a distant uncle of mine, a farmer, selling fruit at an outdoor market in Athens. He had with him a small machine for printing receipts—an unusual sight at a farmers' market, but financial-crime investigators had recently visited to see if the vendors were documenting their sales. I watched him print out a receipt for a lady who bought two lemons for a couple of dozen cents, and I thought it was a pretty absurd sight. My uncle told me he viewed the situation like this: billions for undelivered subs, and receipts for lemons. My uncle, a cigarette-rolling former hippie with a gray beard, was normally a very calm guy, but the submarines issue made him angry, not only with his own government, but the German one too: "They're stomping us with their boot!" Greeks felt still worse about the subs after a German court at the end of 2011 convicted two Ferrostaal managers of bribing Greek officials in order to secure the initial submarine deals. This, it turned out, would be one of several bribery investigations involving European—often German—armaments makers and Greek defense officials. In this case, Ferrostaal was fined 140 million euros.

This time, the alleged bribe recipient was eventually held accountable. Tsochatzopoulos was arrested in 2012 at his home across from the Acropolis. The house proved to be the key that allowed prosecutors to trace the trail of kickbacks in connection with the German subs. A maze of bank account transfers led to Torcaso, the offshore company that had years earlier bought the home. Tsochatzopoulos was first convicted of failing to properly declare his assets and was sentenced to eight years in prison. He was later convicted of laundering tens of millions of dollars worth of kickbacks not only related to the German subs programs but also connected to the deal for Russian surface-to-air missiles that had come under scrutiny years earlier. He was sentenced to twenty years in prison. The penalty was technically for money laundering and not for accepting bribes, prosecutors told me, because as an ex-minister, Tsochatzopoulos was immune from prosecution for the latter crime. More than a dozen other people were convicted of crimes in connection with the case, including Tsochatzopoulos's wife, his daughter, his ex-wife, his cousin, his accountant, and his right-hand man at the defense ministry.

The Tsochatzopoulos case opened up a lot of additional leads for investigators to follow, and, as some of Greece's top prosecutors told me, even though they had caught the former minister, they had barely scratched the surface of the bribery and money laundering associated with armaments spending. The defense ministry had been functioning like a shadowy organized crime network. There was no independent audit agency with the power to review the contracts, and one defense ministry official who resigned in 2010 announced on Greek television that every armaments contract since 1996 was flawed. Prosecutors told me they estimated that Greece had spent some 10 to 15 billion euros on armaments from 1998 to 2002, and that between 7 and 10 percent of the value of the contracts—up to 1.5 billion euros—consisted of illegal payments.

Following Tsochatzopoulos's conviction, one Greek defense ministry official of not particularly high rank testified that he had expressed reservations about a proposal to buy a large number of tanks from the German company Krauss-Maffei Wegmann.

Then, he said, a Greek representative of the German company left a bag filled with 600,000 euros cash in his office. "I indeed ceased objecting to that procurement," testified the official, who said he accrued many millions of dollars in bribes related to various arms deals over five years on the job. Greece—this was in the post-Tsochatzopoulos era—ended up buying 170 German Leopard 2 tanks for 1.7 billion euros. Both Krauss-Maffei Wegmann's German headquarters and their Greek representative—a celebrity in the armaments field whom people speaking with me referred to as "the king" and "the emperor"—denied giving bribes. As of the end of 2014, no charges had been filed, though an investigation into the tank deal was ongoing. Many defense experts questioned the wisdom of the purchase, arguing the tanks would be useful only in case of a protracted land war, which seemed an unlikely prospect. More questions about the tanks' usefulness were raised when the Greek press reported that they did not come with ammunition, leading many to ask what good ultramodern tanks were if they had nothing to fire.

Though Tsochatzopoulos became an object of near-universal scorn, and his fellow politicians joined in deriding him, it is exceedingly difficult to believe that no one outside Tsochatzopoulos's immediate circle knew something was very much amiss in the defense ministry. I tried talking to several high-ranking politicians and defense ministry officials about this, and almost no one was willing to discuss the issue with me. The few officials who initially agreed to speak with me either didn't show up for scheduled interviews or, in one case, contacted me afterward to demand I speak not a word of our meeting. During the prolonged, nerve-racking, and utterly futile effort, I began to feel like I was going around asking master chefs to reveal to me their secret recipes. I wasn't going to get very far.

As he sat in prison, Tsochatzopoulos continued to deny all charges against him and said he was being singled out by "centers of power" for "political and moral annihilation." It's not hard to understand why he may have felt that way. The political system that had nurtured him was now allowing him to become the mascot of its worst ills. Throughout his money-laundering trial, Tsochatzopoulos repeatedly emphasized that a government council consisting of various other ministers and the prime minister had also signed on to the weapons program. For the whole truth to come out, he said, the others, too, must appear in court. That never happened, though Tsochatzopoulos kept pleading for it. "In the climate of the times, everything is in the light," he once told television cameras before his conviction, speaking slowly and deliberately, pausing to look up into the empty space around him as if finding the words there. "All the truth to the people, as they say."

Just as Greece went on the post-Imia weapons-spending splurge, it also launched an effort to enter the eurozone. In order to gain membership, Greece, like all the other members, had to cut its annual deficit to below 3 percent of gross domestic product. Greece was able to meet this requirement—an impressive accomplishment for a country that in 1995, before the Imia episode, was running a deficit of over 9 percent of GDP. Based on its apparent budget discipline, Greece was welcomed into the currency union on New Year's Day 2001. The nation's deficit, as initially reported, stayed well below the 3 percent limit through the first years of its membership. Greece was therefore able to drastically boost armaments spending while maintaining strict budget discipline. How was it able to do this?

Not everyone believed the numbers Greece was reporting. Some investment bankers in London had taken to calling the head of Greek statistics "the magician" for his ability to make deficits disappear. The deficits, however, reappeared later, when

Greek authorities, under the supervision of Eurostat, the European Union statistical office, revised the country's 1997 through 2003 numbers. In reality, it turned out, Greece's deficit had never fallen below 3 percent of GDP, though it came close in 1999—the year its fiscal performance was assessed for eurozone membership. In other words, the Greek government, while having done a lot to improve its finances in the years leading up to its euro entry, had never quite met the criteria. Greece's accounting of military expenditures—or rather, lack thereof—provided a central reason for the big revisions, Eurostat reported in 2004. The data on weapons spending were apparently inconsistent and contradictory going back as far as 1994, or even earlier, according to the agency. Greece at one point told Eurostat that it recorded armaments expenditures when the arms were delivered. At another point, it said such military information was considered confidential, and therefore the people doing the statistics never received information on deliveries. Most weapons expenditures covered by borrowing from 1997 through 2003 were therefore not recorded. The armaments deals were, in short, off-the-books transactions.

On a summer day in Athens in 2014, I visited Yannos Papantoniou, the PASOK politician who was finance minister in the years leading up to Greece's eurozone entry, and who considered Greece's currency-union admission a crowning achievement of his political career. As such, he did not agree with the conclusion that it was accomplished on false grounds. I met Papantoniou at his office at the Center for Progressive Policy Research, a think tank of which he was president. The morning of my visit, not much seemed to be going on at the center. There was no one there but his assistant and a thin old man who had arrived at the same time as I did. The old man wanted to know why his latest retirement check had come in a few euros under the previous one. The assistant tried to be polite, but suggested the appropriate government office where he could find an answer. After the old man left, Papantoniou came out of his office and shook my hand. He had gone to college at the University of Wisconsin in Madison, earned a PhD in economics at Cambridge, and later became part of PASOK's "modernizing" wing. Following his time as head of the finance ministry, he became defense minister, taking over in the place of Tsochatzopoulos.

Papantoniou wore a suit jacket and khaki pants and flashed his broad, well-practiced smile, though it seemed rather forced. He did not appear to be in a particularly good mood, and this was perhaps understandable. He was coming under a lot of scrutiny at the time for some tax-related matters. His wife's name was on the Lagarde List, and financial investigators, it seemed, were finally making some progress probing it. Some months after I met him, Papantoniou and his wife were convicted of failing to declare assets in 2009, and each was sentenced to a four-year suspended prison term. The couple faced additional charges for the same offense in 2008. Papantoniou was also coming under scrutiny for his tenure at the ministry of defense. Around the time we met, prosecutors were making progress on their investigation of the very large Leopard 2 tank deal, which was completed under Papantoniou's reign. Also, the president of the parliamentary committee that had a decade earlier investigated Tsochatzopoulos was quoted in a Greek newspaper as saying the findings back then had shown that Papantoniou too had partaken in the "party" of kickbacks at the defense ministry. Papantoniou, in response, said there was no evidence he was involved in that party, calling allegations that he had engaged in wrongdoing slander.

When I met him, Papantoniou did not want to talk about the accusations involving the Swiss account—though he had declared his innocence when talking to the Greek press—and he did not want to speak about his time at the defense ministry. "You know, because defense has been blurred with all these accusations." He laughed uncomfortably and added, "I don't want to have my name linked in any way to that story, which is not a very nice one." This seemed to me an untenable position for someone who had served as defense minister, particularly following Tsochatzopoulos. After a few efforts to get him to discuss what he had found at the ministry when he arrived on the job, he said he had contributed to "rationalizing structures and policies."

During our talk, Papantoniou rejected the notion that Greece had cooked its books to get into the eurozone. The 2004 deficit revision was a political maneuver by New Democracy to change the accounting methods on defense spending, he told me, in order to make the previous PASOK government look bad and to make itself look more fiscally disciplined. The revision, he said, had unjustly "maligned the reputation of Greece as a country that is cheating and so on." Papantoniou then ruminated on the debt crisis for a while. Despite the difficulties Greece was facing, he said, euro membership remained the country's best hope for progress. "The argument for a country like Greece to join the EMU"—the European Monetary Union—"to us sort of modernizers in Greek politics was that by forcing this country into a system of rules, it would help the country to improve itself and behave better," he said. "And this remains the hope."

3

The Resistance

With my rifle on my shoulder
In cities, plains and villages
I open the road for freedom
I lay palms for her and she passes

—From the anthem of ELAS
(the Greek People's Liberation Army)

In early March 2014, German president Joachim Gauck, a former Lutheran pastor with an oratorical flair that suited his ceremonial position, flew to Athens for a state visit. At seventy-four years of age, it was his first time in Athens, and on the evening of his arrival, he and his partner, Daniela Schadt, went for a stroll on the Acropolis. This was, Gauck said, a special moment for him. Growing up in East Germany, he had taken Ancient Greek in school and imagined what it would be like to behold this citadel of Western civilization. He paused with his partner for a photo in front of the Parthenon. He put his hands on a stone parapet and looked out over the Acropolis's south slope, gazing beyond the Theater of Dionysus Eleuthereus and toward the Temple of Olympian Zeus. "It's now so that the old man sees with his eyes what he before as a young man had dreamed about with spiritual eyes," Gauck told reporters. It was a pleasant evening, but the trip would get far more difficult after that.

The following day, Gauck met with the Greek president and various Greek politicians, including the ninety-one-year-old Manolis Glezos, a member of the far-left Syriza. Glezos was a hero of the Greek World War II resistance, and famous in particular for a spectacular feat he pulled off one spring night seventy-three years earlier, a few weeks after the Germans had entered and occupied Athens. Glezos, who was eighteen at the time, climbed up to the Acropolis with a high school classmate and pulled down the large, swastika-emblazoned Nazi war flag from its place above the city. The following day, a notice went out in Greek newspapers condemning the culprits to death, but the young men were never caught, at least not for that particular act. The deed became known as the first act of resistance in occupied Greece, and Glezos later attained an almost demigod status, particularly among those who shared his leftist politics.

The German president smiled broadly when he met Glezos at the plush Hotel Grande Bretagne, across the street from the Greek parliament building. "It is a joy and honor to meet a hero, a myth that I see standing alive before me," said Gauck, shaking Glezos's hand. Glezos, on the other hand, had a stern look on his face. He wore a baggy, dark suit and no tie. His thin, long white hair was combed back to his shoulders and a thick white mustache reached the creases of his cheeks. Glezos's elderly body was slightly bent, but he nevertheless looked younger than his age, and his wide blue eyes appeared sharply in tune with the world around him. Glezos addressed his response to the translator rather than to Gauck, breaching, it seemed, diplomatic etiquette. "I was expecting him at the shooting range of Kaisariani and he didn't come." The shooting range Glezos was referring to—named after the Athens suburb where it is located—is a memorial where the Nazis executed hundreds of Greek partisans and communists during the occupation. Among the people killed there was Glezos's younger brother, Nikos, who was executed on May 10, 1944, for resistance activities. That day, as Nikos Glezos was being taken away in a truck to the shooting range, he hastily scribbled a note on the lining of his cap. "Dear Mother. I kiss you. Greetings. Today, I'm going to be executed. Falling for the Greek people." Nikos Glezos signed the hat, added his address, and threw it from the vehicle. Someone on the street found it and took it to his mother, who read it around the moment her son was shot dead.

Gauck did his best to maintain his smile as a phalanx of Greek news photographers illuminated his face with flashes. Glezos and Alexis Tsipras, Syriza's leader, then went into a conference room with the president. There, Glezos said, he read the German president a poem he had written for four comrades executed during the occupation. At the time of their murder, Glezos had been imprisoned with the men in Athens's Averoff Prison, a drab stone mass that has since been demolished. The poem began:

> One *Achtung,* two *verboten,* three *raus*
> and one and two and three and four times
> the shrill voices rattle the silence's calm
>
> A building skinned the earth
> And entered the flesh of the wound

Expressing penitence for the evils of the Third Reich is a persistent duty for any German president, and one purpose of this trip, Gauck told the newspaper *Kathimerini,* was to acknowledge Germans' "moral debt" to Greece. Yet, while expressions of moral debt were welcome, what Glezos and many Greeks were really looking for was an admission of material debt. "What does moral debt mean?" Glezos told a Greek radio station before he met the German president. According to Glezos and others, in fact, the amount Germany owed Greece for occupation-era damages and debts was 162 billion euros, not including interest. That sum would have halved Greece's total debt, thereby going a long way toward resolving the country's vast fiscal quandary. The Germans were not exactly open to the idea of paying the Greeks, though. Glezos said he presented his argument about Germany's debts to Gauck in the room at the Grande Bretagne. The German president mostly "said nothing" in response, according to Glezos's account of the meeting, only that he would relay the message to the German government.

    The suggestion that Germany owed Greece money and not the other way around did not sit well in Germany. A summer 2013 article that appeared in the German tabloid *Bild,* the country's largest-circulation newspaper, probably summarized the common German sentiment regarding the reparations claim pretty well: "Have these Greeks gone completely crazy?" To make its case, *Bild* published a graphic laying out the aid payments disbursed to Greece under the bailout agreements, which to that point amounted to about 210 billion euros. This was to emphasize who the real debtors were. The article ran on the occasion of another visit by a prominent German politician—finance minister Wolfgang Schäuble. If there was one politician as disliked in Greece as the German chancellor, it was the cantankerous Schäuble, considered, along with Merkel, to personify punishing policies that had resulted in diminished wages, pensions, and economic output. Schäuble had visited Athens to declare German readiness to contribute 100 million euros to an investment fund that would help credit-deprived Greek businesses borrow money—a gesture, though relatively paltry, meant to illustrate that Germany was promoting more than just fiscal stringency, and was in fact doing something to help spur growth. "But instead of a thank you comes from Athens once again hate and malice," the *Bild* article read.

In addition to the fact that one Greek newspaper greeted the finance minister with the headline "Heil Schäuble!" the main affront, according to *Bild*, came from Syriza's leader, who during the visit made the unbelievable claim that Germany should compensate Greece for wartime damage. Schäuble had already shared his views on the matter with another German newspaper, saying Greece had no hope of getting reparations and that any insinuation otherwise was irresponsible. Greece's leaders, he said, should advocate the reform path rather than "lead people astray with such stories."

The Greek conservative-led government, however, maintained that it would pursue reparations in international courts. Around the time of Schäuble's visit, the Greek finance ministry announced that, under orders of the prime minister, it had assembled a team to go through piles of documents scattered and decaying in various Greek ministry basements—the Greek government version of archives—and it compiled 761 volumes of documents that could presumably be used as evidence in a legal claim for reparations. A secret report on the findings had been sent to Greece's quasi-judicial State Legal Council, which would determine the best course of action, the government said. Speaking in the Greek parliament, the foreign minister at the time, Dimitris Avramopoulos, recounted the suffering of the Greeks during the war, the "economic pauperization, hunger, assault, the theft and destruction of our cultural wealth, the arson and violence of the occupiers." Greece would "claim what belongs to us," he said. Times may have changed, "but memories do not fade."

This was likely for domestic show. The conservative-led government did not want to upset Germany—its most powerful creditor, on whom it was completely reliant and with which it had allied itself. Months earlier, Prime Minister Samaras had hosted a visit of German chancellor Angela Merkel in Athens. It was the first such visit from the German leader since the crisis began, and it marked an important turning point for Greece. Until then, some of Merkel's political colleagues had pushed for Greece's ejection from the euro. Merkel, by the time of her visit, had decided that this would be too risky for the rest of the eurozone. Greece had to be rescued, even if the Greeks didn't deserve it. She therefore silenced Greece's critics in her government and began to praise the Greek reform efforts, despite the fact that they were lackluster. The existing Greek government, after all, seemed to be her only conceivable partner. Syriza, the next strongest party in Greece, vowed to fight her and reject the bailout agreement, which it deemed responsible for the economic catastrophe. The ruling coalition, on the other hand, drew its support from the shrinking plurality of Greeks who calculated that the country was better off cooperating with Germany, because they feared the alternative could mean a still more catastrophic euro exit. These voters revered Merkel's power—providing a political reason for Samaras to host the chancellor—but that didn't mean they liked her. One would be hard pressed to find a Greek who did.

During her visit to Athens, Merkel was greeted by some 40,000 protestors, among them a small, grinning old man who walked around in front of parliament with a poster that read: GET OUT OF OUR COUNTRY YOU BITCH. The protestors were kept at a distance from the chancellor as a large swath of the city center was closed to traffic and pedestrians, except for those with security clearance. Inside the blocked-off area, thousands of police officers lined the streets, one stationed every ten yards. Snipers peered from the rooftops. Helicopters hovered overhead. As this went on, and as the sound of street battles between protestors and police echoed in the downtown Athens air, Greek television showed Merkel and Samaras going for a casual stroll and chatting outside the presidential mansion. One television commentator on a channel friendly to the government remarked at how amiable and relaxed Samaras seemed. It is safe to assume he was not asking her for World War II reparations.

While Syriza, with Glezos as the vanguard, made the reparations demand a main part of its platform, the then Greek government felt the need to pay lip service to the issue. So did all major
Greek parties, for that matter. Golden Dawn, too, demanded reparations, even though its ideological predecessors were the ones
who had inflicted the damage. The parties did this because it was
immensely popular with Greek voters. According to one 2012 poll,
91 percent of Greeks believed their country should use all necessary means to obtain reparations. More than three-quarters of those
polled said Germany was working on building a "fourth Reich."

Opinions like this underscored the vast gap and, often, the
antipathy that had developed between the Greek and German
electorates as the debt crisis strained European cohesiveness. Germans largely viewed the Greeks as overspending, irresponsible,
and corrupt, more deserving of punishment than of help. After
all, the German word for debt—*Schulden*—closely resembles the
word for guilt, *Schuld.* The expression *"Wer den Pfennig nicht ehrt,
ist die Deutsche Mark nicht wert,"* or "He who does not value the
pfennig is not worth the deutsche mark," also summarizes German attitudes on fiscal responsibility rather well, and during the
boom years, Greeks were certainly not valuing their euro-cents.
Merkel tried to alleviate her electorate's moral and fiscal unease
with the penny-denigrating Greeks by emphasizing the painful
reforms demanded of them. As Merkel repeatedly put it to her
voters, the Greeks had to "do their homework" in exchange for
German financial support.

To many Greeks, however, doing their homework meant losing their jobs or seeing their incomes dwindle. If this was the price
for Germany's help, many preferred not to have it. Inevitably, al-
lusions to that previous instance of German domination became
frequent, and images of Angela Merkel with a Hitler mustache
or swastika armband began to appear rather often on the covers
of Greek magazines and newspapers. In Greece, I often heard resentment toward Germany couched in terms of war. I heard it on

the playground with my son, in the supermarket, and in taxis. "This time, it's an economic war," or "This is worse than what they did to us during the war." The latter statement was a particularly ludicrous assertion—one that dishonored those who endured the massacres and famine of the wartime occupation—but one I nevertheless heard often.

As Greece's troubles deepened, so did crass, cross-party expressions of anti-German sentiment. One morning in early 2012, the popular commentator Giorgos Tragas, a round, graying, right-wing populist, began his radio show with this greeting: "Citizens of the German protectorate, good day!" With suspenseful background music, he added: "We don't have a government. We don't have a democracy. The will of our people applies nowhere. We don't have our own laws. We are slaves. Vassals. A colony." His voice rose to a scream. "From Thrace to Laconia, the foreigners are trampling our country. The Germans are torching again! They are burning Greece again!" This was an ordinary morning for Tragas, who also appeared on Greek television giving an ironic Hitler salute. Tragas referred to the Greek parliament as "collaborators," Angela Merkel as the "dog of Berlin," and he was fond of splicing into clips of her speeches archival sounds of Nazi rallies and German crowds yelling *"Sieg heil!"* Nazi symbolism also became a fixture of Greek street protest. I once walked by the German embassy in an upscale part of central Athens and noticed two large banners hanging on the residential building across the street from it. One depicted Hitler's face, a swastika, and a Greek flag covered with a splotch of blood. APRIL 27, 1941, THE GERMANS ENTERED ATHENS. WE RESISTED, it said. The second banner depicted a stern-looking Angela Merkel superimposed over a German flag and pointing her index finger. IN 2013, it said, THE GERMANS ARE IN ATHENS AND WE'RE SLEEPING. Certainly, German embassy workers did not particularly enjoy being greeted with a sizable image of Hitler's face every morning when arriving for work. Greek authorities eventually had the banners removed.

At times, the antagonism turned aggressive. During a conference of German and Greek mayors in Thessaloniki, protestors, some yelling "Nazis Out!," attacked German consul Wolfgang Hoelscher-Obermaier, pelting him with water bottles and iced coffee. The assailants had been incensed by the comments of another German, Hans-Joachim Fuchtel, Merkel's special envoy to Greece, who earlier had told reporters: "One needs three thousand Greeks for work which in German municipalities is performed by a thousand workers." Greeks tend to be incredibly sensitive to frequent accusations—often coming from Germany—that they are lazy, and in fact view themselves as quite industrious. In a 2012 Pew survey of eight European nations, people in seven of them said Germany was the most "hardworking." Only Greece differed with this assessment, saying that Greeks, in fact, were the most hardworking. (Actually, Greeks, according to an OECD report, do work longer hours than all other Europeans, though this does not equate to high productivity.) Fuchtel's statement—perceived as an insult to Greeks' work ethos—was covered with great interest by the Greek media and stirred a lot of fury. Fuchtel later said he was referring to "unproductive structures" in Greek municipalities, and did not mean to imply anything about the Greek work ethic.

Some attacks against German targets were far more serious. One early morning at the end of 2013, gunmen opened fire on the German ambassador's residence in Athens with two Kalashnikovs, spraying some sixty bullets in front of his gated suburban home. A few of the bullets ended up in the room of the ambassador's teenage daughter, the Greek media reported. An organization calling itself the Popular Fighters Group later claimed responsibility for the attack, delivering a long anticapitalist, anti-imperialist manifesto declaring war on the "German capitalist machine." The group also claimed to have launched a rocket at the headquarters of Mercedes-Benz outside of Athens, though the rocket missed and instead landed in a nearby field. Leftist terrorist groups have long operated in Greece—since the fall of its military dictatorship in 1974—and have often targeted Americans. The most lethal of these has been the Revolutionary Organization 17 November, which over nearly three decades killed twenty-three people, including the CIA's station chief in Athens and other American officials. In 2007, one terrorist group fired a rocket-propelled grenade at the U.S. embassy. Now German targets were becoming more of a focus. While these terrorist acts were by no means supported by the Greek public, they were undeniably another manifestation of the rising discord.

Greece's debt crisis was testing European unity, and the results weren't looking particularly good. As European leaders spoke of the importance of solidarity and further European integration, resentments between Greeks and Germans, between the debtors and the creditors, were growing. The vast differences weren't limited to sentiment; they were materially evident in the economic and fiscal conditions of the two nations. As Germany enjoyed the lowest unemployment rate since its reunification, Greece was experiencing the highest unemployment in Europe. As panicked investors bought German ten-year government bonds at interest rates so low that investors were essentially paying Germany to hold on to their money, interest rates on equivalent Greek bonds peaked at around 37 percent. This meant that, for Greeks, borrowing from the market was impossible, while for Germans it was profitable. Germany was able to both increase spending on some social programs and have extra money left over to attain a fiscal surplus, while Greece's debt burden continued to rise despite the fact that it was deeply slashing its expenditures.

In Germany, these differences were largely seen as evidence that Greece ought to try to imitate German policies in order to achieve the same result. In Greece, you could frequently hear an opposing idea: that these disparities proved the Germans were benefiting from the euro at others' expense. Germany, in other words, was plundering Greece again, but this time without an army. It was in this environment that Glezos, "the fighter for democracy" or "the symbol of national resistance," as his admirers called him, appeared to be trying to finish a fight that he had begun when he tore down the Nazi flag from the Acropolis. Contemporary Germans, Glezos often said, bear no guilt for the sins of their forefathers, and the demand for restitution was not driven by bitterness or vengefulness. Still, sometimes a clear tinge of acrimony seeped into his words, one that reflected the tension of the times. "They say we owe them," Glezos said at one point during a visit to the Peloponnesian city of Nafplio. "They owe us. We don't owe anything to anyone. In particular, we don't owe anything to Germany, which owes us for the death of the Greek people."

On a sunny morning in late April of 1941, the Germans entered Athens from the north in a single-file convoy of tanks, cars, and motorcycles. Shorty after their arrival in the city center, they raised a war flag over the Acropolis, the "Holy Rock," as Greeks call it, the place where "human culture found its beginning," as Hitler once put it. The German flag's red and black over the city in lieu of the Greek blue and white confirmed that the "barbarians"—Greeks' term for the invaders—had arrived.

At the time, Manolis Glezos was about to enter college in Athens to study business and economics. He was slender, wore a narrow black mustache, and exhibited a tendency to defy authority. In school, he was a member of an antifascist student group that had written slogans on the blackboard against the authoritarian, farright 4th of August Regime of General Ioannis Metaxas, which ruled in the years preceding the Axis invasion. Now, with Athens under Nazi occupation, Glezos's subversive acts would grow more daring. The night the Germans arrived, Glezos recalled many years later, he went out in his working-class Athens neighborhood of Metaxourgeio with a friend to survey the scene. He noticed that wooden German-language traffic signs had been put up for the benefit of the occupying troops. Glezos thought the signs ought to be destroyed and, without informing his friend beforehand, knocked one down. The friend then decided it would be a good idea to leave, though Glezos stayed and continued to knock down signs. As he was doing this, he heard the footsteps of someone approaching in the street, and hid in a doorway. The passerby was an old man who had seen what Glezos was doing. "Bend down so I can kiss you," the old man said, Glezos recalled. The man kissed him on the forehead. To Glezos, it felt like all of Greece would support resistance.

Over the next couple of weeks, Glezos repeatedly met a friend and like-minded classmate, Apostolos Santas, to discuss what actions they could take against the occupiers. They thought about stealing a pistol from a German soldier, or setting a tank or a plane on fire. At one point, they threw Molotov cocktails at some parked German vehicles, but their incendiary-making skills proved deficient, and nothing happened. Finally, what seemed like a very good idea came to them. From their frequent rendezvous point near the Greek parliament building, they could clearly see the Holy Rock and the German war flag fluttering above it. The pair decided they would climb up one night and take the flag down.

A few weeks later, on May 30, Crete was succumbing to German paratroopers after a bloody ten days of battle. The Germans were declaring the Third Reich's enemies in Greece defeated. "So that's how you are?" Glezos thought at the time, he told me more than seven decades later in his living room. "We'll show you that today, the fight begins." Late that night, under a crescent moon, Glezos and Santas climbed the steep north slope of the Acropolis, pausing in a cave, before reaching the surface near the Ionic-order temple, the Erechtheion, where Athena and Poseidon were worshipped. When they saw the ancient temples of the Acropolis in the faint moonlight, Santas later said, they became emotional with the thought that they were the "descendants of our great pro-genitors."

The pair found no guards, and crept along the citadel's perime-ter to the eastern precipice, where the flagpole stood. They yanked on the cables keeping the war flag in place, and after quite a bit of difficulty and some climbing up the pole, the banner finally fell on top of them. The two friends kissed, embraced, and did a quick dance before heading back down the way they came, with the flag. They threw most of the banner down a dry well, keeping one piece of it—a corner decorated with an Iron Cross—as a me-mento of the feat.

The next day, a notice appeared in Athens newspapers an-nouncing the offense: a waving German flag had been torn down and an investigation was taking place. The culprits would face the death penalty. Printing this was a mistake on the Germans' part, Glezos said later. Otherwise, no one would have known about it. Instead, the act became famed across the nation and abroad, blemishing the sheen of German invulnerability. While Glezos was imprisoned a few times during the occupation, the Germans never found out who took the flag down until after they withdrew. Greece, after the war, fell into another one, a civil war between the communist partisans that had fought the Germans and the right-wing, anticommunist government backed by the United States. Even after that war ended in 1949 with the communists' defeat, the ideological conflict underlying it lasted for a quarter century, during which time communists were persecuted or ex-iled to distant Greek islands. Glezos, for his political activities, spent a total of sixteen years in prison or exile, and was twice con-demned to death as part of the Greek government's fight against what it called "red fascism." He may well have been executed had not the Acropolis feat won him international acclaim and advo-cates like Jean-Paul Sartre, Picasso, and Charles de Gaulle, who once called him "Europe's first partisan." In 1963, while out of prison for at least a while, Glezos traveled to Moscow to receive the Lenin Peace Prize. The same year, *New York Times* journalist C. L. Sulzberger, in an article about the Greek communist threat, called Glezos "heroic but dangerous."

I met Glezos at his home in a tree-lined suburb of Athens on a Sunday morning in the spring of 2014. When I arrived, he rose off the couch in his pajamas from underneath a mound of newspapers, shuffled over to a desk cluttered with books, and cleared a space for me to sit down. He then signed a copy of one of his recent works, *The Black Book of the Occupation*, which contains a grim registry of the massacres, executions, and hangings that took place in Greece during the World War II occupation, beginning in June 1941 with the leveling of the Cretan village of Kandanos, and ending with the hanging of a man and woman in April 1945 on the island of Kos. After signing the book, Glezos outlined for me the argument he said he made to the German president at the Grande Bretagne, breaking down into categories Germany's debts to Greece (he refrained from using the term "war reparations," which he deemed misrepresentative of Greek claims for damages inflicted during the occupation). The categories were stolen archaeological treasures, damage to the economy, a forced loan, and further subcategories stemming from these. He spoke with the rote, drummed-up passion of someone who had given a presentation on the matter hundreds of times. At one point, he stood up to retrieve a folder containing a reichsmark bill, the currency used by German soldiers in occupied Greece and elsewhere. The bill, a fifty, featured images of a Prussian castle and a somber woman in a white headscarf. Glezos pointed to Gothic script on the bill that said *Reichskreditkassen*, or "Reich credit office," and added: "Do you see a signature?" There was none. He waited for me to answer no before proceeding. "It's fake," said Glezos, tapping his finger on it, "counterfeit." Barbers, said Glezos, preferred to give German soldiers free shaves rather than accepting the bills—which were pegged to the local currency. Honoring the bills would have in effect amplified the loss, said Glezos, because change would be given in Greek currency, drachmas, which, at least during the beginning of the occupation, still had some worth. This was another way the Germans stole from the Greek people, Glezos said. I looked at the bill through Glezos's magnifying glass and asked him where he'd found it. He sat in silence for a moment without looking at me, seemingly irritated with the question. "Say I stole it from the Germans," he said. Glezos's younger wife, Georgia, who was sitting on the couch reading a newspaper, emitted the raspy laugh of a heavy smoker. "I was a fighter during the occupation," Glezos went on, starting to raise his voice. "So I could look and find whatever. I had a lot more and lost them." I then asked how he'd lost them. This seemed to him like another stupid question, and he raised his voice further. I was angering Greece's hero of the resistance. "I was caught three times during the occupation! What could I have done? My mother was afraid and burned them."

Georgia intervened. "Quiet down please, Manoli!"

Glezos at the time had announced his candidacy for the European Parliament, and the fact that he was doing so at ninety-one added to his admirers' devotion. His "special reason" for running, said Glezos, was to bring to Europe the "escalating struggle for the claiming of Germany's debts to Greece." While the struggle was escalating, Glezos wanted me to understand he had been raising the issue for a long time. In fact, Glezos said, he had brought it up to East German leader Walter Ulbricht during a visit to the German Democratic Republic in 1965. Glezos at the time was a national parliamentarian for the United Democratic Left—which was formed as a proxy for the banned communist party. "Don't think that because I'm a communist and you're a communist, that you won't pay for everything you did in Greece, what the Third Reich did," Glezos said he told Ulbricht. "You owe us." Like Gauck, Ulbricht remained silent, according to Glezos's recollection.

This point about visiting Ulbricht reminded me of the intrinsic differences between Glezos, his party, and Germany's current leaders. Both Merkel and Gauck grew up in East Germany, and both, to varying degrees, have defined their political careers in opposition to it. That is particularly true of Gauck, who rose to prominence as a dissident of the East German regime. Glezos, though no advocate of authoritarianism and a professed believer in direct democracy, had been on the opposite side of that ideological fight. Syriza, while encompassing a broad cross section of leftist ideologies, from Trotskyism to ecosocialism, largely traces its roots to a rupture among Greek communists following the 1968 Prague Spring and the Soviet-led invasion of Czechoslovakia. The Communist Party of Greece remained unyieldingly loyal to the Soviet Union, and today it pretty much remains that way as it continues to persist with a stable allotment of Greek parliamentary seats. A milder spin-off faction with a European communist orientation evolved into a big part of what is today's Syriza. While Syriza is not awaiting the resurrection of the Soviet Union like its orthodox relative, traces of the Cold War ideological split nevertheless remain. For instance, following the Maidan uprising in Kiev, Syriza leaders expressed concern that Europe and the United States were destabilizing Ukraine for their imperialist purposes. After Russia annexed Crimea and began fomenting unrest in eastern Ukraine, Alexis Tsipras visited Moscow and decried Western sanctions against Russia while warning of neo-Nazi elements in Kiev. In an atmosphere of renewed tension reminiscent of the Cold War, Syriza was taking the side of an old comrade.

Syriza saw itself as pitted in an epic ideological struggle against the German government's neoliberal rule of and for the bankers and big capitalists. In that fight, Greece would provide the spark that would ignite a revolution of socialism and solidarity not just in Greece, but across Europe. ("Greece is showing the way" was a Syriza slogan at the time.) Capitalism, the party's supporters argued, was in its death throes, and Greece was leading the march toward a brighter future. In Glezos's eyes, Greece was once again leading the resistance. "What's happening in Greece right now isn't by chance," he told me in his living room. In World War II, he reminded me, the Greeks handed the Axis a major early defeat by repelling Mussolini's forces, which had invaded Greece from the north. "We destroyed the myth of invincibility of the Axis," he said. "And now, we're again going to make an example. We're asking for another Europe."

This message proved attractive to a lot of humiliated Greeks, who for years had been scorned as the central cause of Europe's problems. Syriza assured Greeks that the crisis was not the fault of the people, but of unchecked capitalism, and the message proved attractive. By the time I met Glezos, the party, which had come very close to taking power in Greece in 2012, was consistently leading in Greek polls, making Greece the only European Union country in which a far-left party was dominant. The debt crisis, it appeared, was providing the Greek left with an opportunity to take power, a goal it had been seeking since the Axis occupation, when Greek communists by far comprised the strongest resistance force. Glezos at one point told me he objected to a Syriza slogan urging voters to usher in a leftist government "for the first time." It would not be the first time, he told me. During the occupation, communist resistance fighters wrested much of the Greek mainland from Axis control—"Free Greece," as the fighters called it. "We had it once before," Glezos told me. "Unfortunately, we gave it up." Now, he believed, they were on the verge of taking it again.

To understand the intensity of Greeks' feelings about reparations and lingering resentments over World War II, once must know something about what happened to Greece during the occupation and its long, bloody aftermath. Greece suffered a particularly brutal occupation. Only Slavic countries had it worse, according to the historian Hagen Fleischer, a German-Greek academic who has written extensively on the occupation.

The war began for Greece in late 1940, when its army defeated

Mussolini, giving the Allies the important, morale-boosting victory Glezos brought up during our conversation. The Italians' defeat compelled the Germans to arrive six months later to do the job of taking Greece themselves. Within two months of the Germans' arrival, Greece was fully under a tripartite occupation of German, Bulgarian, and Italian forces. In contrast to the Third Reich's "rational exploitation" of Western European nations under occupation, in Greece the Germans quickly instituted policies of "plundering and indifference," as the historian John Louis Hondros put it. German authorities purchased Greek businesses, factories, and the merchant marine for fractions of their worth. Ores such as bauxite, chrome, and nickel, used to manufacture munitions, were mined and sent to Germany. Motor transport was commandeered. Food stocks were shipped to Germany. In the first year and a half of the occupation, the Reich "absorbed nearly every useful economic item and gave little or nothing in return," Hondros has written.

The consequences of this treatment, combined with a British sea blockade, quickly became evident. By the summer of 1941, just a few months after the occupation began, the first signs of starvation appeared, the beginning of what is known as the Great Famine. Almost all surviving Greeks can tell stories about the hunger they experienced or witnessed during this time, including my father, who grew up in a village near Corinth occupied by German soldiers. He could not describe the feeling of hunger itself, but rather told me stories about the euphoric feeling in his body after his mother gave him a piece of bread—grain was a rare commodity at the time—dipped in olive oil to eat. He was comparatively lucky. People on the islands and in Athens, far from arable land, had it much worse. Athens was home to "the worst scenes of starvation seen in occupied Europe outside the concentration camps," the historian Mark Mazower has written. Though the number of dead is hard to quantify, and estimates vary, some 300,000 Greeks out of a population of around 7 million are said to have starved to death.

Like other occupied nations, Greece was forced to pay "occupation costs," though in Greece these were particularly astronomical, for a time surpassing the national income. Greece paid by printing money, leading to rapid inflation, to which the occupation costs were adjusted. Price levels in Greece at the beginning of 1946 were more than five trillion times those of May 1941, according to the historian Richard Clogg—a hyperinflation five thousand times worse than the Weimar inflation of the early 1920s, which is so often cited as the scarring experience at the root of Germans' contemporary inflation aversion. In addition to the occupation costs, Greece's puppet government was forced in 1942 to make a 476-million-reichsmark loan to Germany. (In today's money, that equals a very high 54 billion euros, according to Glezos, though the more common estimate is 11 billion.) Near the end of the war, the Third Reich started paying the forced loan back, though repayment stopped with its defeat. "In all its history, until the occupation, Greece had borrowed," Glezos told me in his living room. "And after the occupation, it borrowed again. And now, it's borrowing still more. One time in its life, it was a creditor. When? In the worst period of its life. That was the forced loan."

The privations during the occupation and breakdown of the preexisting social order fueled support for resistance movements, in particular the communist-led National Liberation Front (EAM), and its military wing, the Greek People's Liberation Army (ELAS), which became the dominant partisan force in the Greek countryside, partly by taking out competing resistance groups. As partisan activity increased, the German supreme command mandated that fifty to a hundred Greek hostages be executed for every German soldier killed. Wehrmacht antiguerrilla operations constituted a terror campaign of executions, burned villages, and massacres that led to more than 20,000 civilian casualties. Some one million Greeks saw their homes and farms destroyed or looted. The vast majority of Greek Jews were deported to Auschwitz. Of the up to 80,000 Jews who lived in Greece before the war began, fewer than 10,000 survived. Many Greeks also died from disease. By one estimate, one-third of the population suffered from infectious diseases such as tuberculosis, malaria, and typhus. Making matters still worse, as German and Bulgarian forces withdrew from Greece near the war's end, they systematically destroyed the country's infrastructure—bridges, roads, railways, and tunnels were demolished, and the Corinth Canal was blocked.

Greece's misery was far from over after the Axis withdrawal. A new acrimony—the kindling that would lead to a second eruption of prolonged violence—had already taken hold. During the occupation, internecine conflict between resistance groups had intensified as the outlook turned to the postwar order. The British government, which had sought to organize resistance activity in Greece, became increasingly concerned with the communists' growing dominance, as did the British-backed Greek government in exile, based during the war in Cairo. In an effort to diminish the communists' sway, the British supported a smaller, noncommunist force, the National Republican Greek League (EDES), though its leader appeared to be more of an opportunist than an eager resistance fighter. Fighting eventually broke out between ELAS and EDES. Further internal fighting broke out after the Greek collaborationist government created anticommunist "security battalions" to hunt the leftist partisans. The social fissures generated during this time soon led to a civil war that left tens of thousands more people dead.

For the occupation-era plunder and bloodletting that commenced this decade of misery, top German leaders never apologized, because they feared this would embolden those Greeks demanding reparations, according to the historian Hagen Fleischer. Greece's hardship was also largely overlooked, lost in the greater panorama of unfathomable human suffering unleashed by the war. Gauck took it upon himself to rectify this when, during his 2014 visit, he traveled with the Greek president to the town of Ligkiades in the country's northwest, the site of a 1943 massacre by Wehrmacht soldiers of scores of people, mostly women and young children. Gauck laid a wreath at a memorial for the victims and tearfully told the assembled crowd and television cameras that he was ashamed. "I am ashamed that people who once grew up in German culture were murderers," he said. "And I am ashamed that democratic Germany, even as it processed the past step by step, knew and learned so little about German debt to the Greeks." He wished, he added, that someone responsible for these atrocities had apologized long ago. "It's the unsaid phrases and the lack of knowledge that constitute a second debt, as they even banish the victims from memory," Gauck said. "And so I would like to express today what perpetrators and many political leaders of the postwar period could not or did not want to express: what happened was a brutal injustice. With shame and pain, in the name of Germany, I ask the families of the murdered for forgiveness. I bow before the victims of these monstrous crimes, those who lament here and in many other places." The Greek president, standing beside Gauck, began to weep.

It's safe to assume that many contemporary Germans first found out that their Nazi-era forebearers invaded Greece after hearing about Greek demands for reparations in the news. The occupation of Greece is not a subject featured very prominently in high school curricula in Germany—nor, for that matter, in a lot of other places. Gauck's visit and apology were moving steps toward a greater understanding in his home country of what happened in Greece. But, it seemed, the gesture did not mollify many Greeks. "Those are just words," Panagiotis Bampouskas, the only remaining survivor of the Ligkiades massacre, told a reporter for a German news agency around the time of Gauck's visit. Bampouskas, an infant at the time of the attack, survived a bayonet stabbing in the back; his mother and brother were murdered. His father died shortly afterward—from grief, according to Bampouskas, who did not attend the memorial ceremony. "I want justice, and that means reparations."

One evening shortly after I met Glezos at his house, I saw him campaigning in the working-class neighborhood of Galatsi, a densely populated suburb of Athens, beside some tall, rocky hills that created a vertical pause in the concrete expanse of the city. Galatsi provided a sort of hometown crowd for Glezos. A lot of people from Naxos, the Cycladic island where Glezos was born, moved to Galatsi decades ago. That included a lot of people from his birthplace, a village of stone homes on the island's eastern side called Apeiranthos—Aperathu, in the local dialect. Glezos is particularly beloved in the village, where people sing songs about him with lyrics like: "You had a heart of steel and a breast of granite, and you climbed the Acropolis, gallant one from Aperathu."

When Glezos arrived on the small square in Galatsi where he was to speak, a crowd of people from the island assaulted him with kisses as an organizer of the event, a woman with a stern, almost martial voice, bellowed through a microphone: "So not a single citizen of Galatsi will go hungry. So not a single student will faint in school" (from hunger, she meant). "So not a single citizen will go without electricity." A black-clad widow in her late eighties sat down in a folding chair next to Glezos and caressed his face. "We were best of friends," she told me when I asked her how she knew him. The old woman's daughter, a retired teacher named Katerina Bougiouka, who wore a large silver-heart necklace, then approached me. "He is my spirit, my soul," she said of Glezos. Bougiouka had been a teenager living in Aperathu when she first saw the famous Glezos on one of his visits to the island. "There, I felt God," she said. "I thought he was a mythical person. That he's Proteus," the sea god; "that he's Diogenes," the ancient philosopher; "that he's Karaiskakis," the Greek revolutionary war hero. "This person has never stopped fighting for one moment. He never stopped. He wasn't afraid of disease. He wasn't afraid of senescence. He wasn't afraid of the Germans. He wasn't afraid of the fascists. He wasn't afraid of dictatorships. He wasn't afraid of anything. When you see a person in his ninety-second year standing up in this manner, toiling and getting out front, whether you want to or not, you fight too. You toil. He becomes your hero."

By this point, I'd seen Glezos make a few speeches. He was an eloquent, poetic speaker, and could captivate an audience. He could also speak on a wide range of subjects. I'd heard him expatiate upon gold and mineral extraction (he had read a lot of geology books while in exile, a subject authorities deemed harmless enough for study), irrigation (he has worked on a method to channel rainwater into underground aquifers), and Marxist theories about the nature of money. I found Glezos's energy and passion admirable, and I wanted to admire him—to believe, like so many others, in his heroic virtue. But this desire ran up against the reality that I often found Glezos to be wrong, if not actively misleading, and populist. Greece, he said one night on the campaign trail, had unimaginable mineral wealth, but it had gone unexploited because government officials "execute the orders of the foreigners, who don't want us to create heavy industry in Greece." The foreign powers preferred Greece to be a "resort of Europe," unproductive and dependent. "They want us only to be waiters!" he said. "Do you want every Greek to be a waiter? Or do we want to stand up by our own strength?" This drew applause from his crowd; it was part of an oft-repeated Syriza assertion, expressed in various ways, that Greece was being victimized by foreign powers interested in subjugating it rather than seeing it thrive.

Glezos also made some dubious claims involving his signature issue—reparations. On a few occasions, I watched him tell a crowd that Germany had recently compelled the Czech Republic to recompense the Sudeten Germans—who were expelled from Czechoslovakia at the end of the war—for their expropriated homes: "Germany now obligated them, three years ago, and the Sudeten Germans took back their properties. Is that the past?" This point was meant to underscore the hypocrisy of the German argument that it was too late for Greece to receive compensation for World War II–era damages. Glezos invariably added a second example—"the most important of all." The German government, he said, had recently agreed "not to pay lump-sum reparation to Jewish victims of Nazi atrocity, but to give them pensions," accentuating the part about "pensions" with a syllabic staccato. "In other words, the Jew who became a victim of Nazi atrocity, his descendant, and his next descendant, and his next descendant will continuously receive pensions!" One onlooker shook her head in disbelief. "And that happened three months ago," Glezos went on. "Is that the past?" Glezos said he brought up both these examples to Gauck when the men met, and the German president "had no answer for me." If Glezos indeed made these arguments, Gauck's alleged speechlessness could probably be explained by the fact that both of Glezos's examples were false. Sudeten Germans have never been compensated by the Czech Republic, nor have their properties been returned. Second, the German government had recently chosen to broaden the scope of existing pension benefits for Jews who had worked in ghettos occupied by the Third Reich. Glezos, however, failed to mention that the benefit applied only to Jews who had worked, and therefore were deemed entitled to the pensions. Furthermore, their offspring would not inherit the pensions. By using inexcusable falsities to make his case, Glezos certainly was not helping his cause.

Glezos nevertheless had a considerable talent for appealing

to people's emotions, and I found myself vacillating between revulsion over such populist disinformation and shedding tears of
sympathy for him. The night Glezos spoke in Galatsi, he was particularly energetic and emotional. It was the seventieth anniversary of the execution of his brother, and he began the night by
dedicating the event to him. The speakers were turned up very
high, and Glezos yelled with fervor into the microphone, his voice
blistering the night air. Near the end of his speech, he lowered his
voice. People often asked him if he got tired of doing this sort of
work at his age, he said. "Beloved friends, you think right now the
one talking to you is Manolis Glezos." He paused for a moment and
snapped, "That's wrong!" His voice started to break as he began to
raise it again. "All my dead friends are talking to you! Companions, fellow fighters who I lost in the battles. They come to me and
say: 'Manoli, what's going on? Our dreams. Where are they?' And
my brother is in front, who speaks to me with a hard tongue: 'You,
Manoli, are living, but I didn't even manage to live out the years
of my youth. I want back the years that you live and I don't live.'
How do I answer him?" By this point, Glezos was crying out like
he was beseeching a lover who had scorned him. "How do I answer him? How?" I looked around to see what effect he was having and saw lots of tears on people's faces. Glezos finally answered.
"I say: 'Niko, believe. We are trying. We are fighting. We're in
front. We're not leaving anything behind. And we're building continuously. We're destroying the old and building the new. Niko,
sometime, you'll live your dreams, you'll see them fulfilled. I can't
give you your years back. But I can give you the vindication of
your fight. Yours and the others'.' That's why I'm here. That's why
I continue the fight." The audience applauded. "There's no way
I'm going to die in bed. I will die standing up, close to you, in the
common struggle." Then Glezos finished the speech with a line
I'd heard him utter on more than one occasion. People always said
to him, "We need you," he said. But this was the wrong way of

looking at things. "As long as you tell me, 'Manoli, we need you,' the country is not going forward. When you tell me, 'Manoli, we don't need you,' then the road for everything opens."

Visits from German leaders have always held special significance in Greece, and that was certainly the case in 1956, when West German president Theodor Heuss was invited to Athens by King Paul of Greece, who happened to be the nephew of the last German kaiser. This was the first state visit of the German president since the end of the war, and the Greek right-wing government was very much interested in providing a warm reception. West Germany was seen as an important economic partner and a valuable ally in the fight against communism. Considering Greece had been under German occupation eleven years earlier, the president's welcome in Athens was incredibly positive, at least according to newspaper reports at the time. Crowds welcomed the German president, and battle tanks were positioned around the central Omonoia Square to add to the pageantry. At one point, Greek farmers—perhaps aware that Germans were buyers of their exported tobacco, fruits, nuts, and olives—were said to have laid flowers in Heuss's path. The German president was moved by the Greeks' "simple, great, and genuine hospitality," and their propensity to "not forget the past, but to forgive," wrote a reporter for the German newspaper *Die Zeit*. Like Gauck, Heuss made the pilgrimage to the Acropolis shortly after his arrival. "Europe is built on three hills," he once said. "On the Acropolis of Athens, the Capitoline Hill in Rome, and on Golgotha," the place in Jerusalem where Jesus was crucified.

Behind the official veneer of warm, forgiving relations, however, the reality was far more complicated. The Greek government may not have been interested in holding a grudge, but many

Greeks had not forgiven the Germans for wartime damages. A U.S. embassy account of the visit found "no observable enthusiasm on the part of the Greek populace in Athens," and called applause for the German president "half-hearted and spotty." Greek World War II victims' organizations used the occasion to highlight their demands for German reparations. One group sent a letter to the German embassy saying that "friendship between peoples cannot be established as long as between them lies a chasm, opened by the bitterness, the pain and the injustice, and the recompense that could bridge the divide is not forthcoming." The rising leftist opposition at the time called for German reparations. After all, in the Paris treaties struck in 1947, Greece received a combined 150 million dollars in reparations payments from Bulgaria and Italy, which also ceded the Dodecanese Islands. Why, leftist politicians argued, shouldn't the main perpetrators also pay?

The United States, however, cognizant of the failures of the post–World War I reparations policy, and of the fact that Germany would never recover if forced to pay at a level commensurate with the damage it had inflicted, protected Germany from paying fixed monetary sums. The 1953 London Debt Agreement forgave half of Germany's considerable external debt and put off the question of monetary compensation for wartime damages until "a final settlement of the problem of reparation." The U.S.-backed agreement was vital to West Germany's postwar recovery, giving the country a blank slate that allowed it to build the robust, export-oriented economy that has prevailed since the beginning of the 1950s. (Syriza leaders often underscore the debt forgiveness Germany received at this time, and suggest the Germans follow the same example in Greece's present case.) Greece also experienced an economic boom following the end of its civil war, and it benefited from Marshall Plan aid, which allowed it to rebuild its infrastructure. That, however, did not erase the persistent calls from leftist politicians and victims' groups for compensation from

Germany, and in the late 1950s, the demands grew stronger as Glezos's United Democratic Left party gained popularity and accused the Greek government of a kind of collaborationist stance toward Germany.

The Greek government's domestic image problem over the issue was worsened by what many Greeks saw as another postwar injustice: very few alleged war criminals had been held accountable for atrocities committed in Greece. Greek authorities had agreed to defer to German prosecutors the investigation of German war crimes. Yet, German authorities, uninterested in stirring up the Nazi past any more than was necessary, exhibited little desire to pursue the cases. Around the time of Heuss's visit, the Greek government threatened to reopen its own investigations of German war crimes unless Germany agreed to pay monetary reparations, according to a CIA report at the time. Germany refused. It just so happened that in 1957, one presumed war criminal, a German lawyer named Maximilian Merten, traveled to Greece in order to testify in a civil case involving his wartime interpreter. During the occupation, Merten was the military administrator of Thessaloniki, where nearly the entire Greek Jewish population of some 50,000 was deported to Auschwitz-Birkenau. After the war, Merten was arrested by the Americans, but the Greek government showed no interest in prosecuting him, and he was eventually released. At the time of his trip, however, Merten was concerned Greek authorities might possess a different view on the matter, and so, before leaving he sought assurances from the Greek consul in Berlin that he would not have any legal troubles. Satisfied it was safe, Merten traveled to Greece and was promptly arrested. Why this happened is hard to pin down. The German government was convinced the arrest was politically motivated, and lobbied for Merten's release. A CIA report at the time determined the arrest was simply a mix-up, and said Merten wound indeed soon be released. Undoubtedly, however, Merten's arrest also gave the Greeks a bargaining chip in negotiations with the Germans. While Merten was in Greek custody, Germany and Greece signed an economic agreement that included a favorable 200 million deutsche mark loan for Greece. The German motivation for this was manifold. Germany wanted to help stabilize Greece and ensure it remained under the Western—not Soviet—sphere of influence. It was also a way of providing economic aid to Greece without recognizing any legal obligation to pay compensation for wartime damages—"veiled reparation," in the words of the historian Heinz A. Richter. There was for the German government one additional benefit. In a confidential annex to the economic aid deal, the Greek prime minister at the time, Konstantinos Karamanlis, promised German chancellor Konrad Adenauer that Greece would return Merten to Germany and refrain from prosecuting suspected German war criminals, according to the historian Susanne-Sophia Spiliotis.

At first, however, Merten received what appeared to be stern justice. Two years after his arrest, a Greek military court sentenced him to twenty-five years in prison. Yet, the sentencing was a cosmetic exercise meant to satisfy the Greek public. Months later, the Greek government pushed through parliament a general amnesty for war criminals. The justice minister at the time argued that "agitation of the past" did not serve Greece's interest in building economic and political ties with West Germany. Greece, the minister added, "was truly proud of its sacrifice, but is not resentful." The bill was strenuously opposed by the leftist opposition, victims' groups, and the World Jewish Congress, which called it a "concession to inhumanity and lawlessness." Merten was quietly released and returned to West Germany, where the government granted him compensation for his time spent incarcerated in Greece. At home, Merten accused Karamanlis of having been an informant for the Nazis during the occupation. Karamanlis and his government adamantly denied the charge, though the allegations roiled

Greek politics for some time, becoming known as the "Merten Affair."

A few months after Merten's release, Germany also agreed to give Greece 115 million deutsche marks to compensate Greek citizens persecuted by the Nazis on account of race or creed—an agreement similar to those made with other nations around that time, intended to compensate Holocaust survivors. The German foreign secretary sent a letter to the Greek ambassador saying the language of the agreement meant that Greece would in the future make no further claims with regard to questions of Nazi persecution during the occupation. The Greek ambassador disagreed, however, and in his response said that Greece reserved the right to request reparations based on a future "final settlement" mentioned in the London Debt Agreement of the previous decade.

The time for that final settlement ostensibly came after the fall of the Berlin Wall, with Germany's reunification. In Greece, there were renewed demands for reparations and repayment of the forced loan. During the '90s, Greek victims' groups filed class-action lawsuits against Germany for atrocities carried out during the occupation. Greek courts ruled in favor of the claimants, and ordered Germany to pay damages. The German government rejected the rulings as a violation of state immunity, and warned their Greek counterparts that relations between the two nations could be severely harmed. In response, the Greek plaintiffs tried to expropriate the Goethe Institute in Athens and other German state properties. The assets were to be auctioned off and the proceeds given to the claimants. The Greek government, however, did not allow the seizures to go forward. The arrival of the Greek debt crisis reinvigorated resentment over Germany's so-called debts. Thus the Greek government found itself in a familiar postwar dilemma—how to placate its citizens' demands for reparations while not alienating Germany, the powerful financial benefactor on which it relied.

In early 2014, German parliamentarians, largely from the so-cialist party Die Linke, an ally of Syriza, petitioned the German government to explain why it believed the reparations demands from Greece were illegitimate. One argument the government gave in response involved the 1990 international treaty that rec-ognized a reunified Germany. The Treaty on the Final Settlement with Respect to Germany—signed by East and West Germany as well as the United States, the Soviet Union, the United King-dom, and France—constituted the closest thing to a World War II peace treaty. The German government argued that the treaty was a conclusive settlement on all legal questions arising from the war, including reparations. When I met Glezos in his living room, he pointed out that Greece had never signed that agreement, nor any peace treaty with Germany. Herein lay his plan. After Syriza took power, he would ask Germany to sign a peace treaty which would compel it to finally pay its debts, though he did not want to elab-orate on how. "I'm sure that once we discuss a peace treaty, they will pay," he told me.

On May 25, 2014, Syriza won the European Parliament elections in Greece, beating out New Democracy by a few per-centage points. Syriza supporters considered the victory historic, the first time a far-left party won a nationwide election. Before long, they rightly believed, Syriza would be governing Greece. In-deed, only seven months later, the party took power after winning a snap general election. In the first of these triumphs, Glezos re-ceived 450,000 votes, far more than any other domestic candidate for the European Parliament. It was a clear mandate to take his fight for reparations to Europe. Glezos could not fly due to a heart condition, which made commuting back and forth from Brussels or Strasbourg, the places where European parliamentarians meet, problematic. He would travel north by car and find a place to live in one of those cities.

On a hot, humid night before his departure, Glezos had a going-away party of sorts at a café in the center of Athens. The gathering was for a newly released book of transcribed conversations with Glezos, compiled by one of his Syriza colleagues, Rena Dourou, who had just been elected governor of Attica. At the event, Glezos sat next to Dourou and Tsipras, both of whom spoke to the crowd, praising Glezos's tirelessness and fighting spirit. Glezos spoke last and, unlike the others, stood up from his chair as if commanded by a drill sergeant. He wore an untucked button-down shirt with short sleeves that exposed his long, skinny arms. The outfit and his excitement over the chance to speak to the crowd made him seem boyish. First he thanked members of the audience, in particular two diplomats in attendance: the head of the Palestinian mission to Greece, who received a round of applause; and the Vietnam-ese ambassador, whose people, as Glezos put it, had struggled and overcome the technology of war because of their desire to obtain independence. He thanked the loyal people from his Naxos village who had come to see him off that night and then began speaking of the importance of Syriza's victory for old fighters like him, those who had been struggling a lifetime to see a leftist government in Greece. "We are on the road to vindication. That is a fact," he told the crowd, his voice cracking and rising. "Very many fellow fighters, fighters never subdued, inconspicuous fighters you don't know, they call me, and they cry from joy. We cry from joy. Why? Because the road has opened, Alexi," he said, glancing at Tsipras, the man who would lead the way. Afterward, the woman emcee-ing the event presented Glezos with a small bundle of dirt from the shooting range where his brother was executed. "I wanted you to take it with you," she said, nearly crying. Then she addressed the audience: "He's going one more time to climb a rock, a hostile rock," she said. "And he has a lot of flags to take down."

It wasn't clear what enemy flags Glezos would manage to take down in the European Parliament, an institution that remained a rather impotent fragment of the European Union's sprawling bureaucracy. Glezos had served briefly in the same parliament in the 1980s, before resigning in frustration and moving to Naxos in order to institute a direct-democracy model of governance in his village. The European Parliament had since obtained more powers, but things still had not changed all that much, Glezos would find. He was one of 751 parliamentarians speaking a score of different languages, in debates during which each one of them was afforded only a couple of minutes to comment. The elections that year had ushered in a wave of far-right parliamentarians, with victories for the French National Front and the U.K. Independence Party—two nationalist parties whose ideologies were largely based on antagonism toward European institutions such as the one they had been elected to serve in. Included among the parliamentarians was one from Germany's neo-Nazi National Democratic Party, and three more kindred spirits from Greece's Golden Dawn. Arguably, the European Parliament was kind of a madhouse. Glezos would likely not be able to effectively use the venue to confront Germany on reparations. Nor, judging by the composition of the parliament, had Syriza's rise in Greece yet sparked a socialist revolution across Europe, as he'd hoped.

After the book event was over, Glezos went out onto the terrace and was mobbed by a group of admirers. One large old man, who looked like he must have been formidable in his younger years, walked gingerly past the scene and noticed the undercover police officer standing guard next to Glezos. "Ha!" said the old man, a communist since the days when communists had to be on the lookout for undercover police. "They used to chase us, and now they're kowtowing to you!" A small group of musicians fiddled and strummed their instruments, and people started singing. By this point, I realized that for some people from his village in

Naxos, composing songs about Glezos was an art form. "Courage, indomitable soul, and a will of steel, and with the same strength, you'll fight again. With heart, soul, and strength, like in those years." A few older ladies started improvising on the spot: "You'll be like a bright page of history . . . Because we have Manoli, we're all proud . . . Hero of the Acropolis!" At one point, I leaned into Glezos's ear and asked him if he'd miss Greece. "No," he said. "I'm taking Greece with me."

4

Murder in the Civil Service

And where the rewards for merit are greatest, there
are found the best citizens.

—Pericles

On the night of December 27, 2009, two employees of the municipal treasury of Pangaio, a verdant, mountainous area of northern Greece, lured the mayor, Triantafyllos Koukoudis, to a remote
coastal road with the intent of resolving a pressing monetary difficulty. Over the previous three years, the treasurers, acting jointly
with the mayor, had repeatedly taken municipal money for their
personal use, public prosecutors later alleged. That month, as auditors arrived for a routine check of the books, the resulting gap in
municipal finances had reached beyond 700,000 euros, a circumstance that was apparently causing the three men a great deal of
stress.

That night, the deputy treasurer, Ioakeim Monos, a dark-eyed,
middle-aged man, called the mayor and told him he wanted to
hand over titles to his property, which could be used as collateral
for an emergency loan to plug the financial gap. "Come and I'll
give them to you," Monos said he told the mayor, though the treasurers would later acknowledge that the handing over of titles was

not the true purpose of the meeting. Monos's apparent involvement in such wayward activities came as a surprise to many locals, who described him as taciturn. He was married with four sons, and had worked as a municipal clerk for two decades before the mayor appointed him to work for the treasury a few years earlier. A colleague at the town hall called him a "good person."

The mayor, a tall former gym teacher with a lush crown of silver hair, a low forehead, and a well-groomed beard, was by all accounts a garrulous, friendly man, though some locals say his successful mayoral bid a few years earlier had changed him, giving him an air of import and a politician's manner of speaking. He was divorced, and when he received the call from Monos, the mayor was with a younger woman he'd been dating for a few months. He told her he had to leave for a "professional rendezvous," she later recalled. The mayor then got into his blue Audi and sped off.

The rendezvous point was a parking area off a highway that runs along the sandy Aegean coastline, a stretch of road little trafficked during the winter months. Monos and the municipality's head treasurer, Savvas Saltouridis, drove together. Saltouridis was a stout man in his late forties, and his thin-framed glasses seemed fitting for a keeper of municipal books. Locals said he was outgoing and had lots of friends. He was a former tax collector, and had been appointed treasurer by the mayor at the beginning of the term three years earlier. Saltouridis seemed to have a good reputation among his peers. He was an "impeccable employee," a coworker in the town hall said of him. He was also a musician and played the *lyra*, a fiddle-like instrument common in the jig-like traditional music of the Pontic Greeks, who descend from the region around the Black Sea. He had married a Ukrainian woman, and together with a daughter from her first marriage, they had two boys, both of them still very young at the time of this December night.

The treasurers had brought an Uzi submachine gun along with them for the rendezvous. When they arrived at the parking area, Saltouridis took the gun and hid near a shuttered roadside snack bar, according to a later court decision regarding the night's events. The mayor arrived shortly after 9:00 p.m., and got out of his car. Saltouridis then sprang from his hiding spot, the court determined, pointed the gun in the direction of the mayor's head, and opened fire, hitting him with two bullets in the face at close range. The mayor fell to the pavement, and Saltouridis unloaded five more bullets into his body. The municipal treasurers then stuffed the mayor's body into the trunk of his car, where it was discovered three days afterward.

Three and a half years later, when I first found out about the killing, people in Greece were still talking about it. That was because the two convicted treasurers remained on the municipal payroll—receiving a portion of their salaries—even as they sat in prison for killing the mayor. The case had come to represent in blatant terms the thicket of public-worker job protections that safe-guarded even convicts from losing their government jobs. ("They Murdered the Mayor but Still Get Paid!" ran a Greek newspaper headline.) At the time, Greece's Troika of official creditors was pushing hard for the nation to reform its public bureaucracy, and demanded the government fire public workers deemed unsuitable. The case of the slain mayor showed how challenging that was likely to be.

The perpetuity of a government job in Greece has been considered as incontrovertible as the earth's solar orbit since it was consecrated in the country's constitution a century ago. "Civil ser-vants holding posts provided by law shall be permanent so long as these posts exist," the document says. The constitution technically allows for employees to be fired for acts like murder and embezzlement, but not "without a decision of a service council consisting of at least two-thirds of permanent civil servants." These job protections were initially enacted to keep political parties from a then common post-election practice; new governments would fire civil servants en masse and appoint political adherents in their place. Yet, while the law prevented the mass firings, it did nothing to dampen the hiring aspect of the custom. Politicians therefore continued to allot jobs to their supporters or kin as if distributing breadcrumbs to pigeons, simply adding them to the ranks already on the public payroll. In 2009, about one out of five Greeks in the labor force had a public job, whether directly as part of the government, or for a state-owned entity. That ratio, although higher than in Germany, was still smaller than European nations such as France, and especially Scandinavian countries like oil-rich Norway. The problem with Greece's public sector, however, was not as much size as composition. The public workforce swelled with unskilled clerks and midlevel managers hired without much if any regard for their qualifications, and put into positions created for the benefit of the workers rather than that of the citizens they technically served. Once appointed, no matter your performance, losing your job was virtually impossible, as you could be fired only by a majority decision of colleagues inclined to protect you. This career tenure arguably contributed to a sense of impunity among those public servants who tended to arrive to work late, not to arrive at all, or, once they arrived, to conceive illicit ways to make their positions more lucrative. Those public servants wishing to do an honest, good job were often discouraged by a system seemingly designed to reward the opposite behavior.

The Greek government, under duress from the Troika, was forced to undertake efforts to evaluate workers' performance. A good starting point seemed to be to check whether employees were showing up, and if so, whether they were working full days. The initial findings were not particularly good. In one department of the Ministry of Culture and Sports, for instance, the electronic system for monitoring working hours—which was installed in 1998—became operational only in 2012, and even then it was not fully functioning, inspectors found. Some 70 percent of the employees sampled there in the fall of 2012 flouted their full working hours. The same was found to be true of three quarters of the workers sampled at an auxiliary social security fund. A second inspection there four months later showed a marginal improvement of seven percentage points. The inspectors' report noted that managers at the fund failed to discipline the staff or dock their pay as was formally required, but instead granted unwarranted overtime.

Once the government was forced by its creditors to account for the true self it had for decades kept behind the curtain, a pageant of unpleasant revelations appeared. The highest-profile cases centered around the few politicians caught laundering or embezzling tens of millions of euros. But many smaller-scale corruption cases emerged among civil servants also wishing to partake. For instance, six women working for the nation's largest social security organization were accused of assigning some 11 million euros in fraudulent benefits; they were charged with money laundering and other crimes. Sixty-five urban planning department employees in and around Athens were charged with felonies for systematically and arbitrarily reducing or waiving fines for building code violations (presumably, the disappearing fines did not benefit only the building owners). At the end of 2013, Greece's finance minister wrote a letter to Greek banks asking them to provide account information on hundreds of tax auditors suspected of having undeclared income and assets of apocryphal origins, the Greek newspaper *Ethnos* reported. Investigators found large bank transfers amounting to hundreds of thousands of euros that did not appear to be justified by the employees' salaries. The following year, the government reported that it was investigating more than five thousand civil servants who collectively transferred some 1.5 billion euros to foreign banks over the previous four years. About half of them were teachers, who often have private, cash-only side jobs tutoring students in what they don't learn at school: to pass the difficult exams needed to get into a Greek university. Public doctors and defense ministry employees were also heavily represented.

Not surprisingly, nearly all Greeks think poorly of their public administration. In a 2012 EU survey, 96 percent of polled Greeks characterized it as "bad"—the worst result in the EU. The sentiment is so pervasive that one can assume most of the public administrators share it. The poll result was similar in the years preceding the financial crisis, and therefore cannot be attributed to subsequent cuts in services. Despite Greeks' dissatisfaction with the way their government works, public employees in the decade leading up to the crisis received very large pay raises. During that time, public sector wages per employee grew by over 100 percent, near the highest increase in the eurozone, according to a report published by the European Central Bank. By contrast, in Germany, where people were satisfied with the way the state bureaucracy functioned, public wages grew around 13 percent. (That low rate, when one factors in inflation, essentially meant a pay cut.) Greek civil servants also received an array of benefits that sweetened their jobs. Until 2013, when the Greek government put an end to it, those working in front of computers—a condition considered a hardship—received an extra six days off a year in order to provide them some relief.

In the summer of 2013, a young New Democracy politician named Kyriakos Mitsotakis was appointed head of the Greek ministry overseeing administrative reforms, replacing the previous minister from a small leftist party whom conservatives accused of obstructing rather than fulfilling the Troika's reform demands. Mitsotakis, a high achiever with two Harvard degrees and another from Stanford, belonged to one of Greece's most prominent political families. His father, Konstantinos Mitsotakis, governed Greece for three and a half years as prime minister at the start of the 1990s. The father didn't keep that position for long in large part because he tried to carry out some of the unpopular reforms the Troika later demanded of Greece: to cut government spending and privatize bloated state-owned companies. He, however, also developed a reputation for liberally distributing government posts to his political allies. The younger Mitsotakis was now given the unenviable job of reforming the public administration and implementing another unpopular measure: firing thousands of public workers, something no Greek politician had done in a very long time. The ministry he took over—officially called the Ministry of Administrative Reform and e-Governance—had been created a few years earlier with the purpose of modernizing Greece's public administration, though it was still unclear whether it was doing much to improve government or was simply adding to its girth.

After taking over, Mitsotakis declared he would move quickly to turn the civil service into an efficiently run meritocracy. One good place to start, he said, would be to fire convicted criminals on the public payroll. In a radio interview, he brought up the treasurers in Pangaio, and said stories like it did not "foster honor in our country." He announced that a decision had finally been reached for their permanent removal, and portrayed this as a sign that the government boards reviewing disciplinary cases had begun to function. Such efforts to dismantle an "overgrown client state that is the source of evil" should have been made far earlier, he said. After hearing the minister's interview, I was under the impression the treasurers had been fired, and in subsequent phone calls to the ministry, Mitsotakis's spokesman confirmed that this was the case. Yet, when I contacted the Pangaio town hall, an aide to the mayor told me no one there had heard anything about firings, and in fact the convicted killers still remained on the payroll. At that point, I decided to visit Pangaio to find out why that was the case.

. . .

Pangaio Municipality is a collection of villages in northeastern Greece near the mountain range from which it takes its name and where, locals say, Alexander the Great once mined for gold in order to finance his conquests. About seventy miles to the north is Bulgaria, and just to the south stretches a northern shore of the Aegean. When the mayor was killed, the Pangaio town hall was located in his hometown, a place called Nikisiani, a village of red-tiled roofs on a slope of the Pangaion Hills, covered with fir, beech, and chestnut trees. The town hall was later moved to a larger, neighboring city as part of a nationwide overhaul to reduce the number of municipalities by merging them, though when I arrived in Nikisiani early one evening, a large town hall sign still hung from the former mayor's office. Next door, a group of retirees idled outside a small *kafenio*, sitting in a semicircle under the shade of a chestnut tree. I took a seat with them and ordered a coffee. The retirees looked at me like I had descended to their location in a spaceship. *"Kalispera"* ("Good evening"), I announced. They returned the greeting politely, and then there was silence. Across the road was a small plaza featuring a row of flagpoles without flags. Beside it was another café occupied by retirees. Opposite them was a third café with a few more retirees.

"How do you determine who comes to this café and who goes to the others?" I said to the men sitting close to me under the tree.

"That's where the retirees go," said one of them, pointing to the other cafés. It took me a second to realize that the man, who looked like an older Willem Dafoe, was joking. I then told him he looked like the actor, but he'd never heard of the guy.

"How does this village sustain itself economically?" I asked the group.

"Germany sends us loans," one squinty-eyed man said from behind a cloud of cigarette smoke.

After my coffee arrived, I worked up the courage to ask Willem Dafoe if he had known the murdered mayor.

"Of course we knew him," he said. "He used to come down and drink coffee with us."

"Was he a good guy?" I asked.

"He was very social," said Willem Dafoe.

"We're all good people here," said another man with a bitter-looking grin. It was unlikely I would hear any criticism of the mayor. In addition to the fact that it was his hometown, Greeks tend to abide by the maxim "A dead man is always right." Reproach is instead reserved for the living.

"Did you know his killers?" I asked the group.

No one said anything. One man tossed his *kombolói* and looked pained. "They're from other villages," he said. "They're of different races." I didn't quite understand at the time what he meant. Were people in these mountain villages so tight-knit that they considered their neighbors racially dissimilar? I later realized he was referring to the shooter's Pontic origins. Often, Pontic Greeks are unfairly stereotyped as thuggish in Greece, a regrettable circumstance I was reminded of when I went to a regional courthouse to pick up a file on the murder case. There, a courthouse clerk told me that Pontic Greeks have "criminality inside their blood."

The comment about the killer's origins was followed by more silence. The old men did not want to talk about the murder, at least in front of one another. I finished my coffee. The waiter informed me that Willem Dafoe had already paid for me. I thanked him and started walking to my car. "Hey, American! Come here," yelled someone from across the square. An old man from one of the competing cafés was waving to me. I changed direction toward him and wondered how my biographical details had so efficiently spread to the other establishment.

The old man had pale blue eyes and dyed black hair. Two

fingers were missing from the hand he reached out to me. I shook it and began to introduce myself, but he interrupted as if he'd already been fully briefed.

"Do you know what you should write in your book?" he said.

"No, tell me."

" 'Fuck the Greeks!' "

A friend sitting across from him at the table, an octogenarian with a mullet, made a look of horror. "No! Don't write that," he said, doing the best he could to raise his faint voice.

"Okay, don't write that," said the man with the missing fingers. "Write, 'We need to burn down this whole idiotic country and start with the government.' "

"No! Don't write that," said the octogenarian. "Write: 'I can't make sense of any of it.' "

The man with the missing fingers was Lambros Kotsikaris. He'd worked for forty-nine years as a "guest worker" in Germany, one of the hundreds of thousands of laborers from the Mediterranean rim who in the decades following World War II went to Germany to provide muscle for its booming economy. He'd left his fingers behind in a German auto parts factory, he told me. Kotsikaris complained about various matters of local governance that did not seem serious enough to warrant his outrage. He pointed to the row of empty flagpoles across the street. The municipality had once kept a nice row of international flags there. What the hell happened to the flags? He complained of the noisy engines on mopeds and motorcycles that local teenagers adjusted to make louder. He criticized the twenty-euro fee necessary to reserve a plot in the community cemetery.

He then casually mentioned that his nephew had provided the Uzi that the treasurer had used to shoot the mayor. The nephew, who was described by witnesses in the murder trial as unmarried and marginally employed, testified that he had found the Uzi in an abandoned quarry. "I know it was illegal, but I held on to it," he told the court. "That weapon, I saw it and I had it. It looked loaded." The court found that the nephew provided the gun in exchange for the promise of a 5,000-euro payment, and sentenced him to seventeen years in prison for complicity in murder and for offenses related to the weapon. Kotsikaris didn't have much sympathy for his nephew. "He and the others should be sentenced to a lifetime of hard labor," he said.

"What about the fact that the two others are still on the municipal payroll?" I said. I thought, given his considerable anger over other matters, he'd have something to say about it. To my surprise, it was not among his issues of concern. "It's a way of taking care of their families," he said. "That's the way I see it."

"But is that the proper way to provide welfare to the families?" I said. "By keeping convicts on the municipal staff?"

"What's proper in Greece?" said a heavy man who had come over, taken a seat, and lit a cigarette.

The octogenarian decided I needed to be reminded: "Write, 'I won't make sense of any of it,' " he said.

"People in Germany hear stories like this and ask, 'Why should we send money down there?' " I said, thinking this might provoke a response from Kotsikaris, who at one point showed off his German with the thickly accented declaration: *"Ich spreche Deutsch."* Kotsikaris said nothing. A butcher with a bald crown and a lazy eye who had until then sat in silence was inspired.

"Tell Merkel there's nothing left to take," the butcher said. "The cow has run off! We're holding only the cowbell now." This statement induced a round of laughs. Encouraged, the butcher went on, making a fist and grabbing his wrist in a manner of depicting a penis. "Merkel can come and take this!" he said. There were more laughs. The butcher then invited me to spend the night drinking ouzo with him, but I declined on account of having more work to do.

The octogenarian arose and looked as if the conversation had disturbed his peace. "Write: 'I won't make sense of any of it,' " he told me again, and then hobbled off.

A few days later, I returned to Nikisiani and stopped by the former town hall—which still functioned as a small municipal office—during working hours. One of the clerks was an affable, lanky man who sat at a desk filling out and stamping paperwork for a small group of gathered citizens. After he was done, he offered to show me the dead mayor's office, which, he said, still looked like it did the day he died. We walked up a few flights of wood stairs and entered the office. On the wall behind the desk hung an imposingly large print of Leonardo da Vinci's *The Last Supper* in between Greek and European Union flags. Scattered around were religious icons and a bust of Democritus, the ancient thinker who theorized the existence of atoms. On the wall hung a plaque with a saying attributed to the historian Thucydides: "The city runs well if the citizens are convinced by the rulers, and the rulers by the law." The clerk told me that the mayor used to be his gym teacher. He was a friendly guy, the clerk said, and relations between the mayor and the treasurers had seemed good. "I couldn't believe it," he said of the shooting. "It all happened because of money."

After I left the mayor's office, I visited a man named Apostolos Tsiakiris in his tidy house near the former town hall. Tsiakiris, a retired municipal clerk, had been a friend and political associate of the mayor, and filled in for him for one year after the shooting. Tsiakiris sat on his couch in a pair of shorts under an icon of Mary and Jesus. He told me that when he was acting mayor, he'd stopped sending payments to the treasurers because they'd been jailed for the shooting. At the time, however, stopping their pay was illegal. Employees who couldn't go to work due to incarceration were considered on "automatic holiday" and entitled to half their pay, pending the outcome of a local government disciplinary board decision. A lawyer for Saltouridis, the treasurer, therefore sued Tsiakiris for breach of duty, forcing the municipality to begin paying the prisoners again, and to make back payments. About six months after the killing, the local disciplinary board ruled that the treasurers ought to be dismissed for "undignified behavior." The lawyer for Saltouridis, however, appealed that decision, sending the case to a secondary disciplinary board in Athens. That meant the treasurers would keep getting their halved salaries at least until a decision on the appeal was handed down, which would take a very long time. This very much upset Tsiakiris. "You can't be a murderer and keep getting paid," he told me. "That doesn't happen in any other government." Before I left, I asked Tsiakiris what the mayor had been like. "He always tried to help," he said. "He could never say no to anyone."

On my way out of town that day, I stopped by the local cemetery. Triantafyllos Koukoudis's grave was decorated with a large crucifix, plastic flowers, and three portrait images of him wearing a tie. On a plaque was written a message from his daughter: "I hope you are the closest star up there and your sparkle will hug the whole world as happened when you were with us. You are and will always be my angel."

During their murder trial, Savvas Saltouridis and Ioakeim Monos told the court they never intended to harm the mayor, just to frighten him. "I learned from my parents, both of whom are lost, to not do harm to any person," Saltouridis, the shooter, told the jury. "Never, never did I intend to do something like this." Saltouridis testified that shortly after he was appointed treasurer, the mayor began asking him for municipal money. On the first occasion, Saltouridis testified, the mayor called him into his office and said: "Because we had elections, I had some financial exposures." The treasurer, eager to please, said he forked over 50,000 euros. Over the next three years, the mayor's requests for money kept coming, according to Saltouridis. He said he grew anxious over the growing financial gap, and suffered periods of trembling and high blood pressure. His psychological state deteriorated, and he couldn't play with his children. "I'm near death," he said to himself at the time, according to his testimony. "I'm going to die. I'm certain." In the summer of 2009, Saltouridis said, he reminded the mayor that certified accountants would be coming for a routine check of the municipal books. "Don't worry," the mayor said, Saltouridis testified. "Everything will fall into place." Saltouridis said he complained to the mayor about the situation one day, but the mayor just lay down on his office sofa and began scratching his genitals. "I started to go crazy," Saltouridis told the court.

Monos, the deputy treasurer, described himself to the court as a dedicated public servant. "I did what I could to serve the local citizens and to be okay at my job," he said. "Whatever the mayor told me to do, I did it." Monos said he gave the mayor "some amounts," but added he did not have a complete understanding of the depth of the fiscal gap until November 2009, when Saltouridis informed him. At one point, the mayor called him into his office and asked for the titles to his house, Monos told the court. "But I don't have anything to do with this," Monos testified he told the mayor. "Do what you can to help," Monos said the mayor told him. "Otherwise I will be destroyed, but I'll destroy you both as well." In December, as the visit from the accountants was imminent, Saltouridis proposed a plan to scare the mayor, Monos told the court. "If you think it will change something, let's scare him," Monos said he replied.

Saltouridis said he didn't mean to pull the Uzi trigger that night; he was trembling when he removed the weapon out from under a jacket and said: "Mayor, please put back the money because I don't know what will happen." Saltouridis said he expected the mayor to be frightened by the sight of the gun. Rather, according to his testimony, the mayor said: "Stop, you *tsoutseki*"—an untranslatable, derogatory word thought to be derived from the Turkish for "flower," or perhaps "dwarf"—and lunged toward him, hitting the gun. Saltouridis said he then slipped backward and accidentally pulled the trigger. The gun was set to automatic and sprayed bullets, he testified. "I pulled the trigger once," he told the court. "I regret it. Not once in a million times would I do something like this again. I couldn't understand what I had done. I'm ashamed of it and I should be punished for what I've done," he said. "I apologize one thousand times."

The court did not believe Saltouridis's version of the events. It found the gun was not set to automatic, but to fire one bullet at a time, and that Saltouridis intentionally and repeatedly pulled the trigger. One year after the shooting, the court convicted Saltouridis of intentional homicide "decided on and carried out in a calm mental state." He was sentenced to life in prison. Monos, the deputy treasurer, was sentenced to sixteen years in prison for direct complicity in the murder, and one year for possession of the weapon. The court held that both men acted with intent to kill the mayor as part of a plan to pin on him the full blame for the missing money. At the time of my visit, both Saltouridis and Monos faced additional criminal charges of embezzlement, in which prosecutors said they acted jointly with the mayor to take more than 700,000 euros of municipal money, some 6,000 of which came from a public kindergarten fund. Lawyers for Saltouridis and Monos told me their clients were not responsible for the embezzlement and did not take any of the missing money for themselves. They were also appealing the convictions in the murder case, maintaining they had not intended to kill the mayor and that things had just gotten out of hand.

The mayor, of course, was not around to defend himself from allegations that he partook in the embezzlement or was responsible for it. The mayor's brother testified that the mayor had used some 200,000 of the missing municipal euros to plug a temporary financial shortage elsewhere in the budget, the result of "some community program" being delayed. "That happens in municipalities, that is to say, to use money on other projects," the brother said. The other 500,000 euros, the brother added, was probably misappropriated by the two treasury employees.

One morning in Kavala, a nearby Aegean port city dotted with Ottoman-era buildings, I visited the office of a lawyer for Saltouridis, a man named Vasileios Kagkaidis. The lawyer worked in a dingy office building near the city's harbor, and seemed to have a good business going. When I arrived, I sat down next to a few seemingly down-and-out clients in a small, windowless waiting room filled with their cigarette smoke. In his office, Kagkaidis loudly maintained simultaneous conversations with a client, an office phone, a mobile phone, and a young woman working for him. When he hung up one of the phones, it inevitably rang again within a few seconds. "Those are magic tricks!" he yelled into one phone, smacking the desk with his palm. "Whatever they say, the truth is I opened their eyes!" he yelled into the other phone. Eventually, he yelled to me: "Come inside, big guy." Kagkaidis was a short man with graying hair and large brown eyes. The back of his swivel chair reached above his head. Above him on a bookshelf was a plaque inscribed with an Ancient Greek aphorism: "There is no surer enemy than an ungrateful beneficiary." Two older men, both clients wearing shorts and sleeveless T-shirts, sat at the desk opposite the lawyer. Kagkaidis asked me why I was interested in Saltouridis's case. I told him it was because Saltouridis was still on the public payroll even as Greece's creditors were demanding the country fire civil servants. "So now that the Troika, Europe, are asking us to lay off loads of civil servants, now it becomes an issue," he said. "Otherwise, they would have kept getting paid." He banged his hand on his desk in a way that made it seem he was angry about this, though I soon realized this was his default way of talking. "And they keep searching for civil servants to fire so we can get the next dose." "Dose" had become the common Greek way of describing the bailout loan installments, which came in trickles, like methadone for an addict, based on the fulfillment of the creditors' rehabilitation program.

I asked Kagkaidis if it was right that his client still remained on the public payroll. "Behind it all is a woman and three children," he said, in a plaintive, lowered voice. "The law wisely foresaw, that if he kills someone, what are his kids going to do?" His voice resumed its normal, elevated volume. "Wise is the law that says you'll take half because there's a wife and three children." It seemed important to Kagkaidis that his imprisoned-for-life client be grateful, if not for a less severe sentence, then for the fact that he was still getting a paycheck. Kagkaidis, after all, was the one who had sued Tsiakiris, the acting mayor after the shooting, for having refused to pay his client; and it was his idea to appeal the local government disciplinary board decision, which forced the municipality to keep paying the men, pending the outcome.

"All those babies were paid from me," Kagkaidis said, in reference to his client's three children.

"What was your justification for the appeal?" I asked him.

"What justification?" he said, shrugging, looking side to side and scrunching his face to indicate this was a preposterous, legally irrelevant question. "There is no justification. You took a weapon and killed the mayor? What justification?" The reason for the appeal, he said, was to "draw it out."

Indeed, the disciplinary review process had been drawn out. During the summer of my visit to Pangaio—three years after the appeal—a second-degree review board in Athens decided that Saltouridis and Monos should be dismissed, as Mitsotakis, the administrative reform minister, had pointed out on the radio. When I contacted the ministry to find out why it had taken that long, the answer wasn't particularly illuminating. "It took really long to start functioning properly," a ministry spokesman said. That spokesman also maintained that the two employees had been fired as a result of the appeal decision. I asked him if he was sure about that. Yes, he told me. He was very sure. In Pangaio, however, municipal officials told me that only they could technically fire the employees, and legally, they could not do so quite yet. According to Greek law at the time, the employees had a right to appeal again, this time to the country's supreme administrative court. The treasurers would automatically be given up to three months to decide whether they would file such an appeal. This three-month period could not, according to the law, begin over the summer, due to its being a period of leisure. That meant the convicts would remain on the payroll at least until late autumn, and potentially much longer if they did decide to appeal again. I eventually informed the reform ministry that it had been premature in declaring the treasurers fired, and its spokesman later acknowledged the error.

Kagkaidis, seemingly bored with discussing the case any further, began to talk to me about politics. He said he'd had a poster of John F. Kennedy in his room as a child. Kennedy, Obama, they were human beings, he said. Bush? "He fucked up the whole world." Kagkaidis was a passionate advocate of PASOK, which made him a bit unique for the time, as the party was politically eviscerated, and scorned by most Greeks for its part in the country's downfall. "Tell America that Greece exists," Kagkaidis told me. "That there's freedom in Greece, and that we speak freely." He then proceeded to speak his mind some more. German chancellor Angela Merkel, he said, was like Bush, and she was the one who wanted Greece to fire civil servants. "For me it's a mistake to fire them," he said. "They have families, etc. But the European right is pushing us. Bush, in other words. Bush!" He then paused, and changed tack, like a lawyer able to argue any side of an issue. "But they've got the money," he said, shedding the indignant tone of his previous statements. Kagkaidis then pointed to the two gray-haired clients on either side of him, who'd been listening in reverential silence. "You see these two deadbeats?" Kagkaidis said, pointing in their directions but not bothering to look at them. "Greece has three million pensioners like them. Deadbeats. And illegal pensions, too. Thankfully, Germany pays, and they get their money. If their pensions are cut, they'll start killing each other." The two men remained silent, and one nodded slightly in agreement.

One evening shortly before I traveled to Pangaio, the Greek government spokesman at the time, a politician named Simos Kedikoglou, stood before a television camera in a red tie and announced the first large-scale public worker firings in a very long time. "At a time when the Greek people endure sacrifices, there is no time for delay or hesitation," Kedikoglou said, his dark eyebrows seesawing in the unnatural and exaggerated manner of someone attempting to come off as deeply serious. The state broadcaster, known as ERT, was an overstaffed bastion of plush benefits and incredible waste that could no longer be tolerated; it was necessary to "finish with the deficits and get out of the crisis." ERT had six accounting departments that did not communicate with one another, employed tens of technicians to do the work of two or three, and paid massive, unjustified overtime, added Kedikoglou by way of giving a few examples. The broadcaster represented the quintessence of waste, and the government had the "bold and radical" will to do something about it. It had decided to close ERT through a joint ministerial decision, and would replace it with a more streamlined, high-quality broadcaster. ERT's transmission would be cut off that night, he said. ERT's main television news channel covered the speech live; its news anchors and commentators, though vainly trying to keep a modicum of journalistic objectivity, looked like prisoners awaiting their executions. Soon, as newscasters reported that riot police were on the way to disable their hilltop transmitters, the broadcast went blank. Outside ERT's headquarters in a northern outskirt of Athens, thousands of protesters, to whom the government's action seemed dictatorial, gathered and, through their shrieks of protest, suggested that Greece's military junta—which fell in 1974—was still governing.

Though the levels of waste and nepotism at ERT were probably comparable to those in other parts of the public sector, the government made the broadcaster out to be the most errant embodiment of those ills, in order to justify its closure. ERT was so bad, in other words, a new broadcaster had to be started from scratch. The closure also had the effect of immediately reducing Greece's public workforce by 2,660 workers, thereby going a long way toward fulfilling the wishes of the Troika, which was demanding prompt layoffs—specifically, 4,000 of them by the year's end. The government had to begin those layoffs somewhere, but shutting down the state broadcaster was a very heavy-handed, clumsy way of doing it. In the words of a statement signed by the head of every major European public broadcaster, the move was "undemocratic and unprofessional." While the government assured the public it would quickly create a new broadcaster modeled on the BBC or those in Germany, few believed in its preparedness to do so. Indeed, several months after the closure, an interim public television station aired black-and-white films, cooking shows, and innocuous documentaries. The prime minister had shut down a deeply flawed but nevertheless significant public news source with no clear capacity to replace it. This left Greeks to get their news from the major private television stations, largely owned by oligarchs seeking to influence the public discussion in ways amenable to their interests.

The government was acting under pressure from its creditors to show it was willing to break the taboo of firing government workers. Indeed, International Monetary Fund experts later commended the closure as a sign the government had at last begun to undertake the public sector reforms they had long been demanding. Yet, it wasn't clear the action would help the government's financial situation. ERT's budget, as is the case with other European broadcasters, came from a separate levy taken directly from Greeks' electric bills. ERT employees were also eventually granted generous severance pay, canceling out any initial savings that would come from a more efficiently run replacement. The day after the closure, Prime Minister Samaras gave a speech at a business awards event and presented the move as part of the government's drive to break the sclerotic, Soviet-like insularity of the public administration. An incredible bureaucracy had blocked every effort to improve productivity due to its "grid of petrified ideological obsessions that have died everywhere else and survive only in Greece," he said. The Greek state's "opacity and waste don't exist anywhere in the world today, at least not in Europe." For too long, Samaras added, Greeks had been living with a "sinful ERT."

In response, incensed Greek public sector labor unions announced a general strike. This is what they have done with regularity for decades in order to protect and improve public worker pay and benefits, particularly in the 1980s, when there were nearly 4,500 strikes in Greece; that is more than a strike a day. Greece is by far the most strike-prone nation in the European Union, and after the bailout agreement was struck, strikes became so common that some entrepreneurial Greeks created a website named after the Greek word for strike, www.apergia.gr, which daily informed commuters about which public transportation services had been shut down. On the day of the general strike, I traveled to a large demonstration that was to take place outside ERT's headquarters. Despite sporadic transportation service that day, the metro line closest to the ERT building was running smoothly in order to convey trainloads of protesters. On my train car, a middle-aged man handed out flyers taken from his red backpack. "Do you know this government supports pederasts?" he said as he handed them out.

The flyers were copies of a health ministry document listing the various psychological disturbances, including sexual perversions, for which one could get a disability benefit. Diagnosed pedophiles were deemed between 20 and 30 percent disabled, according to the document. "Do you know why the government supports pederasts?" the man asked me after handing me a flyer. "Because they're all pederasts."

"This government is worse than the junta!" cried a woman from further down the train car.

"And us?" said the man with the flyers. "We know our future. They'll throw us out onto the street."

When the train reached the station nearest to ERT, the protesters spilled out onto a suburban boulevard lined with furniture and electronics stores. Outside the broadcaster's headquarters were assembled a dizzying array of far-left parties and organizations, divided by internecine squabbles yet united in their opposition to the plutocratic government. They all gathered, amid the many banners depicting the hammer and sickle, to chant slogans of support for ERT's *ergazomenoi* ("the workers"), a word that has sacred connotation for the Greek left. The workers, in the left's dualist worldview, were always on the righteous side in the class struggle against the bosses. While Greece indeed had an oligarchical class of crony capitalists that inflicted a lot of harm on the country, the left seemed to possess a lover's blindness when it came to the inadequacies of the *ergazomenoi* that constituted Greece's public administration. The communist party–affiliated trade union was particularly visible in its efforts to protect public jobs, at one point hanging a massive hammer-and-sickle banner from the Acropolis that read: PEOPLES OF EUROPE RISE UP. Outside ERT, I tried to keep track of the number of leftist groups: 1) the Internationalist Workers' Left, a revolutionary Marxist group; 2) the Committee for a Workers' International—a Trotskyist group; 3) the Red Network at the Coalition of the Radical Left, one of the "fronts" within Syriza; 4) the Communist Organization of Greece, a revolutionary Marxist and Maoist party; 5) the All-Workers Militant Front, the trade union of the main communist party of Greece; 6) the Marxist-Leninist Communist Party of Greece, a Maoist splinter faction from the main communist party. There were many more, but I decided to stop counting and made my way to the gate of the ERT complex, where enterprising souvlaki makers had set up stands and were conducting a brisk business.

From the bland five-story ERT building, depressed employee faces peered out through rows of windows and exhaled cigarette smoke. These were the first unfortunates in the public sector to be laid off, and they made it clear they would not go down easily. The workers had occupied the building and refused to relinquish control of it to the Greek state. "We are still alive and we are open," a well-coiffed news anchorwoman standing in front of the building yelled into a microphone. I tried to imagine the workers of National Public Radio or the Public Broadcasting Service in the United States taking similar action. It was hard to conjure the image of Renée Montagne or Charlie Rose doing this kind of thing—though it was also hard to fathom the U.S. government sending riot police to shut them down.

On the lawn in front of the entrance sat an array of supportive unions. The Panhellenic Federation of Employees in Public Financial Services, the Association of Workers in Institutions for the Mentally Ill and Vulnerable Social Groups, the Greek Federation of Bank Employees Unions. Some had impossible acronyms, such as EDOEAP, which was the United Journalistic Organization for Supplementary Insurance Care. Next to a few olive trees sat members of the Association of Waiters, Cooks, and Other Employees of the Catering Industry. Next to them hung their banner: IN RESPONSE TO THE ATTACK OF THE BOSSES WE RESPOND WITH CLASS SOLIDARITY AND ORGANIZING. Satellite trucks nearby continued to broadcast ERT programs, which were being streamed online. Inside, a hastily organized security apparatus of ERT employees checked my press credentials and noted my name; a precaution, they said, to screen out government agents and police. I walked upstairs to the broadcaster's cafeteria, which was full of commiserating employees. Behind the counter were servings of roasted half chickens and boiled potatoes, but people mainly seemed to stick to the coffee and cigarettes. As I watched the small lady briskly working the cash register, I asked her where the money was going, given that the broadcaster officially didn't exist anymore. She glanced at me with a look of disdain. "What money?" she said. "We need to pay our salaries!"

I sat down at one of the tables and met a friendly, thirty-eight-year-old mezzo-soprano in the ERT choir named Maria Karagiannaki, whose blue knit sweater matched the hue of her generously applied eye shadow. She began to defend the choir, although I hadn't asked any accusatory questions. "It's not true that we only perform two or three times a year," she said to me. "Yes, some productions were very expensive, but it's the politicians who signed off on those." She went on to tell me that her choir performed very well despite being short-staffed. "How do you perform a Verdi's *Requiem* with just thirty-five people?" A performance of Beethoven had won them so much praise, she said, that some people suggested they go to Germany to teach the Germans how to sing it. As we talked, I found it hard to think of this mezzo-soprano as the embodiment of the public sector problem. Her take-home pay was 900 euros a month, she told me. To be sure, she said, ERT needed some big changes, and a lot of the things people said about the wasteful spending and the nepotistic hiring were true. "But the politicians made it this way," she said.

She had a point about that. Greek politicians had certainly long cultivated ERT's excesses, just as they had cultivated many of the other excesses they were being forced to rein in. Parliamentarians, after all, were charged with appointing ERT's board of directors, who were then in positions to hire politicians' friends and family, and also to influence the news programming so that it was favorable to the government. Government ministers would routinely call ERT to tell its journalists how to report stories. Some people recognized these problems long before ERT was closed, but met fierce political resistance when they tried to do something about it. In 2011, a then government minister, Elias Mossialos, proposed a plan to improve the quality and objectivity of ERT's coverage by making its leadership independent of the government. In order to reduce the excessive costs, Mossialos also suggested cutting down on much of the television programming, which few people watched anyway. Everyone including the New Democracy party, led by Samaras, the one who later closed ERT for its unredeemable sins, rejected the idea. Simos Kedikoglou, the politician who later announced ERT's closure on television, back then told an ERT reporter that Mossialos's reform proposal was going "totally in the wrong direction." It would result in economic damage, lost jobs, and the transfer of valuable public assets to private interests, he said. Also, he added, cutting ERT broadcasts in border regions would dangerously cede those frequencies to neighboring enemies like the Turks. It's unlikely that Kedikoglou only learned of ERT's problems two years later, when he announced the shutdown. After all, Kedikoglou, a journalist by trade, had worked at ERT earlier in his career.

In addition to its regular employees, ERT hired numerous "consultants" for its programs, but whether many of them did much consulting was questionable. I ran into what seemed an example of this practice while briefly subletting an Athens apartment from a musician couple. As far as I first knew, the couple made a living performing music, and while their endeavors were not very lucrative, they seemed to be well taken care of by a parent. The couple had apartments in Athens, at least one in Paris, and a house on an Aegean island. They had sublet their main Athens dwelling, they told me, because they were struggling to make money playing music, and were planning on moving to Paris to begin anew. This was not unusual. Many young Greeks were leaving the country on account of the near impossibility of finding a good job. After ERT's closure, the musician couple seemed demoralized, and then canceled their Paris plans. At first, I didn't understand what ERT had to do with Paris. One of them explained that they had been acting as consultants for an arts program on ERT. Now that the program no longer existed, they had lost their main source of income, and could no longer afford to move to Paris. The musicians had told me about an aunt of theirs I should definitely talk to for my reporting; she knew *everybody* in terms of politicians. I wondered if that's how they got their consulting gigs, but I never had the courage to ask.

ERT employees widely acknowledged the nepotism and other problems, though no one admitted to benefiting from it. Rather, many reacted to their government's maladroit move to fire them with a high degree of self-aggrandizement. UNEMPLOYMENT AND POVERTY AND NOW LOSS OF CULTURE, read a banner employees hung from the ERT building. THIS IS THE PRICE FOR €. Workers portrayed their occupation of the building as a defense of the "the voice of the Greek people." For months, ERT journalists continued rogue news broadcasts largely dedicated to resisting their demise, as if it was the most important global issue of the time. The reports, to put it euphemistically, lacked objectivity, and were interspersed with public service announcements protesting the closure. On one news program, a reporter summarized an article in *The Economist* that said the handling of ERT had made Greeks more skeptical of their government's ability to implement reforms. The reporter left out that the article also said: "Few Greeks watch ERT's four television channels; its programs are dull and its new anchors are political stooges." News programs also frequently aired panel discussions consisting of ERT employees. A balding ERT technician named Nikos called the government's action part of a "crisis of values." He would not let the government take away the "values passed on from our teachers and our parents," the "values we are struggling for and keep as our North Star." I had met another technician, also named Nikos, during my visits to ERT. He told me to be wary when people told me their baseline salaries, because in reality, many received union-negotiated perks. Technicians, he told me, received a 10 percent bonus for being technicians, a 10 percent bonus for being trade union members, and a 20 percent bonus for doing hazardous work. "It was a party that was going on," he said. "Until the moment when it stopped."

After my conversation with the mezzo-soprano, I found the news television studio and met Kostas Karikis, a short man with a graying buzz cut, a large nose, and small eyes that evaded direct contact with mine. He was forty-three, and his job was to come up with the headlines that streamed across the television screen during news broadcasts. We found an empty office to sit in, and he rolled a cigarette and used a soda bottle as an ashtray. The decision to close ERT, he said, was clearly political. "They want a channel that is more subordinate to the government. That's my opinion." He had not finished university, and he feared that if he lost this job, he'd never find another. He would not starve; he had an aunt who was a doctor and could help him, he said. But still, the thought of losing the job made him extremely depressed.

"I'm not young," he said. "I'm not very handsome. I'm not qualified. I don't have a degree. The only thing I know how to do is to do my job well and to use words to make a living. I don't know what else to do. I don't know if I can live without all these things." Karikis then uttered what I thought to be a pretty fair assessment of the larger political situation in Greece. "This society is a society that has been very dependent on state money," he said, extinguishing his cigarette. "It's a communistic capitalism which gives people a small slice of state money so they will shut the fuck up and continue to bear the stealing. Now they say it's our fault because we received the state money." He paused and snapped: "Bullshit!" Then he added in a calmer voice, "We are bearing the weight of the public deficit because of our very big salaries? That is a myth. That is not half true. It's maybe one-quarter true."

I returned to ERT a few days later and found a stage had been set up on the lawn outside. ERT musicians were giving concerts to draw crowds and keep the protests alive. I walked inside, went through security, and found Karikis in the television control room. It was a big news night. The leaders of Greece's coalition government were meeting to discuss ERT. The two left-leaning coalition parties spoke out against the prime minister's action, and a lot of people at ERT were predicting the government's collapse, a result that could mean they would keep their jobs. In the control room, about a dozen laid-off employees sat in front of about a dozen screens. Karikis stood in front of one of them. His stubble had grown into a beard and he had bags under his eyes. He'd been sleeping on a couch in the ERT building in order to guard against a police raid, which was expected to come in the middle of any one of those nights. Beside Karikis, a young woman sat typing on an oversized keyboard. The control room was loud. Everyone spoke at the same time, and the two people in charge yelled over everyone else. "Write 'No Agreement Between the Three Party Leaders!'" shouted one of the superiors. Karikis repeated the line to the young woman at the big keyboard, who then typed it, and then it appeared on the screen. Karikis yelled back to the superior, suggesting they write that the coalition's survival remained a question mark. The superior shot him down, saying it was premature to speculate about such a collapse. "I said 'question mark'!" Karikis yelled in his defense. The superior yelled back: "All-Night Thriller of Political Developments." Karikis repeated it, the young woman typed it, and it appeared on the screen. One of the bosses, a small man who was the loudest of them all, called for "dramatic tone" to play over the background. He then demanded a split screen that mimicked the private broadcast channels he was monitoring from his terminal. The woman in charge of screen splitting protested. One side of the split screen would be an empty podium awaiting a politician, and that would be stupid, she said. "Split screen! When I say split screen, you split the screen," the little man said. "We're showing the thriller. It's the anticipation. When I say split screen, you split the screen." The underling obeyed, but commanded her boss to "relax" in return. "No, I'll yell," he said. "You just split the screen. Period." At one point, the location where the politician was about to speak was misidentified in an on-screen headline. Karikis reacted as if a baby had been run over, bringing his hands to his temples and unleashing a banshee wail as the woman at the typewriter corrected it.

Several politicians spoke on the screens that night. All that was clear was that the three parties didn't concur on the wisdom or legality of the closure. Still, the possibility of a government collapse and new elections was remote. The previous summer, Greece had undergone two national elections within a month in order for a shaky coalition government to emerge, and in the process, the country nearly fell apart. New elections only one year later would have tipped the country over the brink. By the time I left ERT's studio that night, however, it still wasn't clear how the matter would pan out. Karikis was optimistic, though. As he walked me out of the control room, he predicted early elections. Syriza would take over and reopen ERT. "It looks like we're safe and the government is falling apart."

It would take a while longer for Karikis's prediction to come true. The conservative-led government survived for the time being, though the smallest party of the tripartite coalition, the Democratic Left, which despite its communist roots had joined the coalition due to a competing pro-euro orientation, eventually withdrew over the ERT affair. The two remaining factions—PASOK and New Democracy—held on to power by a handful of seats. Despite its weakened position, the government said the change was positive. It was now free of the departed leftists' meddling, which made it fitter to implement reforms with efficiency. ERT employees continued to occupy the facilities and send pirate broadcasts through the fall. One November morning at 4:00, however, five months after ERT was shut down, riot police entered the building and seized control of it. The ERT employees had fought with tenacity, but now only a Syriza victory could save them.

While ERT employees were the first to be laid off, that is not to say public employees had until then escaped the nation's economic free fall unscathed. The Troika sought to undo the steep pay raises civil servants had received in the decade preceding the crisis, and Greek government workers saw their paychecks cut by as much as 35 percent. This was intended not only to reduce the government's wage bill, but to make the Greek economy more competitive. Since public wage levels have a direct effect on private wages, a reduction in the former would result in a cheaper overall labor force, allowing Greece to export products at more competitive prices, the thinking went. Or as I heard some Greeks put it, the plan was to make wages as low as in China, so that Greeks, too, would one day supplicate for jobs assembling iPads until their fingers went numb. The Troika's plan certainly seemed to work, as average incomes in Greece fell about one-quarter in the years following the outbreak of the crisis. It was not clear, however, that the Greek government would be able to sustain all the public wage cuts it had been forced to implement. Unions took the government to court over the cuts, and by 2014, had some success rolling them back. Greece's highest court, for instance, ruled that wage and pension cuts for police and members of the armed forces were unconstitutional. Judges predictably deemed pension cuts for the judiciary unconstitutional.

While most public employees were having to get used to lower living standards, they were still as a whole doing a lot better than workers left to fare for themselves in the crippled private sector, where, for many, work conditions may have made a Chinese factory job enviable. The great majority of the many unemployed Greeks were sufferers of the private sector. Even those who retained their jobs saw working conditions swiftly deteriorate. Only half of Greek companies paid their workers on time, according to one 2013 study, and when they were paying, salaries were often very low. Even after the public worker wage cuts went into effect, college graduates in their late twenties with government jobs earned nearly double the salary of similarly qualified peers in the private sector, where salaries were severely diminished as a consequence of the high unemployment and deregulated labor market. One out of five salaried private sector workers earned less than 500 euros a month, the Greek labor minister announced in 2013. The relatively disadvantageous circumstances for private sector workers stirred resentment, and many Greeks favored the dismantling of public sector privileges. "It is unacceptable that private sector employees be treated as second-class citizens," the *Athens Review of Books* wrote in an open letter to the Troika in 2011. "Why the difference? Because the Greek political system secured its grip on power by continuously expanding the public sector; it is thus understandably reluctant to downsize it. But enough is enough! For how long will the Greek taxpayers foot the bill for this inflated and dysfunctional public sector that impedes private economic activity and the provision of public goods?"

Despite the civil servant job protections that fueled this sentiment, the public sector in Greece did in fact shrink considerably. That was because, early on in the crisis, tens of thousands of public workers retired early in order to protect their pensions from the effect of wage cuts. The shedding of these workers didn't save the government much money, since there was an inverse relationship between the number of employees remaining on its payroll and the number of pensioners it had to support. Nevertheless, the withering of its personnel put the Greek government on track to meet one of the Troika's central demands—a reduction in the number of public workers by 150,000 by the end of 2015. The Troika, however, was not going to allow Greece to carry out the cuts through attrition alone. In 2013, as a condition of unlocking bailout loan payments it had withheld due to its dissatisfaction with the Greek reform effort, the Troika demanded Greece choose 15,000 workers deemed unqualified, negligent, or unnecessary and fire them. In exchange, the government would be able to hire an equal number of new workers based on their qualifications and usefulness. This was meant to improve the quality of the public bureaucracy.

Since the improvement, however, would be coming at the expense of existing employees, no one in the Greek public sector unions seemed to appreciate the potential societal benefits of injecting new blood into the workforce. Municipal workers' unions were particularly theatrical in their opposition to public worker firings, storming the gates of parliament or occupying town halls around the country. I witnessed one such occupation in a suburban town hall outside Athens. The workers excitedly discussed their resistance strategy—work stoppages, additional strikes, legal action—while in the main meeting room, many of them smoked and some of the men drank *tsipouro*, a pomace brandy. The town hall seemed to have been converted into their personal hangout spot. On another occasion, in the city of Trikala in central Greece, burly union heads burst into municipal offices, shut off the lights, and commanded everyone to leave. "This is a decision of the workers," one of the union members shouted. When one office worker, a woman who wanted to complete some clerical task, tried to turn the lights back on, the union head began screaming. "You should be ashamed," he said, slamming his hand on a desk. "Jackasses!" he added. "No one is working. Out!" Another time, when I was on the island of Lesbos, I witnessed a protest of city sanitation workers who arrived in front of the town hall in the local fleet of garbage trucks, honking the horns and blaring sirens as if to generate some kind of primitive air-raid alert. Seeing this, I thought the workers' willingness to use public property—whether town halls or garbage trucks—for their own purposes suggested they considered themselves to be the public.

By the summer of 2013 and into the following year, public employees around the country targeted for potential layoffs engaged in coordinated rebellion. Public doctors walked out of hospitals. School guards tried to burst through riot police lines into government offices. The laid-off cleaning staff of the finance ministry—the "cleaning ladies," as they came to be called—set up a semipermanent protest camp outside the ministry, clashing often with riot police. At two prominent public universities in Athens, administrative employees went on strike through the duration of the first term of 2013, locking down campus buildings in order to keep professors and students from entering.

One afternoon in November, I visited a meeting of striking administrative employees at Athens Polytechnic, one of Greece's most esteemed universities—though, when I visited its abandoned, very concrete main campus on the outskirts of Athens, I thought it would make a good setting for a movie about the apocalypse. Though the colonnades of idyllic American colleges are modeled on the classical, Hellenic forms, one doesn't tend to find such eulogizing picturesqueness on Greek campuses, where communist and other far-left student groups reign and graffitists decorate accordingly. WE DON'T RECOGNIZE THE DEBT. NOT A SINGLE SACRIFICE FOR THE PLUTOCRACY. In a campus auditorium, I found hundreds of administrative employees sitting under a small portrait of Jesus hung high on the wall above the podium. The mood was jittery. That morning, the government had published a list of 399 Greek university administrative employees who faced potential firing after faring poorly in an evaluation. The workers were discussing their next course of action. Most of them supported the status quo—a simple extension of the campus occupation—but one among them, a bearded, avuncular-looking man, approached

the podium and suggested that some return to work and immediately implement a work stoppage instead. This would represent
a softening of their stance, because it meant reopening the buildings. There were jeers in opposition to the proposal. Arguments
broke out in the crowd. Groups of angered workers stood as if fans
at a soccer match arguing with the referee. "We can't turn back
now!" It was hard to decipher full sentences amid the din of tem-
pers. Cigarettes were lit to calm nerves.

There was a further issue of contention. The employees were
conscious that they had come under heavy criticism in the Greek
media because they had continued to receive paychecks during
the long duration of their strike. This had occurred because the
striking administrators controlled the university payment system.
A further proposal was floated to cut off further paychecks, not
only for themselves, but also for all university personnel, effective
at the end of the month. That would include all the professors,
who, after initially striking in solidarity with the administrators,
had decided they wanted classes to begin. One woman approached
the microphone and declared that she couldn't bear the weight of
suspending paychecks for everyone right before the holidays. "Just
because my house is burning doesn't mean the neighbor's house
should burn too," she said. Passions arose and the din returned.
"Don't you all see what's happening?" one woman screamed in
response before storming outside and taking deep, consoling drags
from her cigarette. Fault lines seemed to be appearing between
those who were on the list of people slated for potential firing and
those who were not, the latter of which seemed to be losing their
militancy. The workers nevertheless voted overwhelmingly to continue striking and stop all university paychecks. After the meeting, I spoke with the vice president of the administrative workers'
union, a petite blonde in cowboy boots named Katia Papanikolaou.
She was on the list. "We're playing for everything," she told me.
"We have nothing to lose," she added. "We're at war."

The next day, I saw Papanikolaou on campus again talking to a group of students in the school of mechanical engineering. Until then, communist student organizations had been occupying campus buildings in solidarity with the administrators. But an increasing number of students, concerned they would completely miss the school term, were pushing for classes to begin. Papaniko- laou and other administrators were therefore dispatched in order to enlist the students' continued support. In a voice strained by cigarettes and the passion of repeated union meetings, she urged the students to fight on, not for the workers' sake, but for their own. The administrators' strike was not intended to inhibit their education, she said, but rather to rescue it. After all, how could they register for classes without the administrative workers? Their historic institution wouldn't be able to function. "Education must remain so that minds remain open," she said in a pleading voice. The students listened to her in silence, a rare respect at such meet- ings, reserved for occasions when someone from the working class came to speak. "Education is the foundation of our society," Papa- nikolaou went on. "Keep doing whatever you can. Not for us. We're out. For you. You don't want to be in our position tomorrow." It was righteous rhetoric, which I found to be lacking in lofty intention and motivated by a naked desire for self-preservation. I expected some students to perhaps call her out on this. But who were the students to question one of the *ergazomenoi*, especially one whose job was under threat due to the Troika? The students applauded, seemingly convinced.

At the time, Athens Polytechnic was marking the fortieth anniversary of a bloody student uprising against the repressive, American-backed military dictatorship. Several commemorations were to take place, including a protest march by leftist groups to the American embassy. The administrative employees married their strike to the anniversary theme of "Bread, Education, Free- dom." In a statement read aloud over university speakers on the anniversary day, the administrators said theirs was a struggle not only to preserve the right to work, but to stop university education from becoming a mechanism to produce "narrowly trained, cheap hands of labor" for big companies that "salary the brightest minds for the business of the depreciation of human existence." The administrators, moreover, had done whatever they could to challenge the face of repression, to resist a force that "although not wearing a military uniform nevertheless creeps all around us, humiliating humanitarian ideals."

The university administrators were largely successful in their resistance to the layoffs, and the schools eventually all reopened for classes. When Syriza took power at the beginning of 2015, the threat of imminent dismissals of university administrators and all other public workers immediately dissolved. The new leftist administrative reform minister, furthermore, vowed to reinstate thousands of public workers the previous government had managed to dismiss despite the mass resistance. In addition, Syriza announced, the old state broadcaster, ERT, would be reopened. Upon learning that they'd be rehired, laid-off public workers rejoiced. The finance ministry "cleaning ladies," who had until then maintained a protest encampment outside their workplace, put on red rubber gloves and celebrated in the streets. "You've been fired!" they yelled in reference to members of the previous government.

Around the time of the anniversary of the Polytechnic uprising, Mitsotakis, the administrative reform minister, sent out a tweet: "Albeit late the murderers of the mayor of Pangaio were fired today period." It was nearly four years after the shooting.

The shooter's wife had dreaded this moment. During my trip to Pangaio the preceding summer, I visited the small town where she and her husband had made their home. The place was called

Chortokopi, after a former Pontic Greek settlement in what is now Turkey, in the mountains south of the Black Sea city of Trabzon. One evening in Pangaio, I drove up to Savvas Saltouridis's home, which like other homes in Chortokopi could have been extracted from a Las Vegas suburb. The residence was an elevated two-story house enclosed by a spacious veranda. A golden retriever panted in the front yard, beside children's bicycles and manicured pine trees. No one answered when I rang the bell, so I stopped by the main village square, which sat in the shade of towering plane trees. There, I settled at a *kafenio*. Two youths, seemingly imploding with boredom, sipped *frapés*—iced coffee—and a few old men sat and flipped their *kombológia*. The snap of beads punctuated the sound track of locusts droning from the trees. I ordered a coffee and asked the server if anyone knew Savvas Saltouridis's family. After a quick phone call, his brother Giorgos was informed of my presence and on his way.

As I waited, I became a bit uneasy about how Giorgos might react to my visit. A day earlier, I had tried to visit Saltouridis and his colleague Monos in prison, but neither wished to see me, according to the warden. Now, a question ran through my mind: Did the police ultimately confiscate that Uzi? A red pickup truck pulled up, and from it emerged a brawny man with sun-darkened skin. He walked toward me with a beefy gait that would have been daunting had it not been for the mitigating influence of a beer belly and peaceable brown eyes. "I would have come sooner," he said, "but I was just getting a haircut." We sat at a table and ordered a couple of coffees. I asked him how his brother's family was doing. "My brother did a stupid thing and should pay for it," Giorgos said. "He should be punished. But how is his family to blame? What will happen to the children? Do they need to die?" The family, he meant, needed his brother's halved salary. Giorgos said he had done what he could to help them, but he was just a farmer with kids of his own. "Do you have any idea what the electric bill is on that place?" he said of his brother's house. Giorgos then showed me a 1998 photo taken of his brother in Boston. It was the first image I'd seen of Saltouridis. He was sitting on a chair, bowing a *lyra* and looking directly at the camera with a birdlike, expressionless face. His eyes seemed sunken, as if preferring to hide. A pile of dollar bills was strewn at his feet. "Do you see all that money?" said Giorgos. "It's a lot of money." His brother had been invited to play the *lyra* for Pontic Greeks in New York, Boston, Munich, all around the world, Giorgos said. It was with the money he earned doing this that he'd been able to build that home with the veranda, said Giorgos, who seemed to think that the house required justification. I got out my camera to take a picture of the photo for the record, and Giorgos waited patiently as I snapped a few images of it. "Make sure you get the money," he said. "A lot of money."

Giorgos, at my request, called his brother's wife, and she agreed to come to the *kafenio*. He left before she arrived, saying they didn't get along, though he didn't want to explain why. Soon, a thickset blond woman in flip-flops and a purple "Angry Birds" T-shirt walked up to me and politely shook my hand. She took a seat across from me, put her keys on the table, and asked for a glass of water. I asked her how she and her children were doing, and she began to cry. She said she still had trouble believing her husband was in prison. "I feel like he's just gone for a visit," she said. Their eight-year-old was dealing with it very badly. He needed therapy, she said, but she didn't have the money to pay for it. Things would get much worse without her husband's halved salary. "With the economic crisis in Greece, I understand they want to cut it," she said. "But how should I live? What support do I have?" She said she had lost her job as a cleaning lady at a language school after the employer was forced to make cutbacks. Now, she was helping to take care of an elderly pensioner a few days a week, and couldn't find anything better. Making matters worse, there was a possibility the municipality could seize and auction off the family house, which, she said, her husband had built long ago with profits he made, not with the *lyra*, but in the stock market. "How can they cut his salary just like that after so many years of service?" she added. He had worked for twenty years as a public servant, she said, and he had a good record until this incident. More tears dribbled down her cheeks. "If they cut that money, I can't imagine what I'll do," she said. "There are no jobs."

5

The Apostate

Our Lady was seized with trembling, and the icons
wept tears.
"Be silent, Lady and Mistress; and you, icons, weep not.
Again in years and times to come it will be ours once
more."

—Song of Hagia Sophia

One night in the year 982, the archangel Gabriel descended
from heaven for an earthly visit, according to Orthodox Christian
tradition. Disguised as a monk, the angel arrived on Mount Athos,
a secluded mountain peninsula dotted with Byzantium's most revered monasteries, to partake in a pre-dawn vigil before an icon of
Mary and Jesus. "It is truly meet to bless thee, O Theotokos, thou
the ever-blessed and most pure, and the Mother of our God," the
archangel chanted with such celestial melody that a monk beside
him understood he was in the presence of a heavenly being. The
archangel then vanished, and for a time, according to some tell-
ings, the icon emitted a divine light.

On a sunny, hot October Saturday in 2012, the same icon was
delivered from Mount Athos to the shore of the northern city of
Thessaloniki, Greece's second-largest metropolis, aboard a Greek
navy gunboat. The occasion was the coming 100th anniversary of

the city's liberation from the Ottoman Empire, and the monks of Mount Athos, a few hours' boat ride away, had it seen fit to enhance the festivities by contributing one of their most venerated icons for a few weeks' residence in the city. There on the paved harborside to receive the icon were a military marching band, scores of Greek soldiers in navy whites and army fatigues standing in formation, and various politicians. I stood sweating among a crowd of a few thousand Greek citizens who had gathered around the city's most prominent landmark, the cylindrical, turreted *Lefkos Pyrgos,* or White Tower, built to fortify Thessaloniki during Ottoman rule. After an Ottoman surrender during the First Balkan War, the city came under Greek control in the fall of 1912, on a day that seemed fated, as it fell on the feast day of the city's patron saint, Deme-trios, a Roman military commander martyred there for his Christian faith in the early fourth century.

On an elevated stage sat the nation's highest-ranking clergy, all clad in black hats and robes. Flanking the clerics were two scruffy men adorned in the customary revolutionary bandit garb—the pleated kilts and pom-pom shoes. They wore tired expressions, as if having been rented out for such festivities one too many times. Offshore, a few clerics emerged from the cabin of the gunboat, their frocks fluttering violently in the wind, followed by a pack of sailors carrying the icon. The revered object was enclosed in a wooden and glass case and framed with white flowers. The sail-ors strained from the weight of the contraption as they boarded a smaller coast guard boat that bobbed alongside the navy vessel. The priests, the sailors, and their holy cargo then puttered toward the harborside. The crowd waited in silent anticipation as the faint, windswept din of techno music echoed from the cafés lining the harbor, where young people carried on with their Saturday, apathetic to the sacred undertaking.

The boat pulled up to shore, and the onlookers applauded its ar-rival. Many held their cameras high with one hand while making the sign of the cross with the other. People seemed to believe that the Virgin Mary herself, or the *Panagia,* as she is referred to in Greece—the "All Holy"—was about to step off the boat. It took a few more hushed minutes of anticipation for the sailors to unload the icon. The priests disembarked first, and then the sailors with the *Panagia.* "Present arms!" yelled a voice through a loudspeaker. The soldiers on land snapped to attention and brought their rifles to their chests. The marching band began to play a tune called "The March of the Flag." Cymbals crashed, trumpets blared. Two priests waving smoking thuribles led the sailors with the icon along a red carpet, passing the soldiers in formation. Those soldiers not holding rifles saluted.

I tried hard to repress what must have looked like an impious grin, inspired by this vision of soldiers saluting the mother of Jesus. My neighbors in the crowd were already looking at me with suspicion, apparently wondering why I was jotting down notes on a small notepad instead of crossing myself. What might seem bizarre to someone who grew up in the United States, where the separation of church and state is more stringently upheld, is for many religious Greeks unremarkable. Greece does not in practice abide by Western concepts of secularism. The nation's Orthodox Church sees itself as the torchbearer of Hellenism through the ages, and the guardian of Greek identity. Since Greece's founding, religion has defined what it means to be Greek. When Greek revolutionaries declared independence from the Ottoman Empire and wrote the first constitution in 1822, Greeks were defined as Christians living within the liberated territory. That is because most citizens of the budding state identified themselves primarily by their religion, having lived for centuries under an Ottoman Empire in which religious belief rather than ethnicity was the nomenclature by which the population had been grouped and governed. Nor was "Hellene" a ubiquitous term of self-identification for the unschooled, pastoral citizens of the new state. The term in previous centuries had carried an unpleasant, pagan connotation, and so people still often referred to themselves as *Romaioi*, or Romans, which had a Christian one.

The continuing intertwinement of the Greek Church in political and civil affairs is partly a vestige of Ottoman rule. Under the Ottomans, the Orthodox Church was charged with administering the Christian population and collecting taxes. Bishop and government official were essentially the same thing, and this cultivated the synthesis of religion and *ethnos*. Today, Greek Orthodox clerics are paid by the state, and Greek politicians, from the prime minister on down, are usually sworn in to office not by a judge, but by prelates, as if the church bequeaths the ultimate authority to govern. In 2015, Alexis Tspiras, the atheist leader of Syriza, became the first Greek prime minister to opt for a secular inauguration, drawing an angry response from some church hierarchs. Until then, prime ministers were sworn in by the Archbishop of Athens and all Greece, and took the oath in the name of the "Holy and Consubstantial and Indivisible Trinity."

On the October day of the icon's arrival in Thessaloniki, the archbishop stood among the other clerics on stage as the icon was taken ashore. A Greek public television station broadcast the ceremony live, giving the kind of commentary one would not hear on PBS.

"The *Panagia* is inspecting the military corps, which is giving her military honors at this time," the program's host explained to viewers.

"She, also known as the New Eve, who rectified original sin with her obedience to the will of the Lord," said the reporter on the ground.

"On top of everything else, she's a general, the *Panagia*, both a defender and a general," the host said. Indeed, Mary is a high-ranking military figure of sorts. A Byzantine chant refers to Mary as the "Champion General," praising her for protecting

Constantinople in 626 from invading nomadic warriors on horseback. In Greece, the *Panagia* is still called upon to ward off all kinds of misfortune, not only to protect the nation from attack, but to remedy droughts and, in more recent times, to save the nation from economic calamity.

"The *Panagia* helps Greece with great vigor," the reporter on the ground said, paraphrasing the words of a venerated monk. Mary, the reporter added, was a "broker" for the nation in discussions with her son. "With great vigor, the saints of the church will help us in the hard times that will come," he went on. "The *Panagia* and all the saints will make a huge circle above Greece in order to protect her. We've seen that time and again with the wars, with the difficulties endured by this small nation, which, if you'd like, other stronger nations have attempted to literally swallow. However, Greece remained standing. She lived on. That is not at all out of luck. We have someone who is protecting us. And that is our Christ and our broker, the *Panagia*."

The icon was taken before the stage where the high clergy had gathered. The marching band ceased and the sailors hoisted the icon higher into the air so that it was level with the clergy. Clerics then began to chant, uttering the same modal song of praise to Mary that the archangel Gabriel had sung one millennium and some decades earlier. The prayers and chants, however, were interrupted by a commotion.

"Accursed in front of us! Traitor!" Two monks, also bearded and wearing black robes, lunged toward the mayor of Thessaloniki, Yiannis Boutaris, a chain-smoking, tattooed, silver-haired man of scant size and seventy years. "Boutaris, you bum!" one of the monks cried as they tried to set upon the mayor. A group of army officers intervened, grabbing the monks. Then police officers arrived and began dragging them away. One monk's robe was torn in the struggle. "You lust after Turks!" one of them cried.

.   .   .

I had first heard of Boutaris several months earlier during a visit to my parents' house on Long Island for Christmas. A front-page article in the *National Herald,* a Greek-American newspaper that happened to be sitting in front of me on the kitchen table one morning, caught my attention with the headline "A Nod to Ataturk, Boutaris' New Epoch Begins." Boutaris had just been sworn in as mayor of Thessaloniki and, according to the story, "was backpedaling from a report" that he wanted to build a memorial for Atatürk, the father of the Turkish Republic, in his city. That report "fired up righteous anger in Greeks and those in the Diaspora," said the article. Atatürk is considered villainous by many Greeks, or as the newspaper put it: "Under his reign Greeks were driven out of Asia Minor and thousands were killed and the Greek city of Smyrna was burned and civilians were massacred."

In an interview for the story, Boutaris said he did not, in fact, intend to build a monument for Atatürk—an action that would for a Greek politician amount to electoral hara-kiri—but that he did intend to lure more Turkish tourists to the home in Thessaloniki where Atatürk is said to have been born in or around 1881. "Let the Turks come to Greece and visit like we go to Constantinople as tourists and give Turkish people money by visiting their country," Boutaris told the newspaper, using the Greek name for Istanbul, which lures Greek tourists interested in seeing the landmarks of the Byzantine Empire. The mayor also said he would work to attract other foreign tourists who could trace their roots to Thessaloniki, including Sephardic Jews living in Israel. "This city needs to find its identity," Boutaris went on. Instead of trying to take advantage of the city's pluralistic past, he added, "we try to cover it up as if we are afraid of something."

I was very intrigued by this mayor. Greek society is born from a wonderfully rich amalgamation of cultures and traditions. This reality should be embraced and appreciated, but instead it has long been suppressed out of fear that it could undermine that nation's founding narrative: that it is the progeny of pure, uninterrupted Hellenic civilization. Since the nation won its independence, academics, politicians, schoolteachers, and clerics have often promoted a stilted, hackneyed version of its history, omitting or altering facts that might adulterate this narrative. It's understandable why they made the effort. Greek independence in the early nineteenth century was not the ambition only of bands of Greek mountain fighters, but of Western Europeans who yearned to free the Hellenes, the Enlightenment's forebearers, from the dark ages of Muslim rule. Among the most famed of the so-called philhellenes—foreign admirers of Greece—was the aristocratic English romantic poet Lord Byron, who so much believed in the cause of a liberated, regenerated heir to Ancient Greece that he traveled south in order to participate in the revolutionary fight. He died of a fever before seeing any battle, but not before writing a few poems about the place, such as "The Isles of Greece," "Where burning Sappho loved and sung," and "Where Delos rose, and Phoebus sprung!"

> The mountains look on Marathon—
> And Marathon looks on the sea;
> And musing there an hour alone,
> I dream'd that Greece might still be free;

The Greek revolution was in great part inspired by this romantic ideal. Educated, mercantile Greeks who lived in Europe and were influenced by its thinkers embraced the romantics' vision and coordinated the rebellion in the motherland. When the revolt broke out, European volunteers traveled to Greece to help the Hellenes in their epic struggle. When they arrived, however, they were often dismayed by what they found. The fighting did not resemble the regular warfare they imagined as noble and gentlemanly. Rather, the volunteers found Greek guerrilla bands led by warlord figures who, in addition to their national fervor, saw the revolution as an opportunity to increase their wealth and power. The Greek rebels began massacring unarmed Turkish civilians, and within a short time, virtually all the Turks living in the Peloponnese either had fled for their lives or were dead. The Ottomans, in order the punish the rebellion, unleashed a similar orgy of terror and violence on Greek civilians living in Turkish-controlled areas. Tens of thousands of civilians on both sides were expeditiously slaughtered. At the same time, rebel-controlled areas of Greece descended into utter lawlessness, and bands of fighters looted and plundered at will. Greek warlords began to fight among themselves over the spoils. In short, it wasn't a very romantic scene.

Seeing all this, a lot of the European volunteers left in disillusionment. Still, the disenchanting reality on the ground did not temper the philhellenic spirit in European capitals. Greek rebel fighters smartly used the idealized image Europeans had of them to their advantage, employing it to enlist material support. "With every right does Hellas, our mother, whence ye also, O Nations, have become enlightened, anxiously request your friendly assistance with money, arms, and counsel, and we entertain the highest hope that our appeal will be listened to," wrote one rebel leader in an appeal for European assistance. That assistance eventually arrived, and in 1832, the Kingdom of Greece officially came into existence—a truncated version of what the country is today, encompassing the southern part of the mainland, including the Peloponnese, and many of the islands. More Greeks, at the time, still lived in the Ottoman Empire than in Greece itself.

Greek thinkers were thereafter charged with promoting a national identity that suited the image in which the country had been created: a fusion of Hellenism and Orthodox Christianity. They often fortified national unity by amplifying the wretchedness and injustice Greeks suffered under Ottoman rule, and in the decades following independence, school curricula were shaped accordingly. The Ottoman period—the *Tourkokratia*, as it is known—was depicted as a centuries-long interruption in the eternal progress of the enduring Greek nation. All one needed to know about it was that the Greeks were cruelly enslaved for centuries before the nation was liberated and restored to its rightful Hellenic dominion. What else about it could be worth knowing?

One example from my mother's childhood education indicates how young Greeks have long been educated on the subject. In a school play audition, she tried out for the role of a Greek beauty, clad in the national colors of blue and white, who attracts the interest of a young Turkish pasha dressed in black breeches and a fez. My mother, the maiden, does not respond well to his flirtatious glances.

"Young, frightened Greek, proud virgin, what did I do to you for you to look at me with teary eyes?" the Turk says.

"How do you require me to look at you?" she replies. "With a smiling glance? You, pasha, who choked our memories with blood, and burned our little houses and all our nice things. And now our mothers cry. Our children cry with them."

The pasha takes a few steps closer. His voice becomes more stern.

"Wed a Turk and you will see what wealth you'll get. Among the Turks you'll live, like the daughter of Ali Pasha!"

The honorable maiden is not tempted. She fearlessly raises her voice and replies: "My mother and my father would rather slaughter me than have their honorable daughter made into a Turk!"

The Turk is not touched by her brave righteousness. He draws his sabre.

"Why, take a look at this knife. If you don't want me, it will be buried inside your heart, and your soul will leave you at once!"

"Onward, thug! Slaughter me with a double-edged blade. My honor is to be slaughtered for my sweet country."

The pasha mercilessly lurches at her and digs the blade into her bosom. My mother drops to her knees. She takes her last patriotic breaths before plopping entirely to the ground.

"I was thin then. I could fall easily," my mom said nearly six decades later, after recalling the performance for me.

She, like many Greek children until today, was taught that the Ottomans forbade Greek youths from learning how to read and write Greek. The young, therefore, would sneak off under the cover of night to underground "secret schools" in churches and monasteries. There, under candlelight, a priest would not only teach them the language and the faith, but inculcate them with the enduring flame of Hellenism and the Enlightenment. Pretty much everyone in Greece can recite the nursery rhyme about the secret schools, normally sung to the tune of "Twinkle, Twinkle, Little Star":

> My little bright moon,
> shine on my footsteps,
> so that I can go to school,
> to learn to read and write,
> to learn God's teachings.

The secret-school story is taught to the children of the diaspora too. On Long Island in the 1980s, when my brother and I regularly attended religion and language classes at a Greek Orthodox Church, he played a secret-school priest in a church play. There, on the indoor basketball court that served as the church's social gathering place, he sat on a stool, dressed in a frock, miming the practice of passing on God's teachings to the boys and girls gathered around him as other children recited poems about Turkish oppression into a microphone.

There is one complication concerning the secret-school story, however. There is no evidence the schools ever existed, contemporary Greek scholars now point out. Indeed, there would be no reason for them to exist. While non-Muslim subjects of the Otto-man Empire suffered discriminatory treatment and were subject to heavy, unfair taxes, Christians and Jews, considered "People of the Book," were afforded the right to practice their religion. Despite the abuses Greeks suffered under Ottoman rule—the conversion of the patriarchal basilica of Constantinople, Hagia Sophia, into a mosque, remains one key sore point—the Orthodox Church was given considerable power to rule over its flock and educate the young. In fact, it was not uncommon for church hierarchs to praise the empire for protecting Christian Orthodoxy from the unholy influence of the Catholic West. Later, when the Greek revolution broke out, the leader of the Orthodox Christians, Ecumenical Patriarch Grigorios V, condemned the rebel leaders and decried the revolt. The Ottomans nevertheless hung the patriarch on Easter Sunday for failing to safeguard Orthodox Christians' loyalty to the empire; he was later dubbed a Greek *ethnomartyras,* a national martyr. After Greece won its independence, its Bavarian king, Otto, decided it would not be a good idea for his Orthodox Christian subjects to remain under the authority of the patriarch in Ottoman-controlled Istanbul. So, in 1833, his regency declared the creation of the autocephalous Church of Greece. Church and the new state were now closely aligned. As part of the nation-building effort, the secret-school story and others like it helped depict the clergy as having led the resistance against the Ottoman tyrants. The reality, however, was more complicated.

Another effort of the new Greek state to cultivate a Hellenic ideal included making the official language *Katharevousa*—a "purified," archaizing form of Greek devised by the revolutionary thinker Adamantios Korais, meant to make the language more antique. Vernacular Greek would become the official language in the 1970s, but not before generations of children were forced to learn a painfully overformal version of their language in schools. There have, in addition, been many efforts to "Hellenize" things about Greece that weren't particularly Hellenic. Village names that did not sound Greek were changed. Other languages spoken in Greece were suppressed. (Boutaris, for example, has some Vlach ancestry—a population of people in northern and central Greece whose language, similar to Romanian, is disappearing.) Even the coffee was eventually Hellenized. When my parents were children, men at the *kafenio* would order "Turkish coffee." By the time they grew old and went back to Greece to visit, people were ordering "Greek coffee," though it was the same stuff. Calling it Turkish coffee today might make strongly nationalistic Greeks angry—just as refuting the existence of the secret school could get you accused of being an apologist, a traitor, or, to use the phrase directed at Boutaris, a Turk lover.

With his invitation to Turks to visit Thessaloniki, Boutaris deeply upset the large number of Greeks who so enduringly revile Turkey that their animosity—like that in all lasting, national rivalries—is both carefully cultivated and accepted as an unquestionable, naturally occurring condition. Some Greek nationalists prefer not to mention Turkey by name, preferring to call it "the neighbor to the east." Boutaris seemed to enjoy antagonizing such nationalist sentiment. Earlier in his life, he had suggested that the small street where Atatürk was born in Thessaloniki be named after the leader as a gesture to improve relations with Turkey. The idea was met with a fierce backlash. Rumors swirled that Boutaris wanted to rename the thoroughfare of St. Demetrios after the Turkish leader. Boutaris abandoned the street-naming idea by the time he ran for mayor, though many still revile him for it.

Atatürk in particular inspires deep resentment among Greeks for foiling the *Megali Idea*, or Great Idea, a longtime Greek aspiration to reclaim from the Turks the Byzantine territories of old, particularly Constantinople. After World War I, as the Ottoman Empire was crumbling and the Allies sought to partition it among themselves, Greek forces tried to realize the Great Idea by invading Anatolia. Turkish troops led by Atatürk, however, eventually beat back the Greeks. For Asia Minor's Greek Orthodox Christians,

this was a disastrous result, as the Turks unleashed a spasm of re-
taliatory killings and expulsions. In the aftermath, the Greek and
Turkish governments formalized a population exchange, based on
religious affiliation. In the end, over one million Greek Orthodox
Christians, many of whom spoke better Turkish than Greek, were
expelled from Asia Minor and resettled in Greece. Smaller numbers of Muslims, many of whom spoke better Greek than Turkish,
were expelled from Greece to the new nation of Turkey. Greeks
refer to these events simply as "the catastrophe." The Turks refer
to the conflict as their war of independence. Since then, the two
nations on several occasions have nearly gone to war. Conflicts
erupted in the '70s over the fate of the island nation of Cyprus—
which has both Greek and Turkish populations, each faithful to
its bigger-brother country; territorial water and airspace in the
Aegean remain a source of perpetual dispute. After the outbreak
of Greece's debt crisis, right-wing politicians warned that Turkey
would attempt to exploit Greece's weakness to improve its position in the Aegean. The Greeks needed to remain vigilant against
the threat, they argued. Boutaris, meanwhile, argued that closer
ties with Turkey and its immediate neighbors would help ease
Greece's enormous financial troubles.

I first met Mayor Boutaris in Istanbul, several months
after his inauguration, where he was visiting as part of his campaign to lure Turkish tourists. He was staying at the Ritz-Carlton,
a guest of a local university that had invited him to speak at an academic conference on Turkish-Greek relations, and we met on the
rooftop terrace late the night he arrived. The mayor was a sharp
dresser with a fondness for suspenders and red socks while at the
same time possessing some of the qualities of an aged rock star. He
spoke with a low, hoarse drone and seemed a bit dazed. Deep lines

in his face suggested many years of hard partying. He smoked unfiltered Camel cigarettes almost continuously, as if his life depended on it. A blue-green lizard was tattooed below the thumb of his right hand, its tail running to the wrist—a reminder, he told me, of the reptile's capacity to regenerate after injury. In addition to his other tattoos, the symbol for his astrological sign, Gemini, appeared on the middle and ring fingers of the same hand. The gold stud in his left ear, he told me, protected him from the evil eye, in accordance with Vlach tradition.

Boutaris had spent most of his life as a winemaker. He had inherited the family winery, which was founded by his grandfather in a mountain village just west of Thessaloniki in 1879, when the area was still part of the Ottoman Empire. Since that time, the region has been known for the sour black grapes that produce a dry red wine called Xinomavro. Boutaris is a recovered alcoholic who for the past two decades has tasted but not swallowed his own vintage. The family business—the Boutari Winery—at one point defaulted, Boutaris told me, and he used a considerable amount of his personal fortune to keep the company afloat, a financial hit from which he never fully recovered. He eventually left the company solely to his brother and started his own, smaller brand, called Kir-Yianni, which is now run by his son. The Boutari Winery, having recovered from those earlier financial troubles, today remains one of Greece's most widely known wine brands. Boutaris was in the company of an aide in a fine suit, Antonis Kamaras, a towering former banker twice the mayor's size, who was educated at the London School of Economics and saw it as his job to soften the mayor's often blunt declarations into cohesive policy jargon. Kamaras's father, a successful tobacco merchant, was a friend of Boutaris, and together, the merchant's son and the mayor emitted an air of old aristocracy and somewhat faded wealth.

The terrace of the Ritz-Carlton looked out over the rippling Bosporus, the strait separating the European and Asian sides of

Turkey, its currents illuminated by streaks of city light. We found a table next to a three-piece band playing an assortment of Latin-flavored New Age music that seemed ill-fitting to our location in the world. Boutaris lit a cigarette and crossed his legs. At one point, a shapely woman wearing a short blue skirt and stiletto heels walked past the table. It seemed like perhaps she had come to the hotel to fish for wealth, and the mayor seemed to be biting. His head swiveled as his gaze followed her path. He made an expression of what seemed like sincere pain, and then looked at Kamaras as if perhaps the aide could explain: Why do such lovely creatures exist, and why do they tempt me so? Kamaras tried to move on as gracefully as he could. "There are lots of leggy blondes here," he said as he, too, crossed his legs and lit a cigarillo. "It's safe to say we won't be seeing many of those types during tomorrow's academic conference." Boutaris's focus turned to the less immediately enticing subject of my interest, the reaction at home to his tourism campaign. "Thessaloniki was a booming city of the Ottoman Empire," he told me in his invariably low-pitched voice. "It was a Jewish city, and a Turkish city."

One may take these comments as simple fact considering that, at the same time Thessaloniki became part of Greece, Greeks were the smallest of the three groups. But to refer to Thessaloniki—originally founded three centuries before the birth of Christ and named after Alexander the Great's half sister—as anything other than a Greek city is to the mayor's detractors a provocation, just the kind of blasphemy that inspires convulsions of anger. Yet, until the city became part of an expanding Greece, Jews composed its largest religious community and referred to it in Ladino (Judeo-Spanish) as *la madre de Israel,* a bit of information Greeks were never taught in high school history classes. As Boutaris put it: "They didn't know because nobody told them."

Thessaloniki's Sephardim began arriving at the end of the fifteenth century after being forced out of Spain during the Inquisition. They were welcomed by Ottoman authorities interested in repopulating the once thriving Byzantine city, whose Greek population had been decimated by the invading Ottomans decades earlier as punishment for resistance. During Ottoman rule, Thessaloniki became one of the largest Jewish population centers in the world and Ladino was heard in the bustling port more often than Greek or Turkish. When the city became part of Greece, Jews were unsure about the change, fearful their liberties would be curtailed by Greek authorities charged with the task of incorporating a large religious minority into a nation that questioned whether one could be both a Greek and a Jew at the same time. The Greek state nevertheless allowed Jews the self-autonomy they had enjoyed during the Ottoman Empire. Jewish schoolchildren learned Greek and swore allegiance to their new nation.

But a profound metamorphosis was under way, one that precipitated a stark change in the religious makeup of the city. Thessaloniki began to overflow with the Greek refugees who had been thrown out of their homeland, the budding Turkish state. The changes were sped by a massive fire in 1917 that destroyed much of the city, particularly the Jewish quarter. Many Jews left after this disaster, but still, around 50,000 remained in the city when the Nazis occupied it during World War II. The first deportations to Auschwitz-Birkenau began in March 1943, and within a few months of cruel efficiency, Jewish life in the city was almost completely obliterated. Fewer than 2,000 of the city's Jews survived the war. For Greece, the question of whether one could be a Greek and a Jew at the same time was now largely moot. The near disappearance of Jewish life in Thessaloniki made it easier for residents of the city to ignore the fact that it had ever existed there in the first place.

One month after taking office, however, Boutaris traveled to Israel. "Not for nothing was it called the Jerusalem of the Balkans," he said of his city in an interview with the *Jerusalem Post*.

"And it could be that again." The mayor also told the newspaper that his first high school girlfriend was Jewish. During the same visit, he spoke to a group of Holocaust survivors originally from Thessaloniki, and asked them to help their city of origin by encouraging people to visit. These efforts seemed to pay off. In the first nine months after he took office, visits to Thessaloniki from Israel quadrupled. Visits from Turkey also increased, though not as dramatically. The mayor was working on it, though. Thessaloniki, he told me at the Ritz-Carlton, is a must-see for many Turks, since it was the birthplace of Mustafa Kemal Atatürk. Sure, Greeks blame Atatürk for the Asia Minor catastrophe. But "whatever you think of him," Boutaris told me, "he's a child of Thessaloniki." Kamaras, the aide, then decided it was time to intervene, making the point that this was a particularly controversial outlook for their city's residents, many of whose ancestors were those Greek refugees kicked out of their villages in Asia Minor. "If you ask me, he is too outspoken," Kamaras said. The aide preferred to boil the mayor's views down to the kind of wise economic policy even his antagonists could understand. "In light of the collapse of domestic demand, what we are trying to do is import demand from outside," said Kamaras. "Openness pays."

The next morning, I watched Boutaris give one interview after another to Turkish journalists on the hotel's terrace. The Turkish public—from leftists hostile to nationalism, to Turkish nationalists pleased with Boutaris's apparent sympathy—exhibited great interest in the mayor, and it struck me that he was perhaps more popular in Turkey than in Greece. The first interviewer was a young woman who employed heavy flirtation as an interviewing method, and soon Boutaris had rolled up his sleeves and was showing her the tattoo on his arm dedicated to his deceased ex-wife. "Our life together was like a fantasy," he told the journalist.

"What is your philosophy?" she then asked him.

"Be a good person," said Boutaris.

She, like each of the Turkish journalists who talked to Boutaris that day, also asked about the Atatürk street-naming proposal.

"Now that you are the mayor, why don't you name the street where Atatürk was born after him?" she said.

"This is a delicate issue," Boutaris said. The idea was a gesture of "moving forward" beyond the historical enmities, he added, but it had not gone over well in Greece.

"Can I say you hope to do it?" she said. Boutaris squirmed a bit, and seemed tempted to answer yes in order not to disappoint her. Kamaras, who was smoking a cigarillo as he listened, saved his boss. "The reaction to this suggestion was so strong, we thought there were better ways to improve the relationship with Turkey," he said. A photographer started snapping pictures of the mayor as the song "Moon River" played over the hotel speaker system. "Can you make a peace sign?" the journalist asked Boutaris. The mayor obliged.

In each interview that morning, Boutaris repeated certain themes: Greece and Turkey have a "very, very common heritage," the Greek mentality is similar to the Turkish mentality, and he feels far closer to the Turks than to Europeans like, for example, Swedes. He mentioned repeatedly that Turkish Airlines offered direct flights to Thessaloniki from Istanbul, and that visitors shopping in Thessaloniki "won't believe their eyes at all the beautiful things they can find."

One television journalist asked Boutaris if he thought the 100th-anniversary celebration would stoke animosities with Turkey. On the contrary, the mayor replied. It was a chance to highlight the two nations' commonalities. The mayor pointed out that the Ottomans conceded the city to the Greeks without a shot fired, and that the first elected mayor of the city after its liberation was Turkish. "I do not believe we have to celebrate the win," the mayor said. "It was not a win. It was a change of situations."

Hearing this, I wondered how the mayor had ever been elected.

Though he'd won the 2010 election by just three hundred votes, his victory in the midst of Greece's deepening economic troubles indicated that many Greeks were craving a new kind of politics. Boutaris, who was supported by a coalition of left-leaning and centrist parties, fused the pro-business tendencies more common on the political right with an aversion to the right's staid, nationalist inclinations. This was a rather unique combination in Greece, and people seemed willing to try it. Of course, it didn't take much to be considered a radical improvement over the previous mayor, a man named Vasilis Papageorgopoulos, who was accused of having a severe embezzling habit. Papageorgopoulos, a former dentist and sprinter who won a bronze medal for his country in European competition and was nicknamed "the flying doctor," had governed the city as a member of New Democracy for a decade. After Boutaris took office, his deputy mayor of finance—the first Jewish elected official in the city since the end of World War II—found that the city was deeply in the red and that the previous administration had apparently falsified the books. Two years later, Papageorgopoulos and two of his aides were convicted of embezzling around 18 million euros and sentenced to life in prison. The severe sentence, which preceded Tsochatzopoulos's conviction, represented the first time in many years a Greek politician had received such a severe penalty for such a substantial crime. Some Greek newspapers optimistically depicted this development as the beginning of a new era in which Greek politicians were to be held accountable for their abundant wrongdoing, though that seemed to be wishful thinking. Papageorgopoulos maintained his innocence and appealed his conviction, saying he was the victim of political persecution. His prison sentence was later reduced to twelve years.

Boutaris's treasurer was able to balance the municipal budget within a few years of taking office. This achievement prompted the interest of Prime Minister Samaras, who, one city official told me, said to Boutaris: "I need that Jew in Athens." Boutaris in-

trigued the international press with his self-proclaimed reform-
ist agenda and many tattoos. Journalists, looking for something
good to say about Greece at a time when all the news was bad,
heaped praise on him. The *New York Times* profiled him with the
headline "Greek Mayor Aims to Show Athens How It's Done," the
U.K.'s *Daily Telegraph* with "Greece's Vision of Hope," Germany's *Süddeutsche Zeitung* with "A City's Last Hope," and Toronto's
Globe and Mail with "This Greek Hero Slays Monsters of the Fiscal Variety." Though the international press made him out to be
a savior, at home the feeling was more ambivalent. Much of his
electorate clearly still despised him, particularly religious conservatives, as the outburst at the *Panagia*'s welcoming ceremony had
shown.

       As the police hauled off the irate monks, voices in the
crowd began to chatter and speculate.

"Surely, Boutaris must have done something to anger them," a
little woman beside me said.

"He didn't let them come close to the icon," one woman's voice
responded.

"Well, if he did that, then they have a point."

"Get out of here, Boutaris!" a woman screamed.

"Boutaris, you're dirtying the place with your presence!" bellowed a male voice.

I asked one man next to me, who told me his name was Nek-
tarios, why the mayor was being heckled.

"Because he's an atheist and a devil," he said.

"Why a devil?" I asked.

"He loves Atatürk."

As the chatter continued, a politician with finely parted black
hair named Theodoros Karaoglou took the stage and began his

speech as if nothing had happened. The icon's arrival would "help stimulate religious and national feeling of our tested people," he said. Greeks, he added, clung steadfastly to their roots, "and for that let's not forget the titanic offering of our church to safeguard our national and cultural heritage." State and church must "walk and struggle together to support all those who are suffering from the economic crisis." There was no doubt how the crisis would end, he added. "Greece will get back on its feet. The *Panagia* is on our side."

I had met Karaoglou, the minister of the Greek regions of Macedonia and Thrace, a few days earlier in his plush, enormous office, located in the imposing building where the city's Ottoman government used to be headquartered. It was also where the Ottoman military officer Hasan Tahsin Pasha surrendered the city to Greek forces a century earlier, Karaoglou pointed out. He told me his ministry had organized a massive celebration on a Saturday later in the month to mark the city's liberation from Ottoman "enslavement." Greek soldiers, seven hundred of them, would reenact the Greek army's march into the city a century earlier, dressed in period garb, with many on horseback. They would march to the ministry, where the president of Greece would raise the same Greek flag erected there in 1912, when Greek forces took control of the city. The soldiers would then continue past a small church where the city's bishop and two hundred priests would sing the Byzantine chant praising the Virgin Mary as the "Champion General." The priests would also sing the Greek national anthem. The soldiers would then march on to the White Tower, where an enormous Greek flag—"the biggest that exists in Greece"—would be raised. There, soldiers would perform a twenty-one-gun salute, which would be answered with cannon volleys by a Greek warship offshore. "Now that we have a heavy climate," the minister told me, "the goal for us is to produce a climate of national pride."

The Ministry of Macedonia and Thrace itself existed for reasons of national pride. It was the only federal ministry in Greece to represent regions of the nation, and persisted by virtue of the fact that it had the word "Macedonia"—the name of the Greek region in which Thessaloniki is located—in its title. A copyright dispute over the name Macedonia has inflamed nationalist fervor in Greece since 1991, when Yugoslavia divided into different parts, one of which called itself the Republic of Macedonia. For most Greeks, there can be no such thing as a country called Macedonia, or a language called Macedonian, because Macedonia is Greek and has been since antiquity. The claim on the name not only reflects an effort to rob Greece of its cultural property, Greeks believe, but could also lead to territorial claims on northern Greece. Furthermore, by claiming the name Macedonia, these former Yugoslavs could also lay claim to the greatest of Greek heroes, Alexander III of Macedon, also known as Alexander the Great. Greek concerns over the issue are somewhat understandable. Memories of battles to win and preserve its northern territory remain fresh in Greece, and nationalist politicians in Skopje, the capital of the would-be Macedonia, have certainly fed Greek anxieties by speaking of the "spiritual unification" of a greater Macedonia. Yet, one could argue, the response in Greece has been disproportionate to the threat. One day in February 1992, schools and government offices in Thessaloniki closed and about one million Greeks, according to some estimates—around one-tenth of the country's population—protested their neighbor's wish to use the name Macedonia. A demonstration of similar size occurred later in the year in Athens. Due to Greece's continued objections, the United Nations refers to the nation that calls itself the Republic of Macedonia by the unfortunate moniker the Former Yugoslav Republic of Macedonia, or FYROM for short.

The ministry's purpose, Karaoglou told me in his office, "is to send a message of national symbolism that Macedonia was, is, and will always remain one and Hellenic." A second reason for its existence, he added, was to fight high unemployment in northern Greece. How exactly the ministry's employees performed this latter goal, other than by persisting on the ministry payroll, remained during my visit a mystery to me. No one there seemed to have much to do. I saw huddled groups of employees sitting in folding chairs smoking cigarettes in the large corridors of the ministry building. Apparently, others also questioned its purpose. The ministry was relegated to a "general secretariat" in 2009 by the PASOK prime minister George Papandreou. The institution was promptly restored to a ministry after the right-wing prime minister Antonis Samaras came to power in June 2012. Samaras, during the height of the Macedonia naming dispute and protest, had split away from New Democracy and formed his own more nationalist party, Political Spring. That party's sole purpose had been a hard-line stance regarding the Macedonia dispute, though later, after some of the fervor over the issue receded, he rejoined New Democracy. "When you close a ministry that has the name Macedonia in it, you send the wrong message," Karaoglou told me. It's like telling Greece's adversaries on the other side of the border "that you don't care so much."

After my meeting with Karaoglou, I called Boutaris to ask him what he thought of the ministry's plans to mark the 100th anniversary. "I'm mad," the mayor told me. First, he said, the ministry had no reason to exist. Second, its anniversary plans were "totally kitsch." Boutaris said he would boycott the parade. After local newspapers later reported that the mayor called the ministry's planned commemorations "fascistic," Karaoglou felt compelled to respond. "It is obvious that the mayor and I have different understandings both of the importance of the 100th anniversary of the liberation of our city from the Turkish yoke, and also about how we should celebrate our historic national anniversaries," he said. "And because historical forgetfulness harms our collective memory, I would underscore that a people who forget their history have no future."

. . .

While the monks were berating the mayor, the bishop of Thessaloniki, a short man with a long beard, had a peculiar look on his face. He peered somewhat sideways at the commotion, resting both hands on his staff amid the other clerics onstage, his gaze not fully committed to the direction of the disturbance, which fell below the dignity of a bishop's full attention. It was hard to discern the expression behind the eyeglasses and gray hair that covered much of his face, but I wondered if perhaps what I was noticing was a slight look of pleasure.

Bishop Anthimos of Thessaloniki did not appreciate Boutaris's talk about the non-Hellenic, non-Christian aspects of the city's past. Nor did the mayor like the fact that the bishop treated his Sunday pulpit as if it were his own cable news talk show, during which he railed against developments in the country that indicated the enervation of its "Helleno-Christian" heritage. The bishop often warned in his sermons of a panoply of threats: territorial threats, whether from the Turks or from the republic that wanted to call itself Macedonia; the threat of allowing gay pride parades in the city; the threat of illegal immigration; the threat of European Union hegemony; the threat of Islam, which seeks to rule Europe.

When Boutaris was still running for mayor in 2010, he said that Anthimos reminded him of the "mujahideen" for his fundamentalist views, and suggested the bishop spend more time helping the poor instead of buying new vestments. After these comments were published, the two men met during a service in the basilica housing what are said to be the remains of St. Demetrios. Boutaris approached Anthimos to kiss a gold cross the bishop held in his hand. Anthimos, unimpressed with the candidate's piety, scolded Boutaris with a protruding index finger. "If you don't recant," the bishop said, "I will make a big effort to make sure you never see the mayor's office."

The bishop and the mayor continued their public feud, to the great delight of the Greek media, which covered it closely. Whenever the two men were in the same vicinity, citizens watched in anticipation of a good spectacle. At one point, Boutaris suggested that Anthimos shave his beard and start a political party if he was so interested in sharing his political views. Yet, after the mayor was elected, the two men—unable to avoid one another in their public roles—did their best to tone down the quarreling and made an effort to keep friendly appearances. "The first person I greet is the bishop with a kiss on the cheek," Boutaris told me of public events he attended with Anthimos. Of course, that gesture could have been perceived as a veiled slight, as the customary way to kiss a bishop is with a reverent peck on the hand. For his part, the bishop seemed eager to use his pulpit to rail against Boutaris's agenda, though he refrained from mentioning the mayor by name.

The mayor may have gone out of his way to invite Jewish tourists to the city, but one Sunday, the bishop warned the congregation about Jewish businessmen intending to buy real estate along the harbor in order to build big hotels. "Without bile, I say this," said Anthimos. "Keep in mind, we love the Jews. We helped them in Thessaloniki and in Athens, and I've explained before we have a common origin in the Old Testament." This seemed like a bit of an odd thing to say, given the city he was in. During the World War II occupation, in Athens and elsewhere in Greece, clerics and laymen did help Jews avoid the Nazis. But in Thessaloniki, things had obviously ended very badly. The bishop went on to warn of an academic conference highlighting the city's Jewish history, coinciding with the 100th-anniversary celebration. He read aloud a list of the events' sponsors, such as the Jewish Community of Thessaloniki, the Hebrew University of Jerusalem, and other Israeli organizations. He raised his voice slightly to accent the words "Jews" and "Israeli," in order to emphasize the Jewishness of it all. The city of Thessaloniki itself was also a sponsor, he pointed out, pausing for emphasis as if deeply disturbed, as if the city were a traitor for participating. "I hope you don't one day remember I was telling you about this," Anthimos said, suggesting that, by then, it would already be too late. The responsible authorities must clarify, he said: "What exactly is going on?" He then came to his conclusion: "The Jews are flirting with Thessaloniki." He let the comment set in for a moment. "You tell me, 'What does that mean?' I'm not going to say it. You all understand. You understand it. We have Europe. We have the immigrants. We have the illegal immigrants. We have the threats," referring to Turkish ambitions in the Aegean. He closed his speech by saying: "I cannot tell you more," as if doing so might incur the mysterious wrath of the Jews.

On another Sunday, the subject of the bishop's outrage was a report that a Macedonian-language radio station seeking to spread "propaganda" was asking for a license to start operating in northern Greece. If this radio station was allowed to open, Anthimos said, "the youth and I and whoever else wants to" would go over there "in forty or fifty buses" and "turn everything into shattered glass and nails." He added, "The job won't get done otherwise." Another time, he called the popularity of Turkish soap operas in Greece an "insult and challenge to our national consciousness," and akin to telling the Turks "we've surrendered." Once, after a visit to Athens, the bishop said he nearly "lost it" after seeing the number of migrants who had "blackened" the place. The migrants, many of them from Muslim countries, must be sent home, he said, in order to combat a Turkish plan to flood the country with Muslims and "Turkify" it. On another occasion, he sermonized on the growing danger from those undermining the sacred ideological pillars of the nation. This was a "leprosy," he said, and it was evident in "attempts to spurn, to strip bare the miracle of thousands of years of the Hellenic-Christian culture of Byzantium." It was a culture of astonishing men and scientists, he said, whose books have filled the libraries of all Europe. "It was a great culture, and it was our culture, and we are the continuation of that culture," he said. "And here, some of our own within the Hellenic realm want to disavow this culture, or to name it something else." Those who do so, he went on, "possess the leprosy of denial, or adulteration of our history." He concluded with what seemed a direct rebuttal of the mayor's efforts. "If we remain Greek and Orthodox, the economics will go better," he said. "I believe we will not be destroyed."

On the day of the *Panagia*'s arrival, the protesting monks were out of sight by the time Boutaris approached the podium. To my surprise, he was not booed. The mayor, clearly on hostile turf, was on his best behavior. He paused and looked at the clerics before beginning to speak. "Your Beatitude," he said, nodding to the head of the Church of Greece. "Your All Holiness," he said to Anthimos. "Your Eminence," he said to another cleric. The icon's arrival "coincides with one of the most critical periods of the post-war history of our country and the hard times our people are enduring," the mayor said, his head pointed down at the text he was reading, his voice weary and seemingly forced. By bringing the icon, the clerics had shown "love, encouragement, consolation, and concern with our city and our citizens, and especially for the infirm and afflicted, those whom the crisis has hit with devastating consequences for their daily lives and their families." He finished by adding, "We are grateful for this gesture and reciprocate with respect and honor." There was a smattering of applause from the crowd.

After that, the *Panagia* was placed on a wagon hitched to the back of a camouflaged jeep for a procession through the city. The icon, flanked by clerics waving smoking thuribles, was led by the marching band, the men dressed like revolutionary bandits, officers in full dress whites with their swords drawn, and soldiers doing a poor job of marching in step. Hundreds more sullen-looking priests and monks trailed behind, and silent, darkly shrouded nuns carried lit candles, the wax dripping on their hands. Politicians in suits followed along with thousands of citizens as the icon was pulled along a street called "National Defense." The procession passed the graffiti-tagged campus of Aristotle University, one of the nation's most well-regarded schools, where slogans like NEVER AGAIN FASCISM and VICTORY TO THE STRUGGLE OF THE STUDENT WALK-OUT were sprayed on the unkempt buildings. The campus is built on the site where hundreds of thousands of graves once constituted one of Europe's largest Jewish cemeteries. The cemetery was destroyed during the Nazi occupation at the urging of Greek authorities eager to free up the huge swath of land for development.

The procession went on, passing rows of unsightly apartment buildings, essentially concrete boxes with balconies, the common architecture of Greek cities. Residents emerged from the buildings to watch the icon pass, making the sign of the cross. Finally, the *Panagia* reached the Church of St. Demetrios and was carried past the green marble columns of the entrance and inside the sanctuary, underneath the high, open timber roof. It was placed before the altar, and a long line of pilgrims queued under the dim arcade and out the doors into the sunlight, waiting for what would be hours for a chance to make the sign of the cross before the icon and kiss the glass case covering it. Others waited to pay homage to the remains of St. Demetrios, kept in a small silver coffin beside a large icon depicting the scene of his martyrdom: several Roman soldiers thrusting spears into his breast. The church is built on the baths where his murder is said to have occurred, and the Roman-era ruins can still be seen in the crypt. Demetrios is referred to as the "myrrh streamer," because a miraculous flow of myrrh is said to have emanated from his tomb. Many claim they can still smell it, though I was unable to detect any fragrance during my visit.

The next morning, I returned to the church as a doleful chant of "hallelujah" came out over the loudspeakers perched on the facade. The queue of worshippers waiting for a chance to kiss the icon had not diminished. Inside, I found Devin Naar, an American historian in his late twenties from the University of Washington in Seattle with a particular interest in Thessaloniki and its Jewish past. I had met Naar a few days earlier at a Friday night Shabbat service at Yad Lezicaron Synagogue, where the more religious of the thousand or so Jews who now live in Thessaloniki go to worship. Naar's ancestors were Sephardic Jews who settled in Thessaloniki in the early sixteenth century, and they founded a synagogue called New Lisbon. Centuries later, before World War II, Naar's great-grandfather took his family to America. The young academic's interest in the city began with an effort to learn more about the grim fate of those family members that had remained. Naar, a lanky man with long, curly hair, spoke passionately on the subject of his study, employing his hands to accent his anecdotes as if he had just emerged from a long visit to unexplored archives, and could hardly wait to share what he had discovered. He was in town for an academic conference on the city's Jewish past—the kind of event Bishop Anthimos had warned was part of the Jewish "flirtation" with the city.

Naar and I passed the line of people waiting to kiss the icon, and descended a steep set of marble stairs into the crypt, where we were nearly alone. We walked past the ruins of the marble fountain that had been part of the early church, and illuminated displays of Roman-era column capitals. Naar didn't pay much attention to the displays. His eyes were directed toward the marble floor, where he was looking for headstones from the destroyed Jewish cemetery. After the cemetery's destruction, the headstones were frequently used in construction projects and could still be found scattered around the city. One suburban home I saw was enclosed by a wall of marble Jewish tombstones, the Hebrew script and dates of death according to the Jewish calendar year plainly visible. As I stood in front of the house staring in disbelief, an old lady who passed by told me the script was "a design" the homeowners had put on the stones recently, though she certainly knew the truth. St. Demetrios Church had been almost entirely destroyed in the massive 1917 fire, and was rebuilt after World War II, when the headstones were in ample supply. Naar told me they were almost certainly used in the church's reconstruction. He spotted a slab of marble where he thought the Hebrew script looked like it had been chiseled out, and took a photo. We then walked to the yard beside the church where a lot of marble slabs were stacked in the tall grass. Most of them had old Greek writing on them, but some were tombstones with Hebrew script. Naar walked through the tall grass, reaching more piles and looking for more headstones. For a moment, as the sound of chanting clerics floated in the warm breeze, a gush of fury seemed like it might break through his exterior, academic calm. Naar later pointed out that the preponderance of desecrated headstones had one unintended consequence: scattered throughout the city as they were, the headstones made accidental memorials, providing unmistakable reminders of the city's nearly blotted-out past.

The monolithic, ossified brand of Greek nationalism that has long concealed evidence of past pluralism has served to denigrate the concept of Hellenism itself, making it trite, insular, and fragile. When coupled with the economic crisis, its logic also proved to have dire ramifications across Greece. Widespread belief in Hellenic purity and superiority manifested itself in the hostile treatment of immigrants and the rapid growth of the fascist Golden Dawn, a party steeped in anti-Semitic, anti-Turkish hate. Yet, at the same time, in Thessaloniki, the signs of a change in thinking were also evident. The city's residents, after witnessing the global attention and spike in tourist visits Boutaris brought, appeared to see the benefit of embracing a more expansive view of their history. In the spring of 2014, the citizens of Thessaloniki reelected Boutaris mayor, giving him 58 percent of the vote, a sizable improvement over his previous victory margin.

On a dreary November day months after his win, Boutaris gave a speech on the campus of Aristotle University, the school built on the grounds of the destroyed Jewish cemetery. The occasion was the unveiling of a memorial that recognized what had been there before. Boutaris stood beside a large bronze sculpture of a menorah. He wore a plaid kippah, a gesture Greek politicians normally avoid—even when stepping foot in synagogues—out of fear the electorate will disapprove. Boutaris told the crowd that the city was ashamed of those Greeks who during the occupation had betrayed their Jewish fellow citizens. The city was ashamed, he went on, that it had taken so many years to recognize where they were standing, the place where for five centuries the city's Jews had buried their dead. His words inspired a round of applause. Thessaloniki, Boutaris added, had taken far too long to break its silence.

6

Europe's Hopefuls

I am an unfortunate foreigner in distress, and do not
know one in your town and country.

—Odysseus, in *The Odyssey* by Homer

Tychero is a somnolent Thracian town close to the muddy Evros
River, which marks Greece's northeastern border with Turkey.
The town, named after the Greek word for "lucky," sits in a humid
river delta dotted with fields of cotton, wheat, and sunflowers, and
the skies above it are trafficked by raptors, pelicans, and other mi-
gratory birds of increasing rarity. On a chilly December morning
in 2011, on a quiet hillside road on the edge of town, I saw a group
of nine people—most of them Africans—walking like weary soldiers in dazed retreat. One of them, a very tall and stunningly
beautiful woman, was dressed in a bright red wool coat and designer jeans. For footwear, she had on gray socks and flip-flops.
The pair of shoes she had been wearing apparently hadn't made it
across the Evros River earlier that morning. At the time, the river
was becoming the primary means by which migrants escaping
the war and poverty that afflicted large parts of Africa and Asia
entered the European Union. In the otherwise uneventful Greek
border towns of the Evros River Valley, scenes like this had become commonplace.

As the group of nine approached me, I asked if anyone spoke English. They took the opportunity to pause and sit down on the redbrick sidewalk. "Very tired," said one young man who wore large aviator sunglasses and a winter cap. "Where is the police?" I pointed downhill in the direction of the police station, a plain white building next to the train tracks where incoming migrants were detained. Earlier that morning, I had walked by the station and seen a painter applying a fresh coat of white to its facade, as if to cloak the poor state of its interior. Conditions in this police station, and in other places where migrants were detained after entering Greece, had drawn the attention of numerous human rights agencies. In this particular station, according to a Human Rights Watch report, migrants said they had slept on cardboard boxes and, because they had no access to toilets, urinated in a corner. Guards from the station were seen escorting detainees into the fields so they could defecate, and children and women were often confined to the same overcrowded, cramped space as men. Some detainees, according the report, said guards at the station beat and kicked them because they'd asked for water. Migrants nevertheless often voluntarily turned themselves in to police. Unlike in the United States, where the law allowed for authorities to more quickly deport illegally crossing migrants with no plausible asylum claim, EU law protected migrants from summary deportation in order to ensure they had an opportunity to apply for asylum. The Greek police therefore would initially detain entering migrants but later release them with a document allowing them to stay legally in the country for a limited period of time—usually a month, though sometimes longer. With that paper, one could travel legally to Athens and apply for asylum—a long process that very rarely ended in receiving it, but allowed migrants to legally extend their stay.

Tens of thousands of people passed through border towns like Tychero that year, their numbers increasing just as the country was entering a high point of its political and economic convulsions.

Greece was never an especially welcoming place for immigrants, but this was a particularly bad time. Afghan asylum seekers constituted the largest number of arrivals that year, though when they arrived, they found Greece did not offer them much if any assistance. At the same time, a large number of Pakistanis and an increasing number of Bangladeshis were arriving, hoping to find black-market jobs just as much of that work was drying up due to the economic collapse. The smugglers the migrants paid to get them to Greece were not forthcoming about the unpleasant realities they would encounter, and many received a very grim education upon their arrival. Those that knew better had no intention of staying in Greece, but planned to sneak on to another European country. They were coming for Europe, and though Greece was technically Europe, it wasn't the Europe they had in mind. Asylum seekers had hopes to get to places such as Germany, Norway, or Sweden, where they had a realistic chance at being granted protection and the benefits this entailed. Unfortunately, getting out of Greece was often a lot harder than getting in.

On the sidewalk in Tychero that morning, most of the migrants were from Somalia. One route into Europe for Somalis at the time involved a flight from Africa to Syria and then an arduous trek on land through Turkey and into Greece. This provided a safer alternative to the common and more hazardous method of crossing the Mediterranean on the shaky, overcrowded boats that departed for Italy from Libya and often did not make it. One of the Somalis, an eighteen-year-old named Abdulkadir Osman, wore a black leather jacket that seemed a few sizes too big for his thin body. He had a slight fuzz of a mustache, and carried with him a large woman's handbag that served as his suitcase. "The situation is so bad in Somalia," he told me. "My country is very dangerous, especially for young people. Greece has peace and stability. It's good to life for me." That was about as much talk as anyone in his group of travelers could stomach. Having taken a short rest, everyone stood up and continued their procession to the police station with the tired urgency of people expecting to be rewarded with a place to recover after a long trip.

Locals had gotten used to seeing migrants emerge from the farmlands to the east and wander into town. On the same road where I met the Somalis, I walked by a large café full of *kombolói*-tossing retirees. This appeared to be one of Tychero's busiest establishments on a weekday. A few of the men sat at a table out front, and as I passed, they guessed my bearded face had come from Afghanistan. "Not exactly," I said to them in Greek. They excused themselves for this mistake, but said they couldn't be blamed, given the situation. "They dirtied up the whole country!" said one man, who was wearing a longshoreman's cap. I probably made a disapproving face, because he felt the need to justify himself. "We're afraid," he said. "If you were an old man and saw fifty blacks walking down the street past your house—and I'm talking *very* black—wouldn't you be afraid?" I told him I had just met a group of Somalis, and there was nothing scary about them. Another retiree intervened, thinking he could broker an understanding. "America is half filled with blacks and so he's used to it," he explained to his cohort. Sure, said the man in the cap, "but America is very big. Here, we're just one handful. They're going to fill the whole country."

I'd heard such comments about the blackness of black skin and the "dirtying of the place" often enough that it no longer surprised me. In fact, shortly after I left the café, I got into a conversation with a stout, middle-aged Greek woman with thick-framed sunglasses as she waited for the bus. "They're blacks," she said of the immigrants she'd seen walking into town of late. "They are black, black." Of course, the migrants didn't bother her, she added, but then she proceeded to say things a bothered person would say. "They dirty up the place," she said. "And the Bulgarians and the Gypsies. We eat their dirt." I asked the lady if she knew anything about the conditions for migrants inside the police station in her town. She said it was "a joy" inside the station. "They have shelter, food, and in the summer, they even bring catering," she said. "And it costs money," she added. "We're working for the foreigners now."

She seemed to be warming into a polemic, but we were both distracted by the presence of a woman in a plaid headscarf and a bandage on her forehead, walking down the street in the company of a boy who seemed about five years old and wore a yellow winter coat that said JUNIOR LEAGUE on it. "Salaam," said the woman as she walked up to us. She was from Eritrea, she told me in pretty good English. I asked her what happened to her head and she explained that she had hit it against the ground when her legs gave out during her journey to Greece. She had crossed into the country several days earlier with her husband and two sons. The older boy, an eight-year-old, was still being detained even though the rest of the family had been freed. When border authorities had asked the boy where he was from, he wrongly answered "Somalia" because it was what he heard the other migrants around him say, the mother said. Because he gave a different answer than his parents, he was separated from them. The mixup meant that they had been waiting six days for their son to be freed, she said. During this time, the rest of the family had been staying in a partially built house up the road.

A bus pulled up and the Greek lady, who had remained silent, said good-bye and stepped inside. I then asked the Eritrean if she would show me the house where she was staying. She agreed and we walked uphill toward it, passing the desolate train station and, beside it, a series of tin-roofed sheds containing improvised cardboard mattresses on which migrants had slept. For their accommodation, the Eritrean family had opted to stay in the red-brick skeleton of a house someone had started building but never finished. Flattened cardboard boxes covered the gaps where the windows and doors were supposed to go. The family slept in a room with a large opening in the wall facing the street. On the ground was a stained mattress they had covered with cardboard to insulate themselves from its filth. A couple of broken plastic yard chairs constituted the rest of the furniture. The neighboring room was blocked off with a pink "Hello Kitty"–themed towel behind which lived another family. Given these circumstances, the Eritrean mother and her child looked dignified and neat. The woman wore a white winter coat that was spotless, and the little boy was playful and smiling. I took out a camera and asked if I could take their photo, and the woman nodded. Standing at the opening to their temporary home, they posed. The boy decided on a standing position that he thought looked the coolest, like he had some boy-band pose in mind. His mother held her hands together in front of her stomach and looked off into the distance. She made an expression that seemed to contain sorrow, resolve, and fear all at once.

Her husband arrived from town, where he said he'd been making a few phone calls. He was a slim, scholarly-looking man. The family had walked from Eritrea to Sudan, he told me, and from there they boarded a Nile riverboat to Egypt. In Egypt, they paid for fake passports and flew to Istanbul, and from there they traveled to the border by walking much of the way. They left Eritrea, he told me, due to some troubles he'd had with the government, which he described as "very bad." He asked me not to mention his line of work, the nature of the trouble, and other biographical details he thought might reveal his identity, because he was afraid for his extended family back home. He then excused himself. He and his wife wanted to go to the police station and visit their son.

In early 2008, an Afghan interpreter in Kabul who had worked for international troops, believing his life to be in danger from the Taliban, decided he ought to leave Afghanistan in a hurry. While working with foreign forces, he had met some Belgians and found them to be quite nice, and so Belgium, he thought, might be a good place to go. The Afghan paid a smuggler 12,000 dollars to get him to Europe. He traveled for several months, passing through Iran and Turkey. In December, he entered the European Union by boat, arriving on the Greek island of Lesbos, a rugged, windswept place off the Turkish coast. In Greece, the Afghan learned that it would be much harder to move on to Belgium than he'd thought. A few years later, the story of his efforts to get there became the subject of a case before the European Court of Human Rights, which was tasked with determining whether Greece and Belgium had subjected him to torture.

On Lesbos, the Afghan, who in court records was identified only as MSS, was detained for one week and released with a piece of paper ordering him to leave the country. The Afghan did so, and arrived in Belgium a few months later, where he applied for asylum. According to a European Union regulation, however, the member country where a migrant first arrives is responsible for handling an asylum claim. For the Afghan, this meant that because he'd entered the European Union through Greece, Belgium could send him back. This practice was a source of resentment in Greece, as well as in Italy and Spain, because it placed a greater burden on them by virtue of their proximity to poorer and more violent parts of the world. Greeks had taken to calling their country "Europe's basement," where unwanted migrants were kept. In the Afghan's case, Belgian officials contacted the pertinent Greek authorities and requested they take charge of the asylum claim. The Greeks didn't respond. The Belgians, after a two-month wait, took the Greeks' silence as an implicit acceptance of their request, and deported him. When the Afghan arrived in Athens by plane, he was detained in a holding center next to the airport. He said he was kept in a small space with twenty other detainees and "was given very little to eat and had to sleep on a dirty mattress or on the bare floor," according to court records. Three days later, the

Afghan was released with a "pink card," a piece of paper indicating he was an asylum seeker. Though it allowed him to stay in the country pending the outcome of a hearing, he had almost no chance of receiving asylum. The year he first arrived, no Afghan asylum seekers in Greece were given protected status the first time they applied for it, while other EU countries, on average, gave Afghans protection half the time.

After his release, the Afghan said, he lived in a park in central Athens. Two months later, he was arrested at Athens International Airport as he was attempting to get on a flight out of Greece with a fake Bulgarian identity card. Police detained him in the same place they'd put him the previous time. This time, the police beat him, the Afghan alleged. After seven days, he was released. About a year later—his asylum case in Greece still undecided—he tried to escape the country again through the port city of Patras on the northern Peloponnesian coast, where migrants often tried to sneak onto departing cargo ships to Italy. Greek police apprehended him there, then transported him across the country to the Turkish border, where they tried to force him and other migrants into Turkey, the Afghan said. Human rights groups had repeatedly documented allegations of this practice, referred to as a "pushback." On this occasion, according to the Afghan, the plan was foiled by the presence of Turkish police on the other side.

The Greek government denied any wrongdoing and argued before the court that the Afghan had provided no evidence to support the allegations of degrading treatment. In a 2011 decision, however, the court deemed the Afghan's testimony credible, citing two dozen reports from human rights organizations documenting repeated allegations of police abuse, pushbacks, the systematic detention of migrants in filthy conditions, and an asylum system whose primary purpose seemed to be to deny asylum. A glance through the reports revealed a dreadful picture. In one case, on the island of Lesbos, the United Nations refugee agency, UNHCR, found more than 850 migrants, including 200 unaccompanied children—most of them Afghans—detained in an old warehouse, and one of the rooms filled with 150 women and 50 babies, many of them sick from the unsanitary conditions and overcrowding. In another case, the European Committee for the Prevention of Torture visited the holding center next to the Athens airport—the place where the Afghan was twice kept—and recorded alleged "cases of ill-treatment at the hands of police officers" and instances in which migrants were "obliged to drink water from the toilets."

The court found that both Greece and Belgium had violated the European Convention on Human Rights' prohibition of torture and inhumane or degrading treatment. Greece, in essence, was the torturer, but Belgium was implicated too, for sending the Afghan there. The court acknowledged that Greece faced a greater migration burden than other European Union countries, but said this did not absolve it of its responsibility to uphold the law. The decision compelled EU nations to suspend the routine practice of sending asylum seekers back to Greece. Still, most migrants had to find a way to illegally sneak out of Greece to another European country in order to benefit from the ruling, and as the Afghan's story made clear, that wasn't always easy. At the same time, European politicians were exerting additional pressure on Greece to control its borders and make sure migrants didn't make their way north. Many asylum seekers—particularly those without the financial resources to pay a smuggler—found themselves trapped by the geographic barriers that separated Greece from the desirable countries of the European Union—the Ionian Sea to the west, and the mountain ranges of the Balkans to the north. As one Afghan living in Athens around this time told me, Greece was like "a big cage."

About fifteen miles north of Tychero, the Evros River bends past Soufli, a hillside town of red-tiled roofs and old brick warehouses. The town, once home to a thriving silk industry, has the rust-belt feel of a bygone heyday, though silk-related tourism allows a faint economic pulse to persist. Soufli's main street is about a third of a mile away from the Evros, and as a result, migrants who had just crossed the river frequently wandered past its bakeries and cafés. During my visit, locals used words like "dramatic" and "tragic" to describe the situation, though sometimes they seemed to be speaking as much for their own experience as for that of the migrants. The mayor, Evangelos Poulios, a man with a plump face who sat at his office desk in front of a large painting of the Last Supper, told me the town hadn't experienced any crime as a result of the migrant influx. Still, he said, "at night, when the residents see someone, they get scared." Also, he would have preferred his town's reputation pertain more to its silk legacy than to its use as a migrant crossing point. "It makes a bad impression on visitors," he said.

One morning, near the town's train station, I met Ahmed Takia, a forty-year-old Algerian who was looking for food in trash cans. He was also harvesting whatever significant amounts of unburned tobacco he could find in discarded cigarette butts, with the goal of accumulating enough to roll a cigarette. Takia was tall and skinny, had a wrinkled, worn face, and wore a hooded knit sweater with a wolf's head image on the front and back. During his travels he had turned his ankle, and was walking with a bad limp. The night before, he had slept on a bench outside the station house, which was locked up and out of use.

Takia didn't speak much English, but we communicated in Spanish, which he had learned while working as a mechanic in Spain, and I had learned, at least rudimentarily, in an American high school. He told me he came from Oran, on Algeria's Mediterranean coast, and had been hoping to get to Germany, where he had a brother living in Leipzig. He had planned to make it to Greece and find a job in order to raise more money to finance the rest of the journey. Things hadn't gone according to plan, though. After entering through the Tychero border station nearly a month earlier, he'd traveled around Greece, hopping on trains in search of work along with a twenty-three-year-old Algerian named Abdullah Takoi, who, as we were talking, was taking a nap on a train station bench underneath a European Union flag. The two couldn't find any work, and had come back to the border broke and much thinner than when they started. Outside the station house was a luggage scale Takia could use to illustrate this. He got on and pointed to the seventy kilos indicated on the scale. He had left Algeria weighing nearly ninety. "I didn't know," Takia said. "My plan was to work and find my way. I didn't know. I was thinking Europe. In the end, nothing."

A bit later, I took a walk into town and bought a bag of *tiropites*, triangular cheese pies, then came back to the station. Takoi, the younger traveler, had woken up, and the three of us ate lunch. They told me they were waiting for a late-afternoon passenger train that would take them about thirty miles north along the Evros River Valley to the town of Orestiada. From there, they would make one last-ditch effort to find work, and then, if that failed, try to go back to Turkey. Takia told me that his traveling companion was a cook. "Mwa," Takia said, kissing the tips of his fingers to indicate the quality of his friend's work. The cook, who was still waking up, didn't talk much, though. This changed when Takia began mentioning the Greek words they'd learned during their travels. *"Skoupidia,"* Takia said, or "garbage." The cook added, *"Malaka,"* the ubiquitous Greek word of disparagement. *"Fige,"* he added, or "leave." The cook then put them together in the order he was accustomed to hearing them. *"Fige, malaka,"* he said, grinning. I asked Takia if they knew any other words. Takia shook his head. " 'Hello?' " I said. "Can you say 'hello'?" Takia shook his head again.

Another young man appeared in front of the station in a

jacket covered with Union Jacks and the words FASHION & JEANS. Blond-dyed locks hung from under his winter cap, giving him the appearance of a misplaced surfer. His name was Mohammad Soltani, and when he saw the cook, he gave him a big hug. I asked Soltani, who spoke English, if they were longtime friends. "No," he said. "I just met him last night. But I'm happy to be alive." Soltani explained that he had tried to cross the river back into Turkey early in the morning. He had wrapped his clothes in blue plastic bags and, wearing only a T-shirt and clenching his backpack in his teeth, waded into the Evros. Before reaching the halfway point, he was up to his chest in water and too tired to go farther, he said, so he turned back. He pulled down his pants to show us the red scratches from the bushes over his thighs and shins, and then sat down on a bench.

Soltani told me he was Afghan, but had been raised in Iran and was a convert to Bahaism. He was hoping his religious conviction would qualify him for asylum, but he hadn't had any luck. Three years earlier he moved to Turkey, and he had recently decided to try to make it to Italy. In the Greek port city of Patras, he had twice hidden underneath a cargo truck that was to board an Italy-bound ship, but police found him both times. *"Malaka, malaka, malaka,"* they said while kicking him, he recalled. The hand with which he'd protected his face still didn't work quite right, he said. He showed me a lump on his left wrist, and the last two fingers were slightly bent out of shape. He wasn't the first migrant I'd met who claimed to have suffered a beating in Patras, and according to a joint report written by German and Greek human rights groups, migrants there were victims of systematic police violence. "Too much bad," Soltani said. "This country not good. I think positive, but I have bad luck."

A taxi driver then pulled up. A day earlier, I'd seen him among a group of eight local taxi drivers waiting outside the nearby Soufli police station for the daily release of detained migrants. The drivers offered migrants the forty-five-minute ride to the nearest city, Alexandroupoli, on the Aegean coast, for a fee of eighty euros, and were not exactly forthright about the more affordable public transportation options that were available. This taxi driver didn't want to tell me his name, but introduced himself as the president of the local taxi association. He was a pudgy man in sunglasses, and some of his bottom teeth were missing. "There's no train today," he said in Greek, expecting me to translate for him. I told him that the Algerians had been informed of a northbound train arriving around 4:00 p.m., which they intended to catch. "If they have no papers, they can't get on the train," the driver said. I told him they had papers. The taxi driver didn't want to leave, however. At one point, he stepped onto the luggage scale. He weighed 100 kilos. He had lost a few kilos on account of a cold, he said; it was good to shed some weight.

A graffiti-covered train appeared down the tracks. The three migrants began to gather their bags and water bottles. The taxi driver tried to pantomime to them that they couldn't get on it. I stood behind the taxi driver and shook my head to indicate to them that they shouldn't listen to him. The Algerians rushed toward the train, Takia limping pathetically. They approached a train car with a large thumbs-up spray-painted on it. Before he boarded, Takia stopped to wave good-bye to me. I waved back. The conductor then disembarked from the train and looked down the platform. "Where are they going?" he asked me. I shrugged. He shrugged too, got back inside, and shut the doors. As the train pulled away, the Algerians waved to me from behind the windows. I waved back again. For a moment, it felt like there was cause to celebrate.

The train had let out a small, fashionably dressed Afghan man with a mop haircut. He looked around as if disoriented and asked me in English if I knew how he could get to Turkey. "I'm so tired," he said. The taxi driver, using me as an interpreter, haggled with him on a price to take him to the border, though they couldn't come to an agreement. "Tell him if he goes back there, the Turks are going to beat him," the driver told me before driving off. "They are not like us over here." I was surprised that the driver showed interest in the welfare of the Afghan, though I suspected the comment was inspired by injured pride over the fact that the Afghan was choosing Turkey over Greece.

The Afghan, who didn't want to tell me his name, asked me if I could show him where the police station was. I pointed down the railroad line, and he asked me if I could walk him over to it. On the way, he told me he had reached as far north as Belgrade, Serbia, where he had hailed a taxi and asked the driver to take him to a neighborhood where migrants lived. Instead, the driver called the police, who then kicked him out of the country. The Afghan ended up in Athens trying to figure out what to do. "Too many refugees," he said. "Very bad living. No money. Sleeping in parks. I'm tired. Now I just go back. I'm finished." We arrived at the police station, a yellow, cube-shaped building with a fenced-in plot in the back where migrants slept outside on dirty foam mattresses. At this point, I said good-bye, but the Afghan asked me if I could come inside with him and help translate. Before I could consider whether or not that was a good idea, an officer walked out of the station and motioned for us to come closer. He was a large man in boots and a blue uniform, though the official nature of his appearance was diminished by the *kombolói* he casually tossed with one hand. He asked what we wanted, and I told him that the Afghan wanted to know how he could go to Turkey. "If he wants to go back, he has to go the same way he came in," the officer said. He then glanced in the direction of the river. Another officer popped his head out of the door and told us to come inside. We entered, and they closed the door behind us.

It was a small room surrounded by security monitors. The officer who had invited us in sat behind a desk. The look on his face indicated boredom more than severity. If the Afghan wanted to turn himself in, the officer said, he could spend the night outside in a sleeping bag on one of the mattresses. In the morning, he would receive a form ordering him to leave the country within thirty days. He could then present this paper to Greek authorities at the border crossing, and they would let him return to Turkey, according to the officer. What the Turks would do with him, he had no control over. The Afghan stood there in silence and contemplated. "Don't be afraid," the officer with the *kombolói* said to the Afghan. The Afghan agreed—though I wondered if they would have just let him go if he hadn't. They unlocked a door leading to the rest of the police station, and an officer met him on the other side. "Thank you," the Afghan said as the door shut with a snap.

"Who are you?" the police officer behind the desk then asked me. I told him I was writing about the situation on the border, and he asked to see my identification card. He wrote down the information on a piece of paper. When he was done, he handed my card back. "Is it the Jews?" he said. "Is it the Americans? I don't know. But someone is behind this," he said of the migration phenomenon the country was experiencing. The officer with the *kombolói* then added: "We've become the basement of Europe." I asked them if Frontex, the European Union border agency, which was increasingly involving itself in operations in Greece, had been at all helpful. "That hasn't helped at all," said the one behind the desk.

He then pointed to a little white trailer house outside the police station. "They just sit in there. They come in in the morning, they take down their information, and then they leave. And they get paid twice as much and more." The Frontex official in the trailer, I inferred, was trained to determine the nationality of the migrants, an important step in determining who was potentially eligible for asylum. "I'm not the one who knows about these things, but someone is behind this," the officer behind the desk went on. "Is it a Muslim jihadist plan?" he said. The one with the *kombolói* added: "They will call for a jihad one day, and then they will stab you. Not with a knife, but with a fork."

The two men wanted to know what I thought. I told them I thought the migrants were coming because their homelands were poor or violent, that they didn't necessarily want to stay in Greece. "It's easy to come here," said the man behind the desk. "The harder thing for you to do is to stay behind and fight to improve your own country." I considered at that point whether I should ask him if his statement also applied to the Greeks—my parents among them—who had emigrated when the country was still poor—and the many Greeks who were again leaving at the time due to rising joblessness. I didn't say anything, though. Before I left, I asked them their names, and they refused to give them to me. "You're not going to write this," the one with the *kombolói* said. "No, write it, write it," said his superior behind the desk. "It's the truth."

The Evros River had become the preferred crossing point into the European Union because it was considered safer than the other common method—the perilous journey across the Mediterranean. Still, the Evros was deeper and its currents stronger than many aspirant border crossers assumed, and it became the final resting place for an untold number of people. During the time of my visit, bodies in varying states of decomposition were commonly found washed up on its thicketed banks. Many of the dead were taken to a burial site on the outskirts of Sidero, a tranquil village, home to a Muslim minority, in the mountains west of the river valley. Most Muslims were ejected from Greece in the population exchange with Turkey in the early 1920s, though those living in Thrace were exempted and remained. Greek authorities assumed most of the migrants who died in the Evros were Muslims, and therefore arranged for the Muslim clerics in Sidero to perform the burials.

From Soufli, I traveled up to Sidero one afternoon in a taxi, which dropped me off next to a lime green mosque topped with a short, metallic minaret. Thrace is the only part of Greece where mosques can exist without the vehement protest of the broader population. Greeks justify this allowance with the common albeit questionable assertion that the area's Muslims are descendants of the ancient Greek Thracians—the fairness of their hair and skin is sometimes pointed to as evidence—and therefore deserve the indulgence of being able to observe their religion. For their part, Muslims in Sidero and elsewhere in the region often self-identify as ethnically Turkish, a circumstance that tends to upset their fellow Greek countrymen.

The town was on a high plateau, and a roof of fast-moving cumulus clouds seemed almost within reach. I didn't see any people at first. A few hens crossed the road. Gray winter forests and brush-covered fields dotted with grazing sheep surrounded the village, a cluster of single-story homes. There were no sounds but for the wind. Greece's crises for a moment felt like distant abstractions. From the mosque emerged a man wearing a white skullcap with a golden wreath stitched to its crown. He had chestnut eyes and a gray beard trimmed to outline his jawbone. He spoke an accented Greek when introducing himself as Hasan Saramet, a village *hodja*, the Turkish honorific often used to describe an imam. Saramet's mother tongue was Turkish. With him was a younger man with a slight mustache and a white skullcap who introduced himself as the prayer caller, Abdulrahim Kuru.

The men said they would take me to the cemetery where the migrants were buried. We hopped inside Kuru's small car and drove a few minutes to the edge of town. On the way, Kuru told me stories about meeting border crossers while driving. Once, he was with his children when he found someone unconscious on the side of the road. "I got out and pushed him a little," Kuru said. "He opened his eyes. It was raining. I gave him a sandwich I had prepared for my kids. I didn't know if it would do him harm, because he hadn't eaten. I picked him up and asked him, 'Where are you from?' 'From Pakistan,' he said. 'Where are we, Turkey or Greece?'" Giving away a sandwich or some clothes was often about as much help as they could provide, the men said. Offering a ride was far more risky. If the police pulled you over with an undocumented migrant, you could easily be accused of being a smuggler.

We pulled up to the burial site, a fenced-in hilltop of brown dirt imprinted with bulldozer tracks. The two men pushed back a heavy iron gate. Rows of dirt mounds marked the graves. The *hodja* estimated that four hundred people were buried there. Once, they buried twenty-five people at the same time. "They think they are going to find a good life," he said. "But they die."

"They should know what it's like here so they don't come," Kuru added. "We see them as downtrodden people. They go to paradise."

The *hodja* smiled—exposing a silver cap on a lower tooth. His expression looked somewhat bitter, as if perhaps he had some doubts about this. He then walked over to one of the fresher mounds of dirt. "Here, a sixteen-year-old girl from Afghanistan is buried," he said. "Oh, how her parents cried." Kuru told me the story. Her parents—a Christian mother and a Muslim father—had gone to Athens first, and then, once established, called for their two daughters, who were waiting in Iran, to follow. One of the girls was never found again. The other, the sixteen-year-old, was discovered drowned and decayed. The parents came to the border to attend her burial. "We told the mother not to look," Kuru said.

On the way back into town, the men told me more stories of migrants they'd come across while driving through the hills. Kuru said that one time he saw three men walking in the mountains in the middle of winter. Though he was afraid to give them a ride, he couldn't refuse that time. "One of them was in very bad shape," Kuru said, near death. "So I took the risk and drove them to the police station."

The *hodja* added: "They wander up to the towns and ask, 'Where's Athens?'"

Nearly all the migrants I met planned to go to Athens. "Athens good?" one African man asked me through the fence of the border police station in Soufli. "Athens not so good," I said. He looked at me like he refused to believe that. "Athens good," he said. Compounding the misery of joblessness and penury that many encountered once arriving in Athens, the fascist Golden Dawn was, to use the words of one of its leaders, launching "a pogrom" against foreigners. Still, despite the extremely challenging conditions, for some, even a meager Athens subsistence was often preferable to circumstances back home. Bangladeshis, for instance, could often be seen pushing shopping carts filled with scrap metal. One Bangladeshi man I met, hauling a large water boiler in his shopping cart, told me he received seventeen cents per kilo for his cargo. This work still amounted to a much better daily wage than he could earn in Bangladesh. Others found better jobs unloading boxes of fruits and vegetables for farmers at outdoor markets, or doing yard work in the suburbs. Migrants rented cheap apartments in the overbuilt center of the city—in areas middle-class families had long ago abandoned for the fresher air of the suburbs—where a 300-euro rent split among several became a manageable sum.

One day in Athens during the summer of 2013, I came across some Bangladeshis who had pinpointed an excellent, albeit illegal, business model. I was walking through the neighborhood of Exarcheia, an unruly, graffiti-tagged area populated by young and aging leftists, anarchists, junkies, and hipsters. Exarcheia is their bastion, and not just in a figurative sense. The neighborhood rests upon a long and at times steep incline leading to the green peak of Strefi Hill, one of Athens's higher summits. Police are not fond of venturing into Exarcheia's narrow streets, but rather tend to remain in the heavily guarded police station as if combatants occupying a hostile land. And it is. Police officers' fascistic visage often inspires some of the Molotov cocktail–equipped youths of the area to launch incendiaries in their direction. On this day, I was walking by the neighborhood's epicenter, Plateia Exarcheion, a small square inhabited by junkies and a semipermanent contingent of revolutionary street punks, enclosed by a ring of more-polished cafés where college students come to meet their friends. A group of Bangladeshi men sprinted past me with expressions reflecting a mixture of panic and amusement. Pursuing them was a far less agile cop wielding a baton and weighed down by body armor and a white helmet that seemed too big for his head. The Bangladeshis ran through the square before scattering into the neighborhood's grid of alleys. Before the police officer reached the square, he stopped, turned around, and walked back the other way. He spotted a large shopping bag filled with cigarette cartons hidden between two parked cars. The officer grabbed it and jumped onto the back of a motorcycle being driven by a colleague, and the pair sped off. Within two minutes, the Bangladeshis reappeared on the same corner. This was where they conducted a brisk business selling black-market cigarettes. Such occasional police chases were a hazard of business to which they had become accustomed.

Mohammed, the twenty-seven-year-old ringleader of a cigarette-selling band of four or five Bangladeshis, immediately noticed the loss of the large shopping bag. "Why did they have to take it?" he said, smarting from the financial loss. The bag contained 280 packs of cigarettes, equaling a loss of about the same number of euros, he calculated. Mohammed was a lanky man with eyes that darted back and forth under the bill of his Citroën automobile cap, a behavior that seemed an adaptation to his business, which required that he always be looking for customers and cops. He wore a shirt that said JAPAN AUTO PARTS and TEAM YOSHIMORI, and featured the red sun of the Japanese flag. He would have looked as if he were about to hop inside a race car had he not held a bag full of tobacco product in a pink shopping bag that said ZIC ZAC, the name of a women's clothing brand. The youngest of the group, a twenty-year-old named Shaheen, who had on a pink-striped shirt and a small red backpack, and had a businesslike demeanor, went to check on the rest of the inventory, which was hidden across the street beneath a row of sewer grates. Shaheen looked both ways before bending down to remove a grate. He extracted a few cartons of their most popular seller, RGD, also known as "black," manufactured in China, according to the packaging. A little lady with curly red hair then walked up to Shaheen and asked for two packages. He forked them over and she handed him a two-euro coin. "As-salaam alaikum!" announced another customer, a gray-haired man with the upper half of his shirt unbuttoned in the heat. He ordered a couple of cartons of faux Lucky Strikes and patted Mohammed on the back before walking off. "Greek people need very strong cigarettes," Mohammed said. He himself did not smoke, and therefore all judgments about the quality of his product were based on imagination and customer feedback. "Customer tell me it's not good cigarettes," he told me. "But because of the Greek economic situation, they cannot buy from kiosk."

Herein lay the business strategy. When it comes to smoking, Greeks compete with Bulgarians for the European Union leadership position; over 40 percent of Greeks smoke. With expendable income disappearing, newly hiked taxes on legal cigarettes, and addiction making for static demand, the Bangladeshis were running a brisk business selling what people needed for far cheaper.

Mohammed's black-market cigarettes went for a euro a pack—about one-fifth the cost of a store-bought pack—though finer varieties went up to €1.30. Exarcheia also provided the Bangladeshis an excellent business environment. The abundance of anarchists, or "students," as Mohammed referred to them, provided his team of salesmen with a degree of protection from the cops. "Students are very crazy," Mohammed told me. "They make firebomb. Is very easy to make. Most of the students have them." Still, the police came by often enough. That spring, Mohammed had been arrested for selling cigarettes and sentenced to ten months in jail or a 3,000-euro fine. "Greek police better than Bangladeshi police," Mohammed said. "Greek police only hit you a little. Bangladeshi police hit you more." Mohammed appealed the verdict and a judge let him go. "Give me one more chance and I never sell cigarettes," he told the judge. Mohammed repeatedly justified his line of work to me, as if he felt guilty about it. It was not as immoral as selling drugs, he said. "Cigarette bad, but not too bad." He would have preferred a normal job, he added, but those didn't exist. "No choice," he said.

Mohammed told me he quit school in Bangladesh in the eleventh grade and got a job at a cardboard box factory in order to help support his family. This was necessary because his father, a retired policeman, had lost the family's money on a bad investment involving tons of potatoes. "That year, potato not selling," Mohammed explained. The 6,500 or so Bangladeshi taka Mohammed earned in a month at the factory—worth about 60 euros, at the time I met him—helped support his three siblings. But still it wasn't enough, so he took off for Europe. "I think then, oh, Greece is Europe," he said while leaning on a parked Peugeot. The journey to Greece took him two and a half years, with stops along the way to work and raise money. In Iran, he worked in a Tehran bakery. In eastern Turkey, he worked in a restaurant, cleaning and cutting up chickens for the equivalent of a few euros a day. When he had saved enough at each stop, he would pay a smuggler to take him on the next leg of the journey to Europe. "My target was always Greece," he said. Mohammed crossed the border in the spring of 2010. He was surprised by what he found. In Bangladesh, he'd seen the Bollywood film *Chalte Chalte*, in which two lovers visit Greece. "Goodness, the signs you make," the leading man sings to his lover in the film as the pair prance around on the whitewashed island of Mykonos, and in front of Athens's finest tourist attractions. "What secrets are you exposing? What are you telling me with your eyes?" In the film, Greece looked clean and shiny, Mohammed told me. "I see the film, I think, Greece is very beautiful. When I come, I saw is very dirty."

For people like Mohammed, Greece's dysfunctional asylum system had advantages. It was very unlikely he'd ever qualify for asylum, but pending the final decision on a request for it, he could legally remain in the country. Since the asylum process was often mired in bureaucracy for years, an applicant ended up with a kind of de facto residency permit. After Mohammed arrived in Greece, he applied for asylum—claiming he faced persecution in Bangladesh for his political views—and landed a job in the kitchen of a Chinese restaurant. Mohammed worked there four days a week for fourteen hours a day and earned 600 euros a month. In 2011, though, business fell sharply, and his boss, "a very big *malaka*," according to Mohammed, said he would reduce his salary to 500 euros and increase his workweek to five days. Mohammed quit instead. This, he realized later, was probably a mistake. He looked around for something else, but couldn't find anything. "Look all over Athens. Greek people all empty"—out of money, he meant. "We are foreigner. Illegal. How do we find job? That time, I go a little bit mad. Madness and crazy." A friend, he said, told him he should look into the black-market cigarette business. "I think it is much better than looking for a job," Mohammed said. He told me he'd been selling cigarettes for about half a year, though I suspected, given his leadership role, that it had been longer. Each member of his crew earned about twenty euros a day, more on good days, he said. They worked seven days a week all day, though Mohammed took breaks on Friday afternoons to pray at a Bangladeshi mosque near Omonoia Square, a traffic hub in the city center surrounded by dilapidated, seedy streets. Mohammed said he'd been able to wire 1,500 euros to his family in Bangladesh, and had saved considerably more. "I think about future," he said. "Greek people like to enjoy themselves. They don't think about future. They spend money. Have good time." Before I left, I told Mohammed that I didn't know much about his homeland, only that it was very poor, that many garment workers had died in factory fires. The mention of his country's garment industry, however, made Mohammed smile with pride. He had once gone to a big Greek store called H&M, he said. "Very great many Bangladeshi clothes. I buy one T-shirt. Expensive, but good quality."

The next morning, a Friday, I came back and found Mohammed and his coworkers running down the street after a blue sedan. They caught up with it at a stoplight and started banging on its tinted windows, though the driver sped off once the light turned green. Mohammed returned out of breath. "Look," he told me, holding up a fake twenty-euro bill streaked with watercolor paint. "Big loss." The beefiest of the Bangladeshi sales crew, a man with a shirt that said PREMIER across the chest, screamed in disgust and shook his head as if trying to exorcise a bad spirit. "We do illegal job," said Mohammed. "But we trust. I never pay with fake note. Never never. He is very bad man. Not good person," he said of the guy in the sedan, an Albanian, according to Mohammed. For the next half hour, Mohammed couldn't think of anything else. "We make little profit. Why people do this to us?" he said. "If he comes again, I will remember his face. And then he will know who we are." I asked Mohammed what he meant by that. "Next time when they come, we will beat him," he explained. Mohammed told me there were between fifteen and twenty Bangladeshis on the block, and sometimes they were forced to apply their numerical advantage to protect the viability of their business. Once a junkie tried to buy a pack of cigarettes without enough money, Mohammed said. There was a big argument. The junkie started getting aggressive. "So we beat him. Kicking. Fifteen people. We not break rib. Fracture." Another time, a junkie gave them a Turkish lira coin instead of a euro. "Many of us scream. I think maybe he was a little bit scared, so he gave the cigarettes. We just protect ourselves. Otherwise we never touch anybody."

Business and traffic began to pick up in the early afternoon. An old man in sunglasses rolled up to the corner in a fine blue 1980s Mercedes. He held up an empty pack of Gold Mounts, which featured a golden image of a mountain on the front and the slogan "Full Flavor Finest Virginia." Shaheen provided a carton. The man forked over a ten-euro bill and continued to creep down the street. "He's very good person," said Mohammed. "He comes back every three or four days. He says nothing. Buys carton. Never gives fake notes." Another man drove up on his moped and looked at the product offerings with a skeptical expression. Mohammed provided advice. The Gold Mount Slims were very light. Raquel was "like Marlboro, but not Marlboro." The moped driver took a carton of each. A nice old lady then walked up. She ordered a pack of RGD. "They're the best ones," she told me. "They don't make your throat hurt."

The time was 1:25 p.m. Mohammed announced that he had to leave for Friday prayers. First he would go home and change into nicer clothes, he said, and then ride his bicycle to the mosque. I asked him if I could meet him there, and he agreed. The mosque was located in a derelict warehouse building on a narrow street inhabited primarily by Pakistanis, Bangladeshis, and some Chinese immigrants. Most of the storefronts on the street were empty, though a South Asian grocery store was doing a brisk business selling paan. I walked inside the warehouse building and went up the dark, narrow set of stairs. On the top floor, Bangladeshi men in white skullcaps sat on a green carpet. An imam in a white robe sat in the front of the room and preached in Bengali through a microphone. A reverb effect gave his voice a holy gravitas. This was one of many unofficial mosques in Athens. Over the course of the previous decade, repeated proposals to build an official one had been undone by fierce local opposition. Mohammed arrived shortly after I did and took a seat on the carpet. Bored listening to a sermon in a language I could not understand, I decided to wait for him outside.

Across the street from the warehouse, I found a fabric store in a crumbling neoclassical building with a plaque on the front that read *L. Konstantinidis.* The store was a holdout from a bygone era in which the neighborhood was filled with textile shops and Greeks. I stepped inside and looked around. A man with frizzy white hair emerged from a back room filled with rolls of fabric stacked to the ceiling. I introduced myself and told him I'd come to the neighborhood to see the mosque. "Are you also writing about the Greeks who are suffering because the Bangladeshis spit everywhere?" he said.

"So they bother you?" I said.

"They don't bother me," he said, seemingly abandoning his displeasure. "Well, they did strip the plumbing out of the building upstairs and the bronze handles off the doors. But they are hungry. Why are they hungry? That is the question." I asked him if he had an answer. "Because we whites are destroying the planet," he said. I was surprised to hear this and asked him what he meant. The shopkeeper told me that humans once inhabited Mars, until whites depleted its resources, and the whites were doing it again now by destroying the earth. He perhaps noticed a disbelieving look on my face. "Don't take me as demented," he said. "Was there water or life on Mars? There are a lot of Greeks at NASA, and they will find out. Of that you can be sure." I changed the subject and asked him about the shop. It had been there since 1959, he told me. His father, a refugee from Asia Minor, had started the business. The man said he had wanted to be an astrophysicist, but his father needed help running the place. "So I grew up and got old here," he said. All the other textile shops began closing down two decades ago, he told me. "Globalization ate them up." His store survived only because he maintained a profitable business supplying fabric imported from China to a manufacturer of police uniforms. The shop owner then shared his theory as to why Greece had gone bankrupt. "Capitalists collect the wealth so it won't spread, because if the worker has money, he won't work. That's what happened here. With borrowed money, we were all rich. So we didn't work. That's how we destroyed the country."

A couple of Greek men walked into the store. One of them had long curly hair and looked like he belonged in an '80s hair band. They were standing around talking about the fact that there were no Greeks left in the neighborhood when, from outside, a small Chinese lady in snug light blue pants and pink roses on her high heels asked them if they could remove the car they had just parked there. "You better do what she says," the shopkeeper told the men. "There's no way she won't get her way." The lady was preparing for a large shipment to be delivered to her residence, a two-story lime green building across the street that was meticulously maintained in comparison to the other buildings on the block. A rainbow-colored garden windmill turned among the potted plants on the balcony. At the end of the street, a flatbed truck had pulled up carrying a very large shipping container with COSCO written prominently on the side, the name of a Chinese state-owned shipping company. A division of COSCO had a few years earlier purchased the rights to operate container terminals at the port of Piraeus, one of the biggest ports on the Mediterranean, located near Athens. The company invested considerably in the port, increasing both cargo volume and the number of jobs. For the Chinese, the port was an important landing point for goods it wanted to sell in Europe. Apparently, that included a large number of tennis racket–shaped electric bug swatters. The shipping container at the end of the street was filled with them. It, however, was too big to fit down the street, so the Chinese lady employed some of the South Asian men that had previously been loitering on the sidewalk to unload the boxes and carry them to her building. The men from the fabric store stood at the doorway and watched as one large box after another of tennis racket flyswatters was loaded into the ground floor of the Chinese lady's building. The swatters were a product I'd seen immigrants peddling on the street. Apparently, this Chinese lady was their supplier. "Globalization in action," I said to the shop owner. "Greeks could learn something from her," I added, half kidding. The men seemed to take me seriously, though. "We once knew, but we forgot," said the guy with the big hair.

I later found Mohammed outside the mosque unlocking his bicycle. I asked him what he had prayed for. "For my happiness. Happiness for my family. Happiness for all Muslims. Happiness for all humans." He hopped on his bicycle and peddled uphill back to his street corner.

Philoxenia, the Greek word for hospitality, means "love of strangers." Greeks are often thought of as some of the world's most hospitable people, and there is truth in this. The number of tourists who visit Greece every year far exceeds the country's population, and indeed Greeks amiably welcome them, and their much-needed money. In my experience, I was often treated with exceptional warmth and generosity in Greece. When my wife and I arrived in Athens from Berlin, for example, we noticed that it was difficult to pass through an outdoor farmers' market without being plied with gifts for our child. This didn't change when people detected that my wife couldn't speak Greek, or that I spoke with an American accent. "Some mandarins for the boy! It will make him healthy!" As we strolled past farmers' stalls, sun-wrinkled faces gazed at our son while making a spitting gesture, a precaution against the evil eye, which can be inadvertently given through excessive admiration. This was not the kind of thing that would happen in Berlin.

Philoxenia, however, generally does not apply to those who arrive in need, to work and to stay. This has been evident since the 1990s, when, after the fall of the Iron Curtain, Albanian migrants began illegally crossing the border into Greece. Greece was not accustomed to receiving large numbers of non-Greek immigrants, and while the Albanians' cheap labor was broadly welcomed by those who benefited from it, the Albanians' personhood was often not. Certainly, Greece is not the only European country to have a deeply ambivalent relationship to newcomers, but Greeks' wariness has manifested itself in some unique ways. For instance, students at the top of the class in Greece are given the distinction of carrying the Greek flag during patriotic school parades. Periodic controversies have erupted, however, in instances when the best student has been of Albanian origin. One Albanian student in a small town in northern Greece was twice the best student in his class in the early 2000s, and was twice denied the honor of holding the flag. "This flag is stained with the blood of our national heroes who fought to liberate Greece, and must not be raised by the hands of a foreigner," a spokesman for a village parents' group said, according to an article in Britain's *The Independent* at the time. Not surprisingly, this reaction seemed to eliminate any desire the Albanian student had to accept the flag honor. "I declare that I give up the right to carry the flag," he said at the gates of his school.

Someone ought to have informed the parents' group that many of the flag-bearing heroes of the Greek War of Independence spoke a dialect of Albanian. The Arvanites, as they are called, arrived in the territory that is now Greece during the Middle Ages, and lived in large numbers in the area around Athens and the northern part of the Peloponnese. After Greece won its independence—with a large contribution from its Arvanite population—the Arvanite language was censored by the Greek state. Still, people spoke it in private, including two of my Peloponnesian grandparents. One of them, my paternal grandmother, descended from an Arvanite mountain village in Corinthia she knew as Dousia, though, when I visited the place, its name had long been changed to the more Hellenic Kefalari. Greeks of Arvanite origin often deny any relation to modern-day Albanians. This is partly for reasons of religion; Arvanites, like almost all Greeks, are Christian Orthodox, while the majority of religious Albanians identify as Muslim. Moreover, to acknowledge a close connection would complicate Greek national ideas of a pure Hellenic lineage. Still, when Albanians began arriving in Greece in the 1990s, some Arvanites who still spoke their fading dialect discovered they could communicate with the Albanians who had come to work on their farms.

It was in great part due to the large number of Albanian immigrants in Greece that in 2010, the Greek center-left parliament passed a bill that made it far easier for children born in Greece to foreign parents to be given Greek citizenship. The law was unpopular, however, with the large number of Greeks who believe that "one is born Greek and does not become Greek," as it's commonly put. When he was campaigning for the premiership in the spring of 2012, Antonis Samaras, the leader of New Democracy, vowed to abolish the law, which he called a "magnet for illegal immigrants." A lot of people seemed to approve of this thinking. At a Samaras campaign rally I attended in Athens, his repeated calls for growth-oriented economic policies were not met with nearly as much enthusiasm as his vow to "remove from this place illegal immigrants, who have now become tyrants of the society." Samaras, around this time, also called the influx of illegal immigrants an "unarmed invasion" and said his election would mean the end of a state that took care of foreigners and forsook its own citizens. After Samaras's election, parts of the citizenship law he campaigned against were deemed unconstitutional by the country's highest administrative court.

At the time of the 2012 elections, Greece was in an acute phase of its debt crisis and teetering on the edge of a euro exit that would have sown sudden and profound economic chaos. It was therefore curious that, with such pressing issues at hand, the citizenship law and illegal immigration played such a prominent role in the election campaigning. This no doubt had to do with the rise of Golden Dawn, which gained a great deal of political traction almost solely due to its anti-immigration rhetoric. Other parties felt the need to compete. The tough talk was not limited to the right wing. In the run-up to the elections, the PASOK minister overseeing the police, Michalis Chrisochoidis, vowed to round up 30,000 illegal immigrants and place them in old military bases. He also announced plans to construct a barbwire fence along several miles of the Evros River Valley border, an idea European officials referred to as "pointless," arguing that migrants would simply find another way in. During a visit to Brussels, however, Chrisochoidis said his countrymen could no longer tolerate the "time bomb" that was threatening social peace.

Greece was indeed facing an immigration problem that required the kind of responsible policy response the government had long proven incapable of mustering. Had the government been able to improve its asylum system, it would not only have created more humane conditions for asylum seekers, but it would have also allowed for faster deportation of those migrants who didn't qualify for it and instead lingered in the country indefinitely. The Greek government could not exactly use its financial troubles as an excuse for its failure to do this. European Union funds were available to make needed improvements. A spokesman for the European Commission told me that it had earmarked 304 million euros for Greece from 2007 through 2012 to be put to use for "migration management." Greece's government hadn't "absorbed" much of that money due to administrative red tape, the spokesman said. Politicians' increasing anti-immigrant rhetoric, however, provided a useful way to deflect the focus from their long-standing failings.

Samaras, after his election win, delivered on his promise to do something about the influx of migrants crossing the border illegally. The tactics the government used to accomplish this, however, raised a lot of questions. Within a few months, the Greek government launched Operation "Xenios Zeus," a nickname for the Greek god that emphasizes his role as the protector of foreign travelers. Authorities began conducting sweeps in which they detained migrants in order to check their papers. Human Rights Watch, which called the name Xenios Zeus a "cruel irony," urged Greek police to stop detaining people based on their skin color. In the first seven months of the operation, 85,000 foreigners were taken into custody in Athens. On a few occasions, nonwhite tourists were also detained by police, prompting the U.S. State Department to warn travelers of "confirmed reports of U.S. African American citizens detained by police conducting sweeps for illegal immigrants in Athens." One Nigerian American tourist detained during a sweep complained of having been beaten by police while handcuffed, telling the BBC that he woke up in the hospital with a concussion. He later filed a complaint with the help of the U.S. embassy in Athens, though a year and a half after the incident, an embassy official told me the Greek government had not yet responded.

In the Evros River Valley, Xenios Zeus meant the arrival of 1,800 additional border patrol officers. As a result, "the situation changed dramatically," according to a report by Frontex. The number of migrants detected crossing the border went from 2,000 per week in August 2012 to ten per week in October of the same year, according to the agency. Questions arose, however, concerning the methods Greek border police were using to accomplish this result, particularly as the civil war in Syria was generating a record number of refugees, many of whom set their sights on Europe.

In November 2013, the UNHCR released a statement asking for clarification from Greek authorities on the fate of a group of 150 Syrians who had reportedly crossed over the Evros River into Greece. Locals in Prangi, a village near the river, told the agency that many of the Syrians had gathered next to the village church. Police arrived in vans and took them away, the locals told the UNHCR. The agency, however, despite what it called "repeated contacts" with the police, was never able to trace the Syrians' whereabouts. Police told UNHCR officials that they had found only thirteen Syrians, a spokesman for the refugee agency told me. The UNHCR called for an investigation and, in pained diplomatic jargon, said it had repeatedly appealed to states "to facilitate access of refugees to safety" and to "avoid returns to countries neighboring Syria."

Around this time, the Council of Europe's commissioner for human rights, Nils Muižnieks, sent a letter to the Greek ministers in charge of the police and the coast guard asking them to investigate the "large number of reported collective expulsions by Greece of migrants, including a large number of Syrians fleeing war violence, and allegations of ill-treatment of migrants by members of the coast guard and of the border police." The boost in patrols along the Evros River meant that most migrants began attempting to cross into Greece over the Aegean, where they often encountered the Hellenic Coast Guard. After Muižnieks sent his letter, on January 20, 2014, eleven Afghans off the Greek islet of

Farmakonisi drowned while the coast guard was towing their boat. Survivors said it capsized after the coast guard tried to drag them back to Turkey at high speed. Coast guard officials denied this, and said they were dragging the migrants toward safety when the passengers panicked, causing the boat to capsize. Eight of the dead were children. The surviving migrants were taken to a coast guard station in the morning, where they were lined up on the harborside. Greek authorities, as if to show how well the survivors were being treated, released a video of men who had just lost their entire families being provided sandwiches by a woman wearing a surgical mask and gloves. The survivors later arrived at the port of Piraeus, where a crowd of journalists waited for them. Television cameras focused on two mournful-looking men, one of whom emitted a high-pitched wail of grief. The man held up five fingers to indicate the number of his family—four children and his wife—all of them dead. He looked at the hand and wept as if it were the only trace of them he had left. Another man beside him looked like his eyes had been sewn almost shut from sleeplessness and sorrow. "Who did he lose?" asked one journalist. "His daughter, two sons, and his wife," a translator said. The children were nine, eleven, and thirteen. "They threw them into the sea on purpose," said the man, before covering his face with his hand.

Muižnieks said the incident appeared to be a "case of failed collcctive expulsion." Greece's minister in charge of the coast guard, Miltiadis Varvitsiotis, denied this was the case and said the coast guard had tried to save them all. In a letter to Muižnieks, he expressed his "deepest sorrow for the lives lost in this tragic incident" and pointed out that the coast guard had heroically saved thousands of lives. In a Greek television interview around the same time, though, the maritime minister's tone was noticeably more hostile. "Look, Mr. Muižnieks and others want to create a political issue in Greece," the minister said. The boat's sinking should not become "the object of dumb political exploitation," he added. "I don't believe anyone wants for us to open the gates for all the immigrants to enjoy asylum in this country."

It was around this time, while walking in central Athens one day, that I met Mohamad Hussien, a twenty-year-old Syrian from the civil war–ravaged city of Homs. Hussien had a boyish face, though the dark circles under his eyes and some stubble made him look weary. He had left Syria with his mother and younger brother—leaving their father and a young sibling behind in Homs. Over a glass of tea in a dingy apartment crowded with other Syrians, he described for me the first time the three of them tried to enter Greece from the Turkish coastline. On an October night, he said, they boarded an inflatable boat with some forty other migrants. The smugglers told them that Europe was the lights flickering in the darkness, the Greek island of Samos. The Syrians steered toward the lights, but what Hussien said was a Greek coast guard vessel intercepted their boat, and men wearing balaclavas emerged pointing machine guns at them. Some of the masked men boarded their boat, Hussien said, and confiscated mobile phones and wallets; his family lost 2,000 euros, and one migrant who protested having his money taken was beaten. Last, the officers removed their engine and left the boat floating idle, he said. "Try and get to Samos now," he recalled one of the masked men yelling as the coast guard boat pulled away. The migrants then used their hands to paddle back to the Turkish shore. Hussien told me his family tried several more times to get to Greece over the Aegean. On five occasions, they met Greek patrol boats, he said. Each of those times, crew members took their engine and left them to drift and be rescued by the Turkish coast guard. On another occasion, a Turkish vessel intercepted them and dragged them back to Turkey. Finally, the family crossed into Greece over the land border. Some days before I met him, the family had tried to fly to Amsterdam using fake identity cards. Only their mother made it through security, though. The two sons were let go, and would try again later.

Greek officials denied the Hellenic Coast Guard did the kinds of things Hussien described. Credible allegations of wrongdoing were investigated, they said. Hussien's story, however, was one in a large chorus of similar migrant testimonies documented by human rights groups. Why, one might ask, would all of these people lie? The Greek coast guard and navy, one must keep in mind, did save thousands of migrants drifting in Greek territorial waters. But if some officers acted with such mercilessness, a patriotic rationale for doing so could certainly be found. An officer, after all, might see such actions as a defense of the country against the "unarmed invaders" Greek politicians spoke of. Greece, after all, seemed to be pursuing an unofficial policy of deterring migrants and asylum seekers from coming or staying. Prime Minister Samaras indicated as much. Speaking in parliament, he stressed his government's willingness to use "additional deterrence tactics that until today were also prohibited," though he did not specify what those tactics were. Other Greek officials also suggested that Greek policy was to make life for migrants as hard as possible. In the summer of 2013, for instance, Adonis Georgiadis, a New Democracy parliamentarian, told a Greek radio station that the purpose of the police practice of apprehending migrants in Athens and releasing them twenty-five miles outside of the city was to make migrants' "lives as difficult as you can so that they understand the time has come to get on an airplane and leave." A few weeks later Georgiadis received a promotion of sorts, becoming minister of health.

While inexcusable, it was not entirely hard to understand why Greek officials advocated such deterrence tactics. In theory, if Greece had built the apotheosis of an excellent and just asylum system according to European law, the country would very likely have become one of the world's prime destinations for refugees—people wishing not just to pass through, but to stay. Greek politicians and their electorate clearly did not want to make their small country a haven for people fleeing the world's conflicts. Nor, for that matter, did other European politicians want that for their own countries. The Italians were deporting migrants who had managed to escape Greece back to Greece. The Spanish were summarily deporting to Morocco migrants who climbed over a twenty-foot-high border fence onto Spanish territory. Northern European politicians seemed intent on keeping a great deal of the burden down south. Greece, however, was making a great effort to avoid bearing it. As with the country's debt troubles, a comprehensive solution to the problem was not up to Greece alone, but would have to come from Europe. The migrants, after all, weren't usually coming for Greece. It just happened to be in the way.

7

The New Spartans

This and no other is the root from which a tyrant
springs; when he first appears above ground he is a
protector.

—Socrates, in *The Republic* by Plato

The Athenians of Agios Panteleimonas Square began their self-
described struggle for liberation from foreign dominion near the
end of 2008. It was at this time that a group calling itself the Committee of Residents sent a letter describing the unbearable des-
peration of their circumstances to the president of the Hellenic
Parliament, various ministers, the mayor, the head of police, and
the archbishop of the Church of Greece. In their area lived one
Greek for every six foreigners, the committee wrote. Did the letter's recipients know that the outnumbered Greeks lived under a
"reign of the fullest and worst forms of violence, crime, fear, insecurity, and all forms of delinquency?" Did they know that the
majestic church of Agios Panteleimonas that is the square's name-
sake had become an "immigrant-dump prohibitive even for the
passage of pedestrians?" Did they know the streets and squares of
the area had become "a daily place of sleeping and a toilet for des-
titute and drunk foreigners?" Did they know that the playground

on the square of Agios Panteleimonas "is held by children of immigrants who are destroying it and, yes, threaten and use force against the few Greek children who try in vain to visit it?" That was not the worst of it, according to the letter. Once, a group of a few hundred immigrants gathered outside the church in a fit of rage. "Down with Orthodoxy!" they yelled. "Down with Christ!" And finally, the letter described the "pinnacle of evil, beyond all limits of imagination." In a three-story building across from the square, where about five hundred foreigners were living, two sheep could be seen on the terrace, and on the first floor, about fifteen hens and roosters. According to those locals with a direct line of sight into the building, its dwellers engaged in "bestiality with the sheep, and moreover, slaughtered the roosters and the hens with unspecified intentions and with a direct impact on public health derived from infectious diseases." The letter concluded by saying the government had done nothing to rectify the situation and so, lately, "more and more people are threatening to take to the streets to 'clean' the area."

The letter was written at a time when locals began to come together in an apolitical demonstration of indignation over these circumstances, according to Thomais Giannatou, a member of the Committee of Residents. "Local governance requires active citizens," she told me, years after the letter was written, as we sat at a café on the square. "It didn't make any difference what party you belonged to," she said. "What mattered to me was that my neighborhood had died." Giannatou, a round, short woman with blond-colored bangs covering her forehead and a deepened, withered smoker's voice, had run a cosmetics shop near the square, but it had recently closed—another victim, she said, of the area's degradation at the hands of illegal immigrants. Across from where we sat stood the towering, bulbous church named for St. Panteleimon, said to be a physician and healer from Asia Minor who, under the reign of Maximian, was tortured and beheaded. The saint's name translates to "all-merciful," and the fortresslike church in his honor is one of Greece's largest, though certainly not its prettiest. The church and the square around it represented the heart of the neighborhood, and the residents' struggle, which, by the time I met Giannatou at the café, had become famous across Greece. The neighborhood, in decades past, had been a middle-class bastion, but as its residents had grown wealthier, and the area congested and overdeveloped, many people moved away to the greener suburbs. This left an abundance of empty apartments that migrants began to inhabit, changing the demographics of the neighborhood rather quickly. Giannatou sipped on her coffee and pithily summarized the change for me like this: "We went to bed in Athens and woke up in Kabul."

Around the time they sent the letter, residents also planned a demonstration. "No to the ghettoization of our area," read a flyer advertising the event. "No to the unconditional surrender of our lives." Leftist groups from the area heard of the planned gathering, however, and, considering the committee's tone to be one of "racism and fascism," planned their own counterdemonstration on the square. These leftists threatened to bring 1,500 Afghans with them to "slaughter" the residents, Giannatou recalled during our conversation. Nevertheless, she said, the "indignant residents," as her group and their supporters came to be known, were determined to deliver themselves from the wretchedness of their situation and would not succumb to such intimidations. One late-fall evening, the indignant residents emerged onto the square. To hear Giannatou recall it, the event marked a spontaneous moment of civic awakening, when locals of various political affiliations, strangers in fact, came together to express their mutual exasperation over their common plight. One protest banner read: WE ARE NOT RACIST, WE ARE DESPERATE. A far greater number of counterdemonstrators also convened on the square, among them local leftists, antiracist groups, a number of Afghans, and some

anarchists from a nearby squat called Villa Amalia. "We're all Afghans," the counterdemonstrators chanted. *"Allahu Akbar!"* yelled
some Afghans. Riot police, in an act that would become routine
over the following years, created a barrier—albeit a permeable
one—between the two camps.

Reinforcements for the indignant residents soon arrived. A
formation of black-clad men carrying Greek flags marched past
the shops and cafés, emerging before the Committee of Residents' supporters. "Foreigners out of Greece," these entrants onto
the scene yelled. "Greece belongs to the Greeks." Many residents
greeted the formation with cheers and whistles. "Bravo! Bravo!"
some yelled, and joined in the chants. "Foreigners out of Greece!"
The entrants tossed leaflets pledging their intention to defend the
homeland and urging Greeks to "wake up" and "resist the ghettoization of our neighborhoods." The black-clad men held up their
flags and sang the national anthem. Some raised their arms in
a manner that looked to newspaper reporters present like a Nazi
salute, but was, rather, as least according to the group the men
belonged to, an ancient Greek salute. Before the men departed,
they chanted: "Blood, honor, Golden Dawn. We will return and
the earth will tremble." On this night the political party Golden
Dawn, until then a very marginal group of neo-Nazis, was finding
a way to establish itself. Agios Panteleimonas Square would be its
first big conquest.

"Blood, honor" seemed like a strange phrase to many locals
who had never heard it before. The words happened to be those in
the motto of the Hitler Youth—*Blut und Ehre*—but the drawing
of such parallels was typical of the slanderous media campaign
against Golden Dawn, or so the party would repeatedly assert
in the following years, as its political popularity soared (it later

changed "blood" to "country"). For those at the time who might have been confused about its ideology, Golden Dawn published a statement on its website titled *Nationalists or Nazis? A Reply.* "We are nationalists and not Nazis, first and foremost, for purely linguistic reasons. Because we are proud to use the language of the Gods, the language of Plato and of Aristotle, and not a foreign language, like German, from which the term 'Nazi' originates." The statement also elaborated on the party's ideas about World War II, adding: "We deny the historical falsehood of the 'good democratic' allies and the 'bad' fascists," rejecting too the "post-war propaganda of the Zionists." The so-called liberators, capitalist and Bolshevik alike, had bestowed spiritual desolation, crime, ignorance, drugs, and corruption on the people of Europe. "With respect to our country, which gave a heavy toll of blood to the so-called Allies, the case is glaring and screams in every direction that we were wronged and we continue to be wronged by those who were the victors of the Great War."

Other party texts at the time linked the National Socialist ideology expounded by Hitler's press chief, Otto Dietrich, with the pre-Socratic philosopher Heraclitus, the "harbinger and the philosophical father of National Socialism." A follower seeking the underpinnings of Golden Dawn's philosophy in Ancient Greek thought, however, was also to heed an important caveat. Hellenism did not represent a set of ideas or cultural works but was "primarily a term of racial substance," Nikolaos Michaloliakos, the party's general secretary—or chief, as his followers called him—wrote in his book *For a Great Greece in a Free Europe.* Anyone wanting to read more about Golden Dawn's racial theories could also visit the Internet portal of the party's "Women's Front," where one could read about motherly responsibilities: "We must ensure the existence of Our Race and the future of our children," a take on the "Fourteen Words" of David Lane, the American white nationalist militant who died in prison in 2007.

This party of not-neo-Nazis-for-purely-linguistic-reasons took great interest in the residents' seemingly spontaneous expression of indignation. With the arrival of the "Greek fighters of Golden Dawn, who stood dynamically at their side, the residents broke out in loud applause, feeling visibly encouraged," the party said in a statement following the demonstration on Agios Panteleimonas Square. Golden Dawn would "continue to support such efforts, which are not party-political in nature, as our Struggle is above all the Struggle for the Enlightenment of our people." The party chief, Michaloliakos, a portly man with a babyish face and ample black eyebrows that stood out in contrasting defiance of his graying head of hair, also appeared on a news television program to express his support for the residents' demonstration, which, he underscored, "abstained from political parties and organizations." On the other hand, he added, the counterdemonstration was of a purely partisan, Marxist nature.

Michaloliakos was born in Athens in 1957, though he traces his origins to Mani, the central of the three peninsulas that jut southward into the Mediterranean from the bottom of the Peloponnese. In Greece, the region of the country your ancestors come from is thought to say a lot about you. For instance, if you are born and raised in Athens, but have Maniot parents, you are a Maniot. Michaloliakos certainly thought of himself as a Maniot, and Maniots often think of themselves as the direct descendants of the ancient, warrior Spartans. A regional flag bears the Spartan phrase *"E tan e epi tas,"* the Spartan mother's command to her battle-bound son to either come back with his shield or be carried dead upon it. Mani, isolated by the towering Taygetus Mountains, was until recently known for its recalcitrance and blood feuds between clans. Its name is often thought to derive from the *mania,* or fury, of its occupants, though scholars doubt that etymological explanation.

Michaloliakos, himself a devotee to the power of fury, joined the neo-fascist, anti-Semitic party 4th of August—named after the authoritarian regime that controlled Greece in the years leading up to World War II—while still in high school in Athens. He studied math in university and served for a while as an army commando. As part of his youthful activities, he was arrested a few times, once for beating journalists and another time for his involvement with a "nationalist revolutionary subversive organization with the aim of overthrowing the democratic polity," as he once put it. This was in the years following the collapse of the right-wing military dictatorship, the Regime of the Colonels, which ruled Greece from 1967 to 1974. Neofascist groups, displeased with the democratic direction the country was going in, were at the time bombing theaters deemed leftist and unpatriotic. Michaloliakos was sentenced to a year in prison for providing explosives for this purpose. In 1980, he started a periodical called *Golden Dawn*.

One 1981 article, titled "We," which described the magazine's values, praised the "German revolution of 1933." In that revolution, "we saw the strength that will redeem humanity from the Jewish rottenness, we saw the strength that will drive us to a new European regeneration, we saw the bright revival of the primordial instinct of the race, we saw the dynamic flight from the nightmarish industrial mass man to a new and simultaneously ancient and eternal type of man, a mankind of heroes and demigods, the pure naive and violent mankind of myth and of instinct." Regarding religion, it stated: "We are pagans because we are Greeks, because it's impossible for us to acknowledge values other than those that arise from the miracle of the Greek Spirit. We are pagans because we can never put dark prophets and bloodied kings of a crass nomadic people in the place of our heroes and philosophers." In a 2006 issue, Hitler's deputy Rudolf Hess was featured on the cover, and a year later, the magazine featured the Führer himself, performing an ancient Greek salute. By the time Golden Dawn had come to the side of the residents of Agios Panteleimonas, though, the party was toning down the Third Reich veneration and paganism for the sake of its electoral viability.

Golden Dawn's very public declarations of support for the Committee of Residents were anomalous. The party, which employed the frequent motto "against everyone," was typically reluctant to so publicly and enthusiastically support an organized entity other than itself. This was partly the reason observers of the extreme right in Greece from early on questioned whether the Committee of Residents was indeed driven by an unprompted expression of indignation, or whether it was a veiled extension of Golden Dawn. These suspicions grew with time and for many were validated when one of the most vocal committee members, Themis Skordeli, a middle-aged former bank clerk with blond hair and a shrill voice, later became a parliamentary candidate for Golden Dawn. Before that, Skordeli often appeared on Greek television above the caption "indignant resident." She was also repeatedly captured on video berating migrants and leftists on Agios Panteleimonas Square and in its immediate vicinity. In September of 2011, she was charged along with two others of inflicting dangerous bodily harm on three Afghans, one of whom was stabbed in the thorax and stomach. By the time I sat down with members of the Committee of Residents at the beginning of 2014, Skordeli's trial on that charge had been repeatedly postponed. She maintained her innocence; so did the party on her behalf.

The Committee of Residents, despite clear ideological commonalities, maintained they had nothing to do with Golden Dawn. (Skordeli, they told me, left their group after joining the party, because that action was incompatible with the committee's apolitical mission.) The two entities, however, rose in symbiosis as Golden Dawn became known for its efforts to come to the side of the indignant residents and "clean" Agios Panteleimonas Square of the mostly Afghan migrants that daily assembled there by the hundreds. In doing so, the party closely mimicked the tactics of

German neo-Nazis who, in the 1990s, had created "national liberated zones" across the former East Germany, according to the Greek journalist Dimitris Psarras, who has written extensively about the Greek extreme right. The party's endeavors in Agios Panteleimonas, with the aid of some sympathetic media coverage, won a great deal of approval from a lot of Greeks who, as other parties were passing bills to cut people's pay, perceived Golden Dawn as acting firmly, albeit perhaps a bit roughly, to help their desperate Greek countrymen.

Golden Dawn's emergence from a negligible party that won 20,000 votes in the 2009 parliamentary elections, to one that received 440,000 of them and a place in parliament three years later, has often been explained as a manifestation of Greeks' outrage over the economic collapse and the maladroit governance that spurred it. While Golden Dawn could not have thrived without a source of abundant rage, rage alone provides an insufficient explanation for its ascendance. The party's performance showed that if it downplayed its Nazism, what remained was an ideology that many regular citizens could embrace. Many Greeks had since their childhoods been inculcated with a sense of Hellenic preeminence—promulgated by their teachers, priests, and politicians—yet also with the belief that Greece has long been victimized and trampled underfoot by foreign powers. At a time of economic collapse and national humiliation, Golden Dawn, with its affirmation of Hellenic supremacy and reproach of foreign oppressors—be they creditors or immigrants—appealed to both the hero and the martyr that had been cultivated in the Greek soul.

Nor were some of its extremist beliefs all that uncommon. Its fervid anti-Semitism, for instance, was by no means unfamiliar or unacceptable; one could hear similar viewpoints uttered by leaders of the Greek Orthodox Church. Far-right nationalist beliefs were already present within the police, the judiciary, and the highest levels of government. Golden Dawn's leadership knew that many of its ideas weren't marginal. It needed only to make itself known and legitimate. For this purpose, the party sensed opportunity in the immigration influx, as did resurgent far-right parties elected into parliaments throughout Europe. But Golden Dawn was far more extreme than most of these, and its electoral success would put it in a worrisome category of its own. Illegal immigration, Golden Dawn said, was the "back door to the castle of Hellenism" and "the most insidious practice against the Greek state." And so, as it imposed its ethos of violence, it was able to portray itself as acting in defense of the Greek people.

One of the early priorities of the Committee of Residents was to do something about the playground on the square, Gianna- tou told me when we met at the café. The playground in ques- tion was right across from us, its gates wired shut. It had been closed for nearly five years, and the equipment inside was stripped bare and unusable—a swing set with no swings, a jungle gym undressed of bars and ladders. "A lot, a lot," Giannatou said of the ills the Afghans had brought to the playground. As she spoke, we were joined by another Committee of Residents member, Gianna- tou's husband, Spiros Giannatos, a tall, lean man with thinning curly hair and narrow, dark brown eyes. Giannatos had become known as a very active watchman of the square, protecting it from activities he deemed inappropriate. On this afternoon, as Gianna- tos sat at our table at the café, he announced that he had just seen a young foreign woman taking pictures of the playground. "I ask her, 'Why are you taking pictures of the playground?' She says: 'I'm a tourist.'" Giannatos assumed she was a journalist, and it upset him that she would lie. The playground by this point had acquired some fame as a symbol of Golden Dawn's control over the neighborhood, though the indignant residents disputed that interpretation of its significance. "I say, 'You care about the playground? You came from wherever you came from to take pictures of the playground? It concerns you that the playground is closed?' " As Giannatos took a seat, the young woman in question nervously walked away from the square with a large camera slung around her neck. "It wasn't a playground for kids," Giannatos went on. Hundreds of migrants had taken up residence inside it, he said, sleeping, cooking, bathing, pissing, and defecating within its gates. "There were moms, dads, grandfathers. They were selling heroin." For these reasons, he said, the Committee of Residents successfully petitioned the city to close it.

While the city had in fact closed the playground, citing the need for its renovation, the chronology of the events leading to this action was a matter of dispute. Members of an area leftist group told me the Committee of Residents—"the fascists," as the leftists called them—had chained the playground shut in advance of the city's decision. Litsa Papadopoulou, a thin, chain-smoking pharmacist with short silver hair who drove a four-wheeler around the neighborhood, was a member of the leftist resident group. One morning, I met Papadopoulou at a café on Victoria Square, a five-minute walk from Agios Panteleimonas and the preferred hangout for the area leftists. She and her peers had tried to save Agios Panteleimonas from the fascists by organizing book reading, theater, and music events on the square, she said. The turning point, however, came in the spring of 2009, on the evening they invited the well-known Albanian writer Gazmend Kapllani to visit the square for a reading of his book about Albanian migration to Greece after the fall of the Iron Curtain. By the time Kapllani arrived, a group of indignant residents had gathered to protest the reading. One woman walked around with a megaphone, accusing the event organizers of being the "henchmen of the system." One of the alleged henchmen spoke calmly through his megaphone in response: "We don't want to scold or argue with anyone, with any resident of the area. We don't want immigrants and Greek residents of the neighborhood to argue. We want to live all together." The indignant residents were not convinced by these words, Kapllani told me years later over the phone from Boston, where he was teaching a course at Emerson College. The indignant residents and some thuggish-looking young men became aggressive and overthrew a table, Kapllani said. He also found it noteworthy, he added, that some of the assailants started chanting: "We fucked you during the civil war, we'll fuck you again." Feeling threatened, he and the organizers fled the square, he said.

Spiros Giannatos of the Committee of Residents also remembered that evening. "They come to present a book where we are enduring woe?" he told me. "Is that even possible? In an area that is boiling from indignation due to what we have to live through every day? For them to bring us an Albanian here in Agios Panteleimonas? Have mercy!" His wife, probably noticing my bafflement, tried to help me understand: "We couldn't bear this drowning of illegal immigration." An extreme-right, Golden Dawn–friendly newspaper called *Stochos* concurred with this sentiment. The night of the attempted book reading, it published on its website the news that indignant residents were able to break up the "anti-Greek gathering, which we all knew to where it would lead." The "counterattack of the residents was terminative," it added. "The river of indignation swells and will lure many. The lies, ladies and gentlemen, are over. THIS IS GREECE. And whoever doesn't like it, GET OUT."

Members of the leftist residents' group told me this event marked the fascist takeover of Agios Panteleimonas Square. After that, they found the playground padlocked shut. Some pointed the finger at Giannatos, though he denied locking it, maintaining that the city closed it at his committee's urging. One person who took credit for the playground closing, however, was the self-proclaimed "section manager" of Agios Panteleimonas for Golden

Dawn, Georgios Vathis, a man who could frequently be found at a café on the square wearing a fedora and a suit with white shoes, puffing his cigarettes through a filter tip. Vathis, appearing in a 2012 documentary called *The Cleaners* by the Greek filmmaker Konstantinos Georgousis, stood in front of the Agios Panteleimonas church and declared the square had been liberated. "A Greek can come with his child and sit," he said. "We've closed the playground." Vathis explained that it was full of foreigners. "The soil and everything has to be replaced because of the filth," he said. "If you touch something in there, you'll get a rash. That much filth. From the foreign people," he said. "We kicked them out, and it's a bit cleaner. But it's not that clean. We have to chase them all the time." Vathis is seen in the film campaigning with Alexandros Plomaritis, a then Golden Dawn candidate with a buzz cut and an affection for aviator sunglasses. Plomaritis, in the film, calls immigrants "primitive, miasmas and subhuman," suggests their babies be "thrown to the Dobermans," and says he is "ready to open up the ovens" and turn foreigners into soap. His buddies in the film laugh as he says this.

The documentary got a lot of attention in Greece and abroad, though when I mentioned it to Giannatou on the square, she told me people had made a big deal out of it. They were just kidding around, she said of the people in the film. "A joke and they made it into a big issue." At one point, I showed Giannatou and her husband a letter to the city from the leftist residents' group that described the playground as having been in "excellent condition" before it was closed. This was a lie, Giannatou told me. She emphasized once again the unsanitariness of the playground. The committee had sent a sample of the playground dirt to a government lab, she said, where it was discovered that it contained staphylococcus. "For someone to reenter the playground, the soil must be replaced at a depth of ten meters due to the germs that are in there," she said. This sounded oddly familiar, I thought. Her husband added, "They had turned the playground into a toilet."

. . .

Father Prokopios, the former head priest of Agios Panteleimonas church, doesn't remember the playground this way. Then
again, Prokopios didn't usually see eye to eye with the Committe
of Residents. He led the church for seventeen years, and left it
in 2009 after being promoted to assistant bishop. "My soul is
still there," he told me when I met him one evening in his office
on the ground floor of a dormitory for theological students in a
working-class neighborhood of Athens north of Agios Panteleimonas. Prokopios was a dark-eyed, bespectacled man in his fifties. His face seemed nearly consumed by a thicket of gray beard
that extended to his waistline. A large crucifix stood in one corner
of his office beside a blinking WiFi router mounted to the wall.
Plastic flowers in vases and framed pictures of his parents lined
the bookshelves. This had been his office for nearly two decades,
and the place seemed like it hadn't changed much in that time.
That evening, an old woman named Maria was visiting. She used
to live near Agios Panteleimonas church and had volunteered
there during Prokopios's reign. She wore a trench coat that had
the effect of elongating her hunched body, though her feet barely
touched the floor when she sat down. She was very old, but giggled
like a teenager when Prokopios told a good story, for which he
had a knack. She had moved away from Agios Panteleimonas, she
told me, to assuage her kids, who, given the changes to the neighborhood, were afraid to leave her by herself in the family home
where they grew up. She seemed ambivalent about the change,
and visiting Prokopios appeared to be a way to reminisce about
happier times.

Prokopios started the conversation by speaking about the in-
compatibility of Greece's recent immigrants with Greek society.
What does a Greek have in common with "the other who lives
next door to you when he is black from Africa, or Pakistani, and
has his Muslim customs, and he doesn't say *kalimera*," or good

day, "he doesn't learn your language, he doesn't accept that which you, in your country, take as self-evident—that Greece is Orthodox?" he said. Maria nodded in agreement. I had expected to hear a different line of argument from Prokopios, because, during his later years at Agios Panteleimonas, he had acquired a reputation as having treated the migrants in the neighborhood with compassion. After a few minutes, though, he pivoted. "We had to think something else, too," he said. "Okay, we're also people of God. We are Christians. We need to see people humanely, from the humane side. We can't just look at them like Greeks, but we have to look at them like people. If the other guy is hungry or suffering, you're not going to think about whether he's an immigrant, an illegal immigrant, a foreigner, or a Greek. He's hungry, and you have to do something to help him to eat," he said. "So, that was the problem. We thought we have to think first like Christians, and afterward to think like Greeks. But there was a very big group of people who thought the opposite. First they thought like Greeks, and not at all like Christians."

One evening, Prokopios recalled, Themis Skordeli, the Committee of Residents member who later became a Golden Dawn candidate, came to church while he was hearing confessions and told him a committee had been formed. They had drafted a letter and were "gathering signatures to throw the immigrants out of the area," as Prokopios put it. She wanted him to sign and include the stamp of the church, Prokopios said. He refused, saying he did not have the authority to use the church stamp as he pleased. Nor would he sign as an individual. "I have an order from Christ to not kick any person out, not to be an enemy with anyone. Christ says to love one another. But he goes further and says, love your enemies. If you tell me that person is an enemy, I love him," he said he told Skordeli. She was apparently not persuaded. "From that day on," Prokopios told me, "a war against me began."

To illustrate this point, he took out a few Greek newspaper

clippings. One of the headlines, from *Kathimerini,* read "Nights of Rage at Agios Panteleimonas." The article told the story of what happened the night of May 26, 2009, when smoke began to billow out of the church basement. Police and fire trucks arrived. A Pakistani was injured on the sidewalk, though no explanation was given as to why, and a raging mob surrounded Prokopios. "You take in the foreigners and throw the Greeks out onto the street!" yelled someone. "We're giving you one last chance: you have one week to throw them all out!" The angry people were the "ladies and gentlemen of the committee," Prokopios told me, and the fire in the basement had started because he was housing homeless people there, and one man's candle fell over and set alight a mattress. The committee members, he said, were screaming: "The Muslims have come and set the church on fire!" But the man who accidentally started the fire happened to be a Greek named Nikos. At this, Maria began to giggle. Prokopios, pleased to make her laugh, tried to keep it up. "Ms. Maria," he said, "they fell on me like dogs. You know how dogs bark? Like that. Like dogs." Maria kept giggling, and Prokopios started making vicious dog sounds. "I stop and think, 'Let them bark at me, our good residents.'"

Prokopios then added something he thought I ought to know. The foreigners saw that the residents hated them, and began to resent it. "They said, 'We risked our lives to come here. We paid money to smugglers. We did a thousand things. Why did we come here? Because Greece has nice sun and we wanted to do sun therapy?'" Maria giggled. "'Did we come to swim on your nice shores?'" Prokopios paused and added: "'Why did we come here? To find a better life. Because where we were, we couldn't live. If we could, we'd leave Greece and go somewhere else. We were forced to come here because it's the first country we meet across the sea,'" he said. "So they started feeling bad, and some got mad." They thought, "'We didn't do anything bad to you. Why do you talk to us this way?'"

The notion that the immigrants didn't do anything bad to the residents directly contradicted the Committee of Residents' account of the situation. I asked him, therefore, if he hadn't witnessed the dreadful criminality of which they had spoken. "The criminality was with isolated incidents," he said. "It wasn't a general blight. We have a saying in Greece: When a mouse eats the cheese, we don't say the mouse ate the cheese. We say the *mice* ate the cheese." Maria giggled again.

So it was not a "reign of the fullest and worst forms of violence, crime, and all forms of delinquency?" I asked, paraphrasing the residents' committee's 2008 letter.

"Lies," he said. "It's all lies. Exaggerations. There were crimes. There were thefts. Yes, it's a crime to go and steal one or two cans of food from a store. That's a crime. But when you, the resident, go to where they've rented a house, and where there are ten or fifteen kids inside, and they're learning the Greek language so they can communicate with the Greeks, and you gather outside and break the windows, and you break inside and throw everyone out, isn't that a crime? What's that?" I asked Prokopios to elaborate, and he explained that some "ladies with sensitivities" had started a Greek language school for migrants in the area. Apparently, this upset some locals.

I asked Prokopios who had closed the playground. He told me it was the Committee of Residents, because they didn't like immigrants bringing their children there. I told him that the Committee of Residents had told me the playground had become a sleeping area for hundreds, a place of defecation and urination, of cooking and of bathing, of child prostitution and drug dealing, of staphylococcus contamination. "It's a lie, everything that they're saying," Prokopios told me. Yes, he said, during the day a few hundred people would gather in the square "trying to figure out where they'd found themselves," but at night, most migrants would disappear into overcrowded apartments, rented to them by locals, often at a per-person nightly rate. A few dozen people without money to pay would sleep near the church doors, he said, but no one slept in the playground.

"It wasn't a toilet?" I said.

Prokopios seemed particularly piqued by this suggestion, because, he said, the same people who made such claims "used to piss on the side of the church." Ms. Maria giggled, and Prokopios raised his voice with a flash of irritation. "It wasn't the foreigners, but the same people who are screaming, the residents of the area! They used to piss, and the piss used to trickle down." He asked Maria to tell me if he was lying.

"No," she said. "I used to clean it up."

He then asked her if any of the migrants who slept in or next to the church ever bothered her.

"Never," she said.

Why then, I asked Prokopios, would the Committee of Residents lie? "That's the secret mystery," he said, though certainly there were political reasons behind all the tumult at Agios Panteleimonas. The foreigners were used to create a fuss: "There had to be a lot of noise, so that some political groups could emerge, to be heard. They found the cause, with these issues, these big fusses, which were created without any reason." And so Golden Dawn, which was hidden in the beginning, began to appear. One small example of this emergence, as Prokopios remembered it, occurred on a Sunday after he'd finished the liturgy. He was walking down the steps of the church when a young man approached him and gave him a Golden Dawn party newspaper. Prokopios took the newspaper, looked at it, and then replied to the young man: "Thank you very much. Take it back now." The young man didn't appreciate this response and insulted the cleric and his place of origin, the island of Rhodes. In response, Prokopios recounted to the young man a phrase attributed to Anacharsis, the sixth-century B.C. Scythian philosopher who migrated to Athens from a region near the Black Sea. When one pretentious Athenian insulted Anacharsis over the comparatively lowly status of his homeland, the philosopher is said to have responded: "My country is a shame. You, however, are a shame for your country." The Golden Dawn adherent just walked away, Prokopios recalled, adding that it was a shame to see such young people "enslave themselves" to the party. He considered the party members, full of rage and hatred, to be possessed by Satan.

My visit to Prokopios's office was a long one. For nearly four hours, he did most of the talking, though for Maria and me, it wasn't too much. We listened as he expounded on his tripartite theory for how neo-Nazis were able to make it into the Greek parliament. First, he said, other politicians had created them by doing a poor job. "If Greece was Sweden, if Greece was Finland, we wouldn't have Golden Dawn." The second reason was anger and revenge. "In the past, people used to applaud the politicians because they were giving them money to live." The politicians said, " 'Take the money! Take it! Take it! Because the machine is making it and handing it out.' " But now, he added, "People want someone to come and whip the politicians. To beat them. To make them eat wood." The third reason for the party's rise, he said, was that Greece had never punished those who had collaborated with the Nazis during the World War II occupation.

Prokopios had a point. Near the end of the war and after it, the Greek government—along with its British and American backers—was more concerned with neutralizing the large communist force that had fought the Germans than it was with punishing the collaborationist "security battalions" the Greek puppet government had sponsored to fight those same communists. The security battalions, outfitted in the traditional klephtic fighter garb of *fustanellas* and pom-pom shoes, thought of themselves as nationalists and were driven by a deep hatred of the communists. The wider population regarded them as criminal gangs, and they were violent and vicious toward civilians. The battalions' crimes and collaboration were overlooked after the war, and in fact battalion members were seen by the Greek government and its backers as a useful counterweight to the communists' strength. After the war, members of the security battalions easily found jobs in the newly formed National Guard or joined shadowy security organizations. When the communist resistance fighters initially laid down their weapons in 1945, the former collaborators, now sanctioned by the Greek state, took great satisfaction in going after them, and communists were subjected to a period of persecution known as the White Terror. The communist fighters eventually regrouped in the mountains and the country slid into civil war.

In 1947, when the broke British government declared it could no longer support the Greek government's fight against the communist insurgents, U.S. president Harry S. Truman, fearful Greece and Turkey would fall under the Soviet sphere of influence, spoke to a joint session of Congress and asked lawmakers to approve 400 million dollars in economic and military aid for the two countries. In his speech, Truman acknowledged the extremism of the Greek right as well as that of the left. Yet the extremism on the right was clearly not of equal concern given the budding Cold War climate. Truman's speech marked the beginning of the Truman Doctrine, the Cold War containment policy that often led the United States to prop up authoritarian governments in order to prevent the spread of communism. In Greece, this later meant the U.S. government backed the dictatorial Regime of the Colonels, which used the communist threat as a pretext to seize power, and tortured and imprisoned dissidents. Members of the regime had close connections to the occupation-era security battalions, and tellingly, one if its early acts was to grant battalion members pension benefits for their wartime service. The regime also banned long hair on men and short skirts on women, as well as literature deemed subversive, such as the works of Aristophanes and Chekhov. After the dictatorship's fall, as Greece reestablished democratic governance, its leaders were put in prison. That was where the future Golden Dawn leader, Michaloliakos, imprisoned for his post-dictatorship political activities, met the head of the fallen regime, Georgios Papadopoulos; later, when the former dictator started an ultranationalist political party—National Political Union—from prison, Michaloliakos became head of its youth section.

During my conversation with Prokopios, I had a sense that perhaps he did not quite fit into the clerical establishment. The church in Greece is seen as an intrinsically right-wing institution—many point out its ties to the military dictatorship, which embraced the mantra "Greece of Christian Greeks"—and some of its clerics deliver nationalist, anti-Semitic sermons not entirely dissimilar to Golden Dawn political speeches. Prokopios, it seemed to me, may have paid a price for standing out. He was, by ecclesiastical standards, in his professional prime. Yet, despite his bishop's rank, he seemed to have been relegated to the hierarchical backbench. When Prokopios was moved from Agios Panteleimonas and promoted to bishop in 2009, he was assigned to serve as an assistant to Bishop Amvrosios of Kalavryta and Aigialeia, a man with a white beard comparable in length to Prokopios's. This coupling struck some people at the time as an odd choice, because Amvrosios was known for his nationalist views, and subsequently wrote what might be considered a defense of Golden Dawn on his personal blog: "I am not able to understand how and why the ideas of Golden Dawn are subversive and why the ideas of Syriza or the Communist Party of Greece are not similarly subversive or dangerous." Michaloliakos returned the apparent sympathy, and once listed Amvrosios as one of the "worthy" bishops of the Greek Church, placing him in the company of prelates such as Bishop Seraphim of Piraeus, who once, on a popular television talk show, said Hitler was an "instrument of global Zionism" financed by the

Rothschild family in order to make Jews leave Europe and "go to Israel to establish the new empire."

Things predictably did not go well between Prokopios and Amvrosios, and in the falling-out, Amvrosios, on his blog, accused Prokopios of "wanting the title and the . . . money!" Prokopios was moved again, and became assistant to the bishop of Nikaia in the western suburb of Athens, but this appeared to be a ceremonial position. When I met Prokopios, he seemed a man underutilized, without a flock to shepherd, and trying to come to terms with this circumstance. Despite his charitable deeds at Agios Panteleimonas, he had gone from heading a large congregation to, as he put it to me, possessing "no power" and "no responsibility." At his office on the ground floor of the dormitory, he seemed to cater primarily to four cats he'd taken in, one of which, by the time I left, had pissed on the floor.

Following the playground's closure, one of the next actions of the Committee of Residents was to publish its own newspaper every two months: *The Voice of the Residents of Agios Panteleimonas*, a self-funded venture, Giannatou told me, devoid of any party financing. The newspapers featured pictures of rickety ships overflowing with migrants, "ships that come and go from the depths of Asia and Africa" filled with the people that will "steal wages and will force you to lock your child inside the house, to live imprisoned." The tone was exceedingly urgent. "The country is being driven to chaos," ran the headline of the second edition. "The secret plan of Kissinger is being implemented. The ATHENIANS are PRISONERS of FOREIGNERS." Underneath appeared a picture of the Germans entering Athens in 1941, and next to it, a picture of Muslims in the street holding up the Koran. The text urged Greeks to resist the migrants as they had resisted the

Nazis: "Hellenes. The invader illegal immigrants are within Athens. Brothers! Keep well inside your souls the spirit of freedom. The invaders entered without resistance with the help of ethnic nihilists of our terrorized city. Hellenes! Your hearts high!" The time had come for a "counterattack," declared the third edition, calling for "EVERYONE IN THE STREETS to defeat the tyrants of our people." Underneath another picture of an overcrowded boat of migrants, it said: "They aren't illegal immigrants. They are the fifth column. Among them are found trained commando-saboteurs that impersonate poor illegal immigrants, and at the right moment, they will take an order from the globalizers for enemy actions against our country."

The Voice of the Residents of Agios Panteleimonas seemed to be preparing Greeks for war. It was for this reason among others that, during my conversation with Giannatou at the café, I found it odd when she told me the media had exaggerated the criminality of the area around the square, portraying it as "totally different from what it is." I asked her to elaborate. "When you say you can't walk around Agios Panteleimonas because they're stabbing and the rest, the other becomes afraid," she said. "Do you know how many apartments are unrented?" So, I asked, it wasn't as dangerous as people were making it out to be? "Certainly not," she said. "Those who were dangerous were those that came against us," she added. "Against us simple residents." I asked her who that was. "Anarcho-Syriza people," she said, conjoining "anarchists" and "Syriza" into a compound word that was reminiscent of the way the military dictatorship in Greece once referred to leftists as "anarcho-communists." These people weren't real Greeks, Giannatou told me. They just happened to speak Greek.

It was noteworthy, I thought, that an apolitical organization like the Committee of Residents would have a particular problem with Syriza. Giannatou's husband tried to explain the reason for the antagonism to me. "All of them are creating these problems and calling us racists and fascists, because they couldn't enter these squares inside here to create a core group," he said. "They couldn't do it. Because there was resistance from us. They couldn't enter, because wherever else you go, they go in and talk and make speeches, meetings. Here, they can't do those things," he said. "We won't accept it and there's no way we ever will." Why, I asked, couldn't they ever accept it? "Because we don't accept them," he said. "Because they are against the Greeks. It is racism against the Greeks. Can I make you understand? Someone hits an immigrant. They get together and make antifascist and antiracist chants and demonstrations. Greeks die, and no one demonstrates. We simply can't tolerate something like that."

The indignant residents therefore opened up a second battle-front against Syriza politicians. In October 2010, in the run-up to municipal elections, Alekos Alavanos, a former Syriza leader, vis-ited Agios Panteleimonas with a group of supporters and an escort of riot police who didn't do a particularly good job of protecting him from what was about to happen. Video and photos taken of the incident show what occurred. As Alavanos, a gray-haired econ-omist, approaches the steps of the church, he and his supporters are pelted with yogurt, eggs, and tomatoes. Committee of Resi-dents member Giannatos walks up the church steps and picks up a blue plastic bag already lying there. Inside are flyers advertis-ing Michaloliakos's mayoral candidacy as part of "Greek Dawn for Athens," the name of Golden Dawn's local ticket. As Alava-nos is pelted in the face with yogurt, Giannatos begins throwing the flyers in the air over the leftists. His wife, Giannatou, arrives beside him and joins the leaflet tossing. Alavanos calmly wipes the yogurt off the left side of his face as his companions begin to shout. "Greeks, foreigners, and workers united!" In response, their opponents begin to chant: "Greece belongs to the Greeks," and afterward a few people yell: "Blood, honor, Golden Dawn."

Some of the people captured on camera protesting Alavanos's

presence would later become known as famed members of Golden Dawn. Among them, on the megaphone leading the indignant resident chants, was Ilias Panagiotaros, long a key Golden Dawn figure and a future parliamentarian for the party. Panagiotaros, a plump, bald man with a goatee, had the kind of fieldwork experience that could qualify him for this kind of action. He had long been the leader of Galazia Stratia, or Blue Army, an organization of nationalist football hooligans implicated in beatings of Albanians and other foreigners. The Blue Army was essentially a wing and recruitment tool of Golden Dawn, though Panagiotaros, in a 2004 interview, maintained they were two distinct organizations, albeit with a "very good" relationship. Giannatou, during our talk, had kind words for Panagiotaros, and smiled fondly when I mentioned his name. He was always there and on our side, she said. "He gave us courage." Her endorsement of the man, however, did not mean an endorsement of the party. Giannatou told me her political allegiance was deeply New Democracy. Her husband, too, told me he was not affiliated with Golden Dawn—"Our party is Agios Panteleimonas," he said. I later asked Giannatou why, then, if they didn't support Golden Dawn, they were seen throwing Golden Dawn leaflets at Alavanos and his supporters that day. "I wasn't holding any leaflets," she said, though a photo of her holding the leaflets appeared in one prominent Greek newspaper. She also suggested the leftist visitors to the square that day had framed them by planting Golden Dawn leaflets on the steps. The leftists, she said, did this to make it seem like she and her husband were Golden Dawn supporters.

Shortly after the Alavanos incident, another then Syriza-affiliated politician, a mayoral candidate named Eleni Portaliou, also visited Agios Panteleimonas with a police escort and was greeted with a similar bombardment of edibles. Following the two pelting incidents, a series of Greek media reports wholly embraced the narrative that residents, propelled by their profound indignation, were behind the attacks. One television news report on a now-defunct channel began with a Committee of Residents member, Loukia Rizou, a woman in her late fifties who was a retired employee of the Hellenic Statistical Authority. "Residents threw it," Rizou told the camera. "Indignant residents." The reporter then summarized the meaning of the incidents: "The yogurt for Alekos Alavanos and the eggs for Eleni Portaliou pulled back the curtain and showed the depth of the problem at Agios Pantaleimonas." On the screen again was Rizou. "We simply can't live," she said. A woman with a puffy face then appeared on camera. "There aren't any extreme elements here," she said. The reporter's narrative continued: "Most of them were born in Agios Panteleimonas. They've had their homes here for decades. In the last years, however, their lives, as they say, have become insufferable due to criminality, the insecurity, and the degradation at their every step." The woman with the puffy face reappeared. "Can't they leave us in our pain?" she said of the leftist politicians who'd come to visit. "We can't even go outside."

Another example of the Greek media's embrace of the indignant residents' story came when the egged mayoral candidate, Portaliou, a middle-aged woman, appeared on Mega, one of the main television channels in Greece, and was interviewed by two men in suits and ties of various shades of blue. The host of the program, Nikos Stravelakis, who appeared to be heavily caked with television makeup, asked Portaliou if she hadn't been wary of going to Agios Panteleimonas given that Alavanos had just been egged before her. Portaliou told him that the attacks by "extreme racist elements" had not discouraged her from reaching out to her fellow citizens in the area. Stravelakis interrupted, displeased with her characterization of the attackers. "Why, Ms. Portaliou, are you talking about extreme racist elements?" he said. She answered: "They are extreme racist elements because they are in a time of crisis and poverty and real problems involving a large section of the working class trying to—" Stravelakis interrupted her, and read a statement from Syriza that called the attackers "thugs"; he took issue with this: "I don't see thugs, or racists, I see retirees, old people, men and women," and they say, "We are afraid to leave our homes, and people can't come here to support the rights of the immigrants and not the rights of the residents." He later added: "Is a retiree who is afraid to leave his house, who they've robbed three or four times, an extreme racist element? Or rather a resident who wants to disagree with the positions of the candidates?" It was "an issue of security," Stravelakis told her, but Portaliou, it seemed, just didn't get it.

General fear of crime, a criminologist will tell you, does not necessarily correlate to actual crime levels. The perception of risk is greatly influenced by the information people receive from their neighbors or from the mass media. It is also influenced by faith in the competence of the police. (The Greek police rank near the bottom of the European Union when it comes to citizen faith in their job performance.) Fear of crime can also be caused by nebulous feelings of insecurity. It so happens that Greeks, when compared in surveys to their European Union peers, express a relatively high degree of insecurity and are among the most afflicted by fear of crime.

Despite the comparatively high level of fear, there is less reported crime in Greece than there is on average in the European Union, and compared with other European cities of its size, Athens is considerably less violent. That is not to say crime has not been a problem. Beginning in the mid-1990s, robberies in Greece began to increase, and there was a sharp rise in burglaries as the debt crisis set in. Drug trafficking has also been a growing scourge. In Athens, there are rough and seedy neighborhoods where, in the shade of abandoned buildings, one can find groups of junkies

pricking the parts of their bodies they estimate will most efficiently ingest the contents of the syringe. While this has gotten
worse of late, in great part due to the prevalence of new cheap
drugs and cuts to social services, it's largely been that way since
the 1980s. Prostitution, technically legal within a licensed establishment, most often occurs in unlicensed establishments, and a
few streets near Agios Panteleimonas Square are known as main
drags for this kind of business.

In short, crime and seediness exist in Greece and in Athens,
but not at levels that would justify not being able to leave your
house, as the indignant residents and people on television often
suggested. In fact, around the time the Committee of Residents
began their struggle, Greece was experiencing a notable drop in
the total number of reported penal crimes, with a reduction of
about 28 percent from 2006 to 2010. For Golden Dawn, however,
that didn't matter much, because dangers can be exaggerated or
imagined. The indignant residents fueled the fear, and the fear
fed Golden Dawn.

In his Athens mayoral bid in November 2010, Michaloliakos,
propelled by vows to undo the "reign of terror from the illegal
immigrant criminals," won 5.29 percent of the vote. Around the
polling stations of Agios Panteleimonas, the party won around
20 percent of the vote. The result earned Michaloliakos a seat on
the municipal council. In an interview with a Greek news website some months after the election, Michaloliakos credited his
success in Agios Panteleimonas and nearby neighborhoods to his
party's "wholehearted support" for the residents' committees—by
then a plural phenomenon, as other such self-declared nonpartisan
groups had emerged. The high level of support from those areas
created an obligation for the party to stand with the committees in
their struggle, he added. The struggle of the residents had reached
Attica Square, down the block from Agios Panteleimonas Square.
And very soon, he hoped, it would take off on Victoria Square.

These three squares happened to be the places Human Rights

Watch later described as "particularly dangerous areas for anyone who does not look Greek." The organization documented fifty-one "serious attacks" on migrants that took place from August 2009 through May 2012, more than half of them occurring on or near Agios Panteleimonas Square. Indeed, just before the municipal election of 2010, Ilias Panagiotaros, the bald Golden Dawn leader who helped orchestrate the yogurt attack on Alavanos, told a reporter from the Greek newspaper *Ta Nea* that if Golden Dawn won a seat on the city council, "there'll be a pogrom." The party seemed to be making good on this promise, unleashing "assault battalions"—knife- and baton-wielding men on motorcycles—to terrorize and attack migrants. The attacks only accelerated as Golden Dawn's support grew, and the Greek police and judiciary allowed them to go on with remarkable impunity.

One Afghan mother, Razia Sharife, described to Human Rights Watch how, at the beginning of 2012, her ground-floor apartment in the neighborhood of Agios Panteleimonas had been attacked repeatedly. Once, while she was inside the apartment with her three-year-old and her eleven-year-old twins, a group of men entered and broke beer bottles over the furniture, she told the organization. She'd complained to the police three times, she said, and wondered why, when she could identify some of her attackers frequenting a café on the square, the police did nothing to stop them. At one point, while a Human Rights Watch researcher was visiting Sharife in her apartment, a group of people outside started beating the glass front door with some kind of blunt object. For three minutes, the researcher said, everyone inside watched as the thick glass was cracking. After the banging stopped, the researcher said, they called the police, who arrived and took statements, but they did not find the attackers. The next day, the researcher and Sharife went to file an official complaint at the Agios Panteleimonas police station. There, an officer initially informed them there was a 100-euro fee in order to file a complaint, though the officer eventually processed one without a charge, according to the report. The following day, Sharife said, a neighbor broke her front window and sprayed tear gas inside the apartment. Police came twice to take her statement, Sharife said, and both times they urged her to relocate.

One Afghan man, Safar Haidari, told Human Rights Watch he was punched, kicked, and beaten with clubs by a group of ten to fifteen men wearing helmets and hoods roughly two hundred meters away from the Agios Panteleimonas police precinct. Afterward, Haidari said, he called the police, and about fifteen or twenty minutes later, two motorcycle cops rolled by and asked for his papers. The officers, he said, then told him to go to the police station. There, other officers told him they were busy, Haidari said, despite the fact that he could see five policemen sitting in an office drinking coffee and chatting. Haidari said he waited for twenty minutes and then left.

Mina Ahmad, a twenty-year-old Somali woman, was six months pregnant and walking near the Agios Panteleimonas church with her infant daughter near the end of 2011 when a group of men in black stopped her and asked where she was from, she told Human Rights Watch. They then hit her on the head with a wooden club and ran away, telling her to "get out of the country." She said she fell down bleeding, thinking only of the well-being of the baby inside her, and of her infant daughter, who was crying beside her. No one in the neighborhood helped her, she said; rather, she called friends who came to her assistance, but with no documents at the time, she didn't go to the hospital.

The UNHCR and other human rights organizations documented hundreds more such attacks. The attackers often targeted squares and bus stops, and were sometimes accompanied by children. On a few of my visits to the neighborhood of Agios Panteleimonas, I met people who told me they'd in fact seen children participating. One woman with an apartment directly overlooking the square—she asked me not to publish her name, out of fear of making enemies in the neighborhood—told me she witnessed a man being kicked and smacked around by a group of adults who had brought their children as if to teach them how this sort of thing was done. Another woman told me she once saw several children near Attica Square wielding wooden clubs and chasing a South Asian–looking man. The children returned from the chase laughing with a group of men on the square—presumably their tutors. "It was like a game," the woman said. In both cases, the women told me they felt they couldn't do anything to stop the attacks. Though there was a police precinct a few blocks away, the thought of calling it seemed like a bad joke.

Of course, all of this raised a question that, while many Greek media outlets were reporting on the unspeakable criminality suffered by the residents of Agios Panteleimonas, not enough Greeks had considered: Who were the real criminals?

Golden Dawn's involvement in the defense of Agios Panteleimonas came to a dramatic apogee on a Saturday afternoon in January 2011. It was a sunny, cool day, and leftist groups planned a march to the square. Indignant residents weren't going to allow this, and planned their own counter-rally. Riot police once again arrived to separate the two groups, keeping the leftists from getting too close. The events that followed were captured on video by one apparent supporter of Golden Dawn, who referred to the happenings as a "defense of Greek territory against the mercenary anti-Greek battalions." As indignant residents took turns speaking into a microphone on the square that day, Michaloliakos arrived surrounded by his entourage of bodyguards and took the microphone. "One comment only," Michaloliakos began, as a large portion of the crowd applauded. Pumping his right arm in a manner reminiscent of the fascist orators of yore, he praised his fellow Golden Dawn fighters, who in defense of Athenians were being "stabbed by the Afghans" as other political parties were voting for the bailout program "so they could enslave you to the foreigners." Most people in the crowd cheered and applauded louder. Greek flags were waved. "Blood, honor, Golden Dawn!" the crowd chanted. "Foreigners out of Greece!"

Amid the crowd that day, in his flowing black vestments, was the man that had replaced Prokopios as the head priest of the Agios Panteleimonas church, Father Maximos, a younger man than his predecessor, with a still-black beard. Maximos was born in the late '60s in Leverkusen, Germany, the son of Greek immigrants, and was by this point a rising star of the church. He would soon after this event become deputy to the highest-ranking cleric in Greece, the archbishop of Athens. I later met with Maximos twice, once at the Agios Panteleimonas church, and once in his large office at the archiepiscopate of Athens, an all-white building close to the Acropolis, beside the ruins of the Roman market. The indignant residents had a far more favorable opinion of Maximos than they did of his forerunner, and it was not hard to see why. The conditions in the neighborhood were nightmarish, Maximos told me, and he verified for me the Committee of Residents' account of the playground. It had been a "source of contamination," he said, "a place of defecation." I asked him how he knew this, because by the time he came to Agios Panteleimonas in 2009, the playground had already been closed. "The residents told me," he said. He assured me that the Committee of Residents was a trustworthy source of information. I wanted to ask him if he was sure about this, and I tried to recite to him the content of the committee's 2008 letter— the one that alleged the immigrants were having sex with animals—in order to see if he found it credible. But he interrupted me, and told me the letter did not concern him because he could vouch for the fact that the neighborhood had been blighted by drugs, theft, prostitution, and a "health bomb" of unsanitary conditions. Of course, that did not justify acts of cruelty, he told me.

"It's one thing to express your rage at something and to express a demand that a problem be faced in a proper way, and another thing to take it out on poor people, to chase them, to treat them badly, to hit them and the rest." Maximos, during our conversations, expressed frustration that Agios Panteleimonas had become associated with Golden Dawn. This, he said, was a stereotype. Yes, Golden Dawn had tried to exploit the residents' plight for their own political aims, but then again, he said, so had leftist groups from outside the neighborhood that came to stage antiracist protests. They, too, had imposed their presence, he said, provoking and insulting the residents by calling them racists.

On the day of the gathering at Agios Panteleimonas, Maximos walked amid the crowd, speaking in his typically composed, neutral manner and trying to instill a sense of calm, though it did not seem to have much effect. Riot police wanted to clear the square and began to close in. A police helicopter hovered above. A feeling of tension began to set in, and a big part of the crowd began to leave. About a hundred or so men, many of them hoisting Greek flags, remained, however. They lined up in four rows and banged their flagpoles on the tiled square. One man paced up and down as if riling the men for combat. "What do you want?" he screamed. "Blood!" replied the men in formation. They repeated this a few times and began to chant: "Blood, honor, Golden Dawn." Riot police with tear-gas masks drew closer. It was unclear why they were doing so. The police were known for their very accommodative stance toward Golden Dawn, and generally saw them as an ally in their perpetual street fight against the anarchists. Also, as would later be shown, the police were among Golden Dawn's most ardent political supporters. Golden Dawn, in any case, was enthusiastic for the chance to fight. Men in the square donned motorcycle helmets and carried black shields decorated with the white Celtic cross—a symbol that is popular with neo-Nazis and white supremacists. Then the fighting began. Flagpoles and truncheons met helmets and limbs in a frenzy of beating. The riot police dispersed their supply of stun grenades, tear gas, and chemical spray, which resulted in the prompt retreat of the combatants from the square, and many of them sought refuge in the church.

As tear gas wafted into the heavens, a brief silence governed the square and people began to trickle back out of the church. Standing amid the combatants on the steps was Spiros Gianna-tos of the Committee of Residents, holding a Greek flag over his shoulder and surveying the scene, though not taking part in the fighting. Further away from the church, a man with a shaved head, a Greek flag, and a napkin placed over his nose to allay the effect of the tear gas, stood over the slogans that had long been prominently painted on the square in patriotic blue and white: GREECE, MY COUNTRY!!! and FOREIGNERS OUT OF GREECE. The man stood there, heroically keeping the flag aloft like he was the last man defending the fort. Then fighting broke out again.

Amid the smoke and combat, a cluster of future parliamentar-ians of Golden Dawn could be seen, avoiding direct fighting but seemingly in command of the troops. There was Ioannis Lagos, an excessively brawny man with a handlebar mustache who perpet-ually maintained the erect, ready-to-pounce posture of a bouncer and frequently wore a tight-fitting white T-shirt in order to stress the presence of his muscles. Lagos walked up to the riot police and challenged individual officers to fight mano a mano. "Is any one of you a man? Hand to hand? Any of you? Are there any men here?" No one took him up on the offer.

Also strutting calmly among the combatants, in a black leather jacket and black shades, was Ilias Kasidiaris, a man with a large swastika tattooed on his left shoulder. His existence later became known to the wider world when he slapped a parliamentarian of the Communist Party of Greece, a middle-aged woman, on the face on live, national television. Kasidiaris hit her with a wide, exaggerated swing of his right arm, and then followed with two more swings. When I heard about this, I thought his political ca-reer was over. But I was naive. In Greece, a lot of people—even women—seemed to admire him for putting the communist in her place, and Kasidiaris went on to become one of the party's most prominent figures.

On the steps of the church, the combatants, moved by patriotic sentiment, began to sing the national anthem. Their voices, as they sang of Hellenes arisen, were deep and not particularly harmonious. Then, at a loss for what to do next as a lull in the fighting set in, they sang it again. As riot police approached them on the steps, the combatants sang the anthem a third time. Among them stood Maximos, appearing at one point to try to calm Lagos, the beefy future parliamentarian, from seeking more volunteers among the riot policemen for a one-on-one faceoff. I later asked Maximos how it felt to be caught in the middle of this. "I wasn't in the middle of it," Maximos told me. "I was in my sanctuary. For me, they're all my children. I don't separate people. Nor am I in the middle between anyone," he said. "My job isn't to be with one side or the other. My job is to be there. To be present."

At one point, the police began to march up the church steps. By the door, under the marble arches, the two sides started to beat one another. Many of the combatants fled inside the sanctuary and one of them placed his Celtic-cross shield in the doorway, blocking the police from entering. Maximos then thrust himself toward the door, and as a chemical cloud wafted into the air, he blocked the entrance himself. The police reverently backed away from the cleric. All of this was unnecessary and could have been prevented had the police acted differently, Maximos told me later. He said he asked the police "to not start hitting and the rest" because nothing of severity was occurring, just the screaming of some Golden Dawn slogans. The police unfortunately did not listen, Maximos said. "The truth is, they pushed me, too. And they went toward the church. That's when I got in front and said, not in here. Here no. Here, that's not permitted."

After the police backed off, men with their shields and Greek flags began to trickle back outside, repopulating the church steps and watching the police march around on the square. "They want to take the square!" yelled one combatant in a Paul Revere–like plea. The combatants sang the national anthem again, louder this time. "Greece belongs to the Greeks," they chanted. "Greece, they're selling you, they're kneeling before the foreigners." Paul Revere began to chant again: "We're protecting it. We're protecting it. The square. We're protecting it."

After nearly two hours of this, the two sides seemed to agree to a truce. Police backed away and gave their opponents a chance to honorably remove themselves from the battlefield. The combatants lined up into four rows and, holding their shields and their Greek flags, sang the Golden Dawn anthem. "Followers of mighty progenitors, children of resplendent fighters, we are the new Spartans, with our brave heart," the men sang in a gruff unison, followed by the chorus: "Forward, always forward, a new glorious era is rising. Forward, always forward, the light of Hellenism guides us." They then sang the second verse: "We were the ones to light the torch, to us was born the wrath. We want a new Greece, that will cover all the earth." After they finished, their drill leader yelled, "Hail victory!" which in German happens to translate to *Sieg heil.* "Hail!" the formation responded. The remaining onlookers near the square applauded, and the combatants then marched off in formation, chanting: "Greece belongs to the Greeks."

The events of the day were subsequently overblown in the press, according to Maximos. "In my judgment, I don't think anything important happened," he said. "Again, the television made it a much bigger thing than it really was. Who was it? Some kids they brought to yell slogans, whether they believed them or not."

Those most interested in inflating the significance of the day's events, it so happened, were indignant residents and members of Golden Dawn. Following the battle, a news talk show program called *Makeleio,* or "Carnage," on an Athens channel not known for its high journalistic standards, dedicated a program to the fight on the square. The host, Stefanos Chios, a volatile man who introduced his program as the "freest show on Greek television," began by insulting various politicians as the "scum of the society" and then dared the "bastards in power" to sue him, if indeed they had the manhood to sue him. The source of his anger that day was the shameful beating police had unleashed on the Greek citizens on Agios Panteleimonas, and the desecration of the church, the insult to Orthodoxy. The program that night would "smash the bones" of the politicians, he said. Then, pausing as if he could sense potential legal consequences for saying that, added: "Not their physical bones, but their political and policing bones."

One of the guests that night was "a witness" to the day's events. He wore a tight-fitting black T-shirt and black cap, and looked and spoke a bit like Rocky Balboa. He was among those guarding the square from immigrants and leftists who had planned the demonstration, he explained, and then came the vicious police attack. The police went inside the church, broke windows, and threw chemicals, the witness said. He then held up his right arm and pulled back the white gauze that was wrapped around his wrist, revealing a gash. "This is my wound," he said. He then suggested the politicians governing the country leave "before it's too late." The rage of the people was boiling over, he said. "This can't go on. The people have reached the end. The end. Period. They will rise up. We'll take weapons and go out onto the streets. It can't go on. Period."

Chios told the witness that there were reports Golden Dawn had participated in the residents' demonstration. He wanted to know if this was accurate. "Can you tell me what information you have so we can understand some things? And how the residents gathered and who were these residents who gathered at Agios Panteleimonas? Because they equate everyone with the far right. This thing needs to be cleared up."

"We are extreme right," said the witness. "Nationalist, extreme right, and proud of it," he said. "What are we, murderers? We don't go out to steal, nor do we kill." The people on the square, he said, were "Greek Golden Dawn members." He added, as if an afterthought: "And residents of the area."

A series of callers began to phone in. The first was Loukia Rizou, the retired statistics employee I had met in her capacity as Committee of Residents member. The police attack, she said, was sudden and excessive. The worst part of all of it was the damage to the church. Chios thanked her for her account, and then took several more calls from people who seemed to be reading lines someone had given to them, though Chios said that the callers weren't "made up." One caller said that after witnessing what took place on the square that day, she had decided to take her children and leave for Australia again. "Unfortunately, unfortunately, Greece isn't governed by Greeks, but by foreigners, masons, and Jews." Another woman called and said that unless politicians resigned, the people would "have to go out in the streets with sticks and rocks and with everything to chase whoever gets in front of us." One male caller said he was ashamed to be Greek. "Isn't there a general that can take care of these shit dogs and send them to hell? Isn't there a general? At some point, there were generals with eyebrows," he said, a kind of way of saying "with balls" and an apparent reference to Greece's military dictatorship.

As if on cue, a man with big eyebrows called. It was Michaloliakos, the Golden Dawn chief. The police attack was totally unprovoked, he said. "We're talking about a deep state, about a shadow state that has recruited bums who beat old ladies and children and disperse chemicals," he said. "They even got to the point of throwing stun grenades at the church candle stand."

It was noteworthy to hear Michaloliakos's ostensible offense at such impiety. The party had long shed its preference for the paganism of the ancient Hellenes, knowing that such sacrilege would not get it very far in Greek politics. Golden Dawn, by this point, actively sought to associate itself with the church. During the feast day of St. Panteleimon the following year, for instance, a formation of men wearing black Golden Dawn shirts carried an icon of the saint during a procession around the church as priests with long beards, girls wearing white dresses, and altar boys in sparkling robes watched from the church steps amid ringing bells and chants of *"Kyrie eleison,"* or "Lord, have mercy." Maximos later told me he was out of town when this happened. Had he been there, he wouldn't have allowed it, he said, and he considered it a sacrilege for a political party to exploit a church service. "Simply, there was no one there to tell them, 'Stop. You can't come here.' "

Michaloliakos went on, telling the television viewers that the police actions of the day illustrated how Greece was enduring the most horrible dictatorship that had ever existed. Yet he also expressed hope. Despite all this, despite this unprovoked police attack for which there was no reason, the Greeks who were on the square that day, proudly holding the flag of their nation, did not budge. "The people faced them with simple hands, with bare hands."

One Sunday in early May 2012, I met Khalid Abdulrahman and Mukhtar Jama next to a basketball court by the train station in central Athens, a ten-minute walk from Agios Panteleimonas. Abdulrahman was in his early thirties, wore a Che Guevara baseball cap, and seemed tired. He'd come to Greece five months earlier from Sudan, and things hadn't gone well. He was living in a defunct train car and subsisting off food from a Catholic charity soup kitchen. In a plastic bag he carried a few half-eaten chunks of bread. "I will try and go back to Sudan now," he told me. Jama, on the other hand, had just arrived from Somalia, and appeared to be still processing the difficulty of his new circumstances. He was lanky and twenty-two, and looked bookish in eyeglasses and neat clothes. He said he had sold a piece of land in Mogadishu for $1,500 in order to pay a smuggler to get him to this point. First, they put him on a flight to Damascus, Syria. From there, the journey was one and a half months through rugged topography, most of it on foot. Sugar water kept him from passing out. Jama's "dream" had been to go to a European university, he said, but the idea now seemed fanciful in retrospect. The Somalis who had come before him were dejected and told depressing stories. "They're, you know, what's the word." He scanned his English lexicon for a moment. "Fucked," he said with a wide grin, pleased to have found the right way to put it.

Our conversation was interrupted by the sound of an explosion. Several others followed. A cloud of smoke appeared from around the corner, followed by a chorus of male voices chanting in a deep staccato: "Blood, honor, Golden Dawn" and "Greece belongs to the Greeks." Jama decided it would be a good time to leave and disappeared in a hurry. Abdulrahman lingered long enough for me to buy him a couple of meat-filled hot pockets, his choice among the scant options available at the closest fast-food restaurant. He then shuffled off in the direction of his train car.

A bit later, Michaloliakos marched down the same street surrounded by an entourage of muscled disciples. Voting had just concluded in national parliamentary elections held to replace the unelected, technocratic government that had pushed through the second bailout agreement. The first results had come in, and Michaloliakos, it appeared, had just received a promotion from Athens city councilman to parliamentarian. The loud booms around the corner had been celebratory explosives being tossed off the balcony of the party's main headquarters. His party, having established a foothold with the migrant issue, was now riding a wave of anti-bailout feeling. The party won 7 percent of the national vote, a result that had placed Michaloliakos in the pantheon of short, dangerous men throughout history who, in their pursuit of power, had surpassed expectations of how much of it they could get.

Michaloliakos was on his way to a nearby hotel conference room where a few dozen journalists waited to hear him speak. He strutted passed Hellenic busts in the hotel lobby and entered the meeting room, where a plump party official with a shaved head named Giorgos Germenis instructed the journalists to rise from their chairs and stand at attention. Germenis was also the bassist and guttural grunter for Naer Mataron, a Greek death-metal group of modest acclaim, or, in the band's own words, "the most dangerous satanic band in the world." Naer Mataron was just about to release a new studio album, *Long Live Death*, which one metal reviewer called a "wicked piece of venomous black/death," containing insane drumming and a "brutal vomiting of assaulting vocals." Germenis, known by his stage alias, Kaiadas, the name of the gorge into which ancient Spartans tossed executed criminals, was also about to become a parliamentarian and the party's point person on issues pertaining to decentralization and local governance.

Most of the journalists obeyed Germenis's order to rise. I was fortunate to already have been standing against the back wall, thereby avoiding the predicament of how to react. One woman, whom I could not see behind the phalanx of cameras being hoisted in the air, refused to stand up. Germenis walked in her direction and began waving his hand to indicate she should stand immediately. "Rise! Rise! Rise! Rise! Show respect!"

"What happened?" Michaloliakos said as he walked into the room and encountered the commotion. Behind the cameras, I heard the woman explain to him the nature of the disagreement, as if he might arbitrate in a reasonable manner. Instead he told her she could leave, and she did. Michaloliakos then sat down beside the red party flag, which featured at its center a black meander design. Despite the banner's unmistakable resemblance to the

German Nazi flag in both color and design, anyone making this connection was misguided, according to party officials. In fact, any allusion to it as a Nazi flag, they said, was "ridiculous" and "calumnious." Beside Michaloliakos sat the largest man in the room, Ioannis Lagos, the one who on the day of the Battle of Agios Panteleimonas had persistently challenged the riot policemen to fight. "No one talks," Lagos instructed the room as Michaloliakos sat down at a table in front of the journalists. The party leader placed both hands on the table, as if he were an angry teacher about to scold the classroom, and thanked—"with all the strength of my Greek heart"—his voters. The party would continue its resistance to "the slavery of the bailout program" and fight the "social jungle" of illegal immigration. He then uttered to his political opponents a phrase attributed to Julius Caesar: *"Veni, vidi, vici"*—I came, I saw, I conquered. (For a pure Hellene, Michaloliakos possessed a peculiar oratory fondness for Latin.) "A new golden dawn of Hellenism is rising," he said. "For those who betray this homeland, the time has come to be afraid. We are coming." He then paraded out of the room surrounded by his burly associates.

In front of the party's headquarters a few blocks away, supporters had begun to gather in the street. Police arrived and blocked off traffic in order to provide room for celebration. A couple of motorcycle cops revved their engines as they rolled by. At this discreet but clear endorsement, the Golden Dawn adherents whooped with glee. Golden Dawn's core constituency, it turned out, was not so much the people of Agios Panteleimonas, where the party had come in third, winning between 12 and 14 percent of the vote—a smaller portion than in the municipal election years earlier. Rather, its greatest support came from the neighborhood of Ampelokipoi, a more prosperous area of the city to the east, which happened to be the location of the Greek police headquarters. Greek police, unlike other citizens, voted where they worked, and in several Ampelokipoi polling stations where police were among the voters,

Golden Dawn did exceptionally well, capturing in some stations nearly a quarter of the vote. In area polling stations where police did not vote, the party's performance was on par with the national average.

Men in black shirts lit flares that emitted the blue hue of the Greek flag. Explosives were tossed intermittently. "Foreigners out of Greece!" Though the event was out in the middle of the street, the party had determined it was closed to unapproved journalists, and I watched as a few hefty men turned away a dejected German public television news crew. I kept my notebook and a voice recorder in my pocket. The growing crowd applauded with excitement as they waited for Michaloliakos, who was to emerge onto an upper balcony and speak.

Soon, Michaloliakos appeared next to two large Greek flags. He was greeted with cheers, ear-piercing firecrackers, and car alarms triggered by the explosions. Beside him in the shadows stood someone he introduced as a monk from Mount Athos. "Whoever thinks that now that we are entering parliament, we're going to become good boys and girls, we answer: the streets await us!" Competing chants of "Foreigners out of Greece" and "Greece belongs to the Greeks" merged into a repulsive cacophony. "At some point, the roads will open up and Greece will once again become ours," he said. "They criticized us nationalists, the Golden Dawners, because we had the bravery to protect neighborhoods, to liberate the squares." After thirty-eight years of fake democracy, he said, a nationalist movement had been born to save Greece. The crowd shouted in near ecstasy: "Hellas! Hellas!" followed by the Spartan *"E tan e epi tas."*

Over the course of the next year—as Golden Dawn continued its attacks on migrants—its stature continued to rise, and polls showed it to be the country's third most popular party. Its good fortune went on unimpeded until a mid-September night in 2013 when Pavlos Fyssas, a thirty-four-year-old antifascist rapper known as Killah P, went to a café in Piraeus with some friends to watch a soccer game. There, Fyssas exchanged words with some members of Golden Dawn, who called for reinforcements. Some thirty or so men equipped with clubs arrived on the street outside, according to witnesses, and shortly after midnight, when Fyssas tried to leave, he was attacked. A Golden Dawn member drove up, got out of his car, and stabbed Fyssas in the chest, killing him. This was self-defense, the accused killer said after he was arrested. The next day, the Greek news media heavily covered the murder. The attack, investigators said, appeared to have been ordered through a chain of command, implicating Golden Dawn leaders. Many Greeks were upset. This time, the victim was one of their own—a Greek, a *"palikari,"* to use the affectionate term for a good young man.

The Greek government then acted quickly to crack down on the party. The minister in charge of police ordered raids of Golden Dawn offices and homes, and requested that prosecutors bring a case against the party for being a criminal organization. Before long, the Greek parliament voted to revoke immunity for Golden Dawn parliamentary members, and the party's public funding was cut. As Prime Minister Samaras was about to take a planned trip to the United States, Michaloliakos was arrested along with several other Golden Dawn parliamentarians. Some were later released, though Michaloliakos remained in jail.

In order to crack down on the party, the government decided, it would also have to purge police ranks of party sympathizers. High-ranking police officers across the country resigned for personal reasons, and several others were removed from their positions. The head of a division of Greece's national intelligence agency was removed, and though the government did not provide a reason for this, the Greek press alleged a connection to Golden Dawn. Additionally, the police internal affairs division sifted through police ranks and accused ten police officers of having criminal connections to Golden Dawn. One of them was the man who for seven years had been "head of security" at the Agios Panteleimonas police station, apparently providing insight into how Golden Dawn was able to establish itself in the area. Investigators arrested him for abuse of power, money laundering, and illegal weapons and drug possession, among other charges. Found in the officer's home and residences was an arsenal of weaponry—pistols, many shotguns, a great deal of ammunition, knives, axes, swords—and 700 grams of cannabis.

In New York, after the first arrests were made, Prime Minister Samaras spoke about Golden Dawn before an audience at the American Jewish Committee. "It's important for me to deracinate this group," he said. "Now, everyone realizes who they really are." The Greek government, however, clearly knew what Golden Dawn was before Fyssas's killing. If it was important for Samaras to deracinate the group, a lot of people in Greece were asking why the government hadn't acted sooner.

At a café next to the neighborhood police station in Agios Panteleimonas one morning around this time, I got an answer to this question from a finely dressed man the proprietor of the establishment introduced to me as "Boss." Boss wore a suit and tie, multiple gold rings, a thick silver watch, and wingtip shoes. He had a long nose and spiky gray hair. I'd come to the right place, he told me, after I introduced myself and told him the subject of my interest. "I am extreme right." He was indeed dressed a bit like the shadowy right-wing henchmen portrayed in Greek movies about the postwar period, the men who showed up in the middle of the night to kidnap some leftist from his bed. "People you see licking themselves at a café next to the police station are always from the rightwing realm," Boss told me. "You won't see a single leftist." Boss, a retiree who didn't want to tell me his real name, paced back and forth while I sat at a table by the window. He occasionally bent down to stick his face directly in front of mine for emphasis as he explained to me a few things about Greek politics. Boss then began to clap; during the military dictatorship in Greece, he told me, a lot of people were doing this. "Where do you think they all ended up?" The answer, according to Boss, was that most of them went to New Democracy, the party he, too, had long supported until switching to Golden Dawn a few years earlier. "New Democracy is extreme right," Boss told me. "At least a big piece of it." New Democracy and Golden Dawn, he said, were "cousins," and it's hard to clamp down on your cousin.

Some apparent evidence of the family ties Boss was talking about surfaced a couple of months after our conversation, as prosecutors were working on the Golden Dawn case. Kasidiaris—the Golden Dawn parliamentarian with a swastika tattoo on his arm—released a video of a secretly recorded conversation he'd had with Samaras's senior aide, Panagiotaros Baltakos, in which the aide suggested that Golden Dawn's prosecution was purely political. "First of all, he's afraid for himself," Baltakos said of Samaras. "Because you're hitting him, giving Syriza the lead."

"And because we take his votes, he puts us in jail?" said Kasidiaris.

"The motherfucker. Incredible thing. Unbelievable," said Baltakos about his boss.

Samaras condemned Baltakos after the video surfaced, saying he did not know his aide had close contacts in Golden Dawn. Baltakos resigned, and in an interview on Greek radio he said he was telling Kasidiaris what he wanted to hear as part of a strategy to stay in touch with Golden Dawn and get information about them. This had to be done for the good of the country, he said. "New Democracy is a center-right party that for two years has been in danger of losing its right wing," he said. "And if that happens, it will fall completely out of the primacy of the political spectrum. That should not happen."

The episode helped explain why the conservative-led government did not move against Golden Dawn earlier. Samaras had long been advised against a crackdown on the party out of concern it would alienate New Democracy's nationalist wing, and in the beginning, that logic seemed to have won out. Samaras initially tried to defeat the political threat that Golden Dawn posed to him by getting tough on illegal immigration and anarchist street protesters. This, Samaras hoped, would make those far-right voters who had defected come back. Instead, the strategy just seemed to help legitimize and strengthen Golden Dawn. Samaras's government then turned to Plan B: prosecution. The killing of a Greek *palikari,* and the revulsion this stirred among Greeks, provided the window of opportunity.

Samaras's conservative-led government was by no means solely to blame for Golden Dawn's unhindered rise. Golden Dawn had begun its political ascent and violent tactics long before he took power, and the state's tacit consent ran far deeper. The fact that sympathy for Golden Dawn flourished within the ranks of the Greek police and in the upper echelons of the government lay bare the nationalist extremism that had skulked inside the organs of the government since the end of World War II. Had Greece's police and judiciary functioned as one imagines they ought to in a modern European state, Golden Dawn members would have faced prosecution far sooner. The complicity also extended to the wider Greek society. The mainstream Greek press largely ignored Golden Dawn's violence, inflamed fear of immigrants, and sometimes praised the party for defending Greeks. Church clerics did not speak out forcefully enough against the party's violence, and some echoed its rhetoric.

Even if the government's belated drive to outlaw Golden Dawn proved successful, changing the large part of Greek society that stood by and acceded to its xenophobic reign of violence would be a far lengthier and more challenging undertaking. The crackdown on the party had one immediate and valuable benefit, however. The attacks on migrants in the center of Athens all but stopped.

Prosecuting a popular political party in a democracy is a delicate matter. The Greek government knew that the effort could backfire politically if Golden Dawn retained its popularity. So, as prosecutors prepared their case, the government made an effort to undermine the party's support. Documents, photos, and videos revealing Golden Dawn's unseemly activities were leaked to the Greek press—pictures of Golden Dawn members with guns in what looked like paramilitary boot camps (camping trips and fitness routines, the party explained), a photo of someone dressed in Ku Klux Klan garb and doing a Hitler salute in front of a Golden Dawn flag (a Halloween costume gag, and furthermore, an ancient Greek salute). The leaks were intended to convince the voters that Golden Dawn was not, in fact, simply nationalist, as the party claimed, but Nazi. Still, a lot of voters didn't seem to mind. With its political leadership in jail and its Nazism now underscored in the press, the party's voters did not go away. In the first elections following the arrests—the European Parliament election of May 2014—Golden Dawn won 9 percent of the national vote. In national parliamentary elections several months later, the party won some 6 percent of the vote, nearly as much as it had received in 2012, when it first entered parliament. This outcome made Golden Dawn the third largest party in Greece.

One spring evening just before the European election, Golden Dawn held a rally at the spot where their self-described "struggle" began—the square of Agios Panteleimonas. When I arrived, Golden Dawn's martial-sounding music was blaring through speakers, and a podium draped with a party banner was already set up on the steps of the church. As the crowd arrived, groups of burly young men patrolled the area, telling people who looked foreign to go away. At one point, a solemn tune sung by Nikos Xilouris, a famous Cretan musician of the '60s and '70s, came over the speakers. The song that played, about the apathy of citizens to the presence of an enemy in their midst, is thought of as a protest ballad against the military dictatorship, though Golden Dawn, fond of that dictatorship as it is, seemed to have had another interpretation. As the song played, the church bells began to ring, marking the beginning of the evening vespers inside. "They entered the city, the enemies," sang Xilouris. "They broke down the doors, the enemies. And we laughed in the neighborhoods, on the first day."

I sat down on a bench with a few old ladies who seemed bothered that the party gathering had disturbed their evening bench-sitting session, and after a while they decided to move to a calmer place. One lady grimaced as she gingerly stood up with the help of a cane, taking with her the piece of cardboard she used as a seat cushion. "Don't care to watch?" I said to her. "My love, what's there to see here?" she said before shuffling away. Then, two young Golden Dawn apostles unraveled across the marble columns of the church entrance a large banner of their dear jailed leader, raising his arms in victory.

The candidates for municipal elections began speaking from the steps of the church. "We continue a struggle, the holy struggle that the residents of the area started," said one city council candidate. Another addressed his words to the heroic residents, those who struggled to prevent the Athens of Pericles, Solon, and Socrates from becoming Islamabad. A woman read a letter from Themis Skordeli, the pioneer Committee of Residents member, who had been jailed in connection with the crackdown on Golden Dawn, though she was running for city council anyway. "It was six years ago that here, in our area, we first yelled the slogan 'Greece belongs to the Greeks.' " Then, "Only Golden Dawn stood beside you in your struggles and protestations."

While the speeches were addressed to the residents of the area, there weren't very many of them there. Those residents that had come out to stand with Golden Dawn in previous years now seemed afraid to be associated with the party, given the ongoing prosecution. Of the few hundred people in attendance, most of them—judging by the preponderance of Pit Bull Germany and Lonsdale brand clothes, favorites of European neo-Nazi groups— were core supporters brought in for the event. Though the party later declared that thousands of residents had come to the square that evening, one of the speakers that night, a heavyset parliamentarian named Dimitrios Koukoutsis, acknowledged the lack of turnout. "What's your fear? Is one who is wet afraid of the rain?" he said. "Shame on you! What we're asking for is your action, at the very least, your vote for a movement that matured here on this square."

At one point, I saw Spiros Giannatos of the Committee of Residents. During the battle for the square, he had stood among the Golden Dawn combatants with a Greek flag in his hands. On this day, he passed by on the sidewalk with his shaggy black dog, pausing for a while as a few people petted it, but he did not stay. I later asked his wife if she attended the rally. No, she said. If she had, this would only make people think she was a supporter of Golden Dawn. Besides, she said, the party had taken credit for the successful struggle of the residents, and all the fuss about Golden Dawn and its assault battalions was just a bunch of lies.

Speaking last that night was swastika-tattooed Kasidiaris, the main face of the party following its leader's jailing. He recalled to the crowd the day, a few years earlier, when he and his fellow combatants had clashed with riot police on the square. It was a day, he said, when young kids and elderly citizens, residents, had gathered to show Greeks the meaning of national resistance. Agios Panteleimonas, he said, was the flame that burned in the heart of every Greek. As he spoke, a young boy stood on the steps of the church and waved a Greek flag. Kasidiaris looked at the boy and said he'd never seen a more beautiful sight. The coming fight, he said, would be for the survival of Hellenism itself.

Epilogue

On the January night in 2015 when the leftist Syriza was elected to lead a new Greek government, Alexis Tsipras, the incoming prime minister, gave his victory speech in downtown Athens in front of a young, exuberant crowd. Bruce Springsteen's "We Take Care of Our Own"—a song Barack Obama had used extensively during his second presidential campaign—blasted over the speakers. Tsipras trotted onto the stage, raised his arms in triumph, and declared that his country had turned a page. The election meant Greece was "leaving behind fear and domination, leaving behind five years of humiliation and suffering." Some in the audience responded in unison: "The time for the left has come!" Tspiras did not name Greece's longtime oppressors, as he had done so often during the campaign, but the implication was clear. A woman in the crowd held up a large sign that read, in German, "This is a really **Good Night Frau Merkel**." Another supporter held up a blunter message, addressed to the Troika: "Keep Calm and Go to Hell!"

Tsipras had chosen to give his victory speech in front of the

University of Athens's imposing neo-classical facade. It was a picturesque spot for the occasion. As Tsipras spoke in front of the illuminated Greek columns, it looked, on television, as if he were being broadcast from some nerve center of Hellenism. One glaring irony, however, seemed to go unnoticed. The building had been constructed during the reign of Otto—Greece's first king, installed by European powers. A colorful frieze on it depicted a mustached Otto on his throne, dressed in classical Greek garb. Pictures taken of Tspiras waving his hands in triumph that night show King Otto hovering directly above him, as if having risen from his Bavarian grave to remind Greeks that they remained, as so often in their history, utterly dependent on their more powerful neighbors.

In the following months, the ghost of Otto certainly seemed to haunt the new Greek government as it tried to negotiate with its creditors. The day after the election, immediately following his inauguration, Tsipras took a ride to the suburban Athens shooting range where, during World War II, occupying German forces executed hundreds of Greek partisans—among them, Manolis Glezos's brother, Nikos. There, Tsipras lay red roses on a memorial as a crowd of teary-eyed supporters gathered behind him and shouted slogans of praise for the communist-led war resistance. He stood for a few moments with his hand over his heart before turning to leave. "Bravo!" people in the crowd shouted as they rushed to kiss and embrace him.

Syriza leaders offered various explanations for this first prime ministerial action. Some called it a protest against Golden Dawn, whose strong election performance unnerved many Greeks, some of whom feared the neo-Nazi party would be next in line should the Syriza-led government fail. One of Tsipras's top aides, however, offered a more obvious explanation, calling the visit a symbol of Greeks' desire for "liberty from German occupation."

In Germany, many interpreted the act as a provocation. "Did Tsipras with the blood-red roses want to say: 'Hey, we don't owe these nasty Nazis anything anyway'?" asked one commentator on German public radio before condemning the visit as an attempt to give Germany—the creditor—"guilty feelings," and to make the Greeks—the debtors—out to be morally superior. "These are fatal signals. No one likes to give money when they feel blackmailed."

The public debate between the two governments soon devolved into a feud. Germany's finance minister, Wolfgang Schäuble, was unable to conceal his disdain for Syriza. The austerity and reform regimen had put Greece on the right path, Schäuble told a German radio interviewer, until Syriza came along to derail the progress and "insult those who have helped Greece in recent years." Schäuble added: "I feel sorry for the Greeks. They've selected a government that is at the moment behaving quite irresponsibly." Tsipras felt obliged to respond to this statement in the Greek parliament, suggesting it would be more appropriate for Schäuble to feel sorry for people "who walk with their heads bowed" rather than those "who lift their heads with pride."

Despite their declarations of renewed sovereignty, Syriza's leaders soon found themselves in the same position as their predecessors: struggling under agonizing pressure to scrape together cash for debt payments and to satisfy their creditors' reform requirements in hope of getting some financial relief. To bolster the national mood, the new government resorted to semantics; instead of referring to the hated "Troika," it dubbed its creditors "the institutions." While many Greeks embraced Syriza's narrative of successful resistance, not everyone was convinced, and some of the most strident criticism came from within the party itself. Manolis Glezos wrote a dispirited letter from Brussels after the government agreed to extend the bailout program. "From my side, I APOLOGIZE to the Greek people for having cooperated in this illusion," he wrote. "Between the oppressor and oppressed, there can be no compromise, just as between the slave and the conqueror, the only solution is freedom."

In the following months, Syriza's leaders would face the

impossible task of appeasing "the institutions" while keeping more strident elements of the party from defecting because of it. Tsipras tried to please both sides by promising bold, though not very detailed, reforms—"to build a country from the beginning." The government would crack down on tax evasion by the rich (with a special focus on the Lagarde List), rein in government waste, improve the civil service, launch an unprecedented fight against corruption, improve treatment of migrants. At the same time, Syriza's leaders backed off some previous stances. Years earlier, for instance, the party had criticized the conservative-led government for arresting the restaurateur on Hydra. Now, in a letter to the creditors, the Greek finance ministry proposed a crackdown on businesses that did not give receipts by employing undercover tourists supplied with hidden cameras, a slapdash idea met with great skepticism.

Despite the intensifying climate of antagonism and mistrust, Greece and the eurozone were unlikely to split up, at least intentionally (the threat of an accidental break-up, spurred by failing banks or missed debt payments, still loomed). European leaders, despite their disapproval of the new Greek government, did not want to undermine the euro and the European project by cutting Greece loose. For their part, many Greeks, despite their resentments, were cognizant that from the time of the revolution and King Otto, they had frequently benefited from Europe's intervention. Despite the misery of the previous years, Greeks maintained an almost religious faith in the euro, and the majority rejected one clear path to more independence: a voluntary exit from the currency, fearing it would only generate greater woes. Greeks' disregard for their creditors, moreover, was rivaled by their lack of confidence in Greece's shambolic government institutions. The only thing worse than remaining under Europe's stern sway, many Greeks seemed to believe, was for their country to be left alone to fend for itself.

Acknowledgments

For all the considerable problems and gloomy subjects addressed in this book, I hope that my fondness for Greece and many of its people still comes across. I am grateful for the opportunity I've had in recent years to visit the country often and get to know it better. My family and I were treated with generous hospitality during our travels in Greece, and now that we've been away for several months, we miss it. Greece, of course, is a beautiful place, and if you haven't been there, you should visit. If you, like me, one day find yourself standing among the spring flowers on a rocky hill overlooking the ruins of the sanctuary of Hera on the Corinthian Gulf, and observe the brilliant light and puffs of mist drifting over the azure water, you too might feel like you're dreaming.

This book wouldn't exist if it weren't for a few people in particular. One of them is Joshua Yaffa, a great journalist and still better friend. During a bout of professional anguish a few years ago, I sought his career advice, as I often do. "Why don't you write a book?" he suggested, and then put me in touch with people who could help make a book happen. For his advice and help on this occasion and many others, I am grateful.

Much of the research for this book was connected to stories I reported for the *Wall Street Journal*. For the chance to write for the *Journal* from Greece, and for much else, I'm grateful to Matthew Karnitschnig. I've benefited a lot from his thoughtful editing and guidance in recent years, and he also kindly dedicated time to look at parts of the book manuscript. From Brooklyn to Berlin, he and his wife, Katharina, have been great friends to us.

David Patterson, my agent, has been a terrific advocate, and has provided smart counsel throughout this process. I'm thankful to him for his conscientiousness and for believing in this project from the start.

Many Greek journalists generously offered their advice and help. I am indebted in particular to Dimitris Psarras, Tasos Telloglou, Marianna Kakaounaki, and Nikolas Leontopoulos. Anastasia Moumtzaki also helped with some challenging reporting, and was patient with my frayed nerves when things didn't work out as we would have liked. I also owe thanks to documentary filmmaker Konstantinos Georgousis for sharing with me his incisive observations on Greek fascists and a number of other issues. In Thessaloniki, Antonis Kamaras was a source of numerous great conversations about Greek history and politics.

A few Greek public prosecutors, who wished not to be named in this book, graciously took time to talk to me about some important, ongoing cases. They are engaged in a difficult fight to bring more accountability and justice to Greece. For their efforts, they deserve the gratitude of the Greek people. After meeting with some of the prosecutors undertaking crucial investigations, I was convinced that Greece's best hope rests with an underutilized resource: its women.

During the course of my research, I benefited greatly from excellent work done by scholars and historians of modern Greece.

Acknowledgments

Susanne-Sophia Spiliotis and Devin Naar kindly offered their personal help. In addition, I've learned a great deal from the works of Mark Mazower, Hagen Fleischer, John Louis Hondros, Richard Clogg, William St Clair, Michael Herzfeld, and Heinz A. Richter.

I'm grateful to the dedicated people at Crown Publishers who worked on this book. In particular, Jenna Ciongoli, Meagan Stacey, Emma Berry, and Mark Birkey played crucial roles.

My extended family in Greece provided good company and logistical support, and stuffed us with delicious food on many occasions. My parents and brother, as always, provided steadfast support and encouragement. I thank my parents in particular for teaching me about Greece while I was growing up, and for forcing me to go to Greek school despite my spirited childhood protestations. Most of all, I am indebted to them for their courage and determination, which have served them well in the New World.

My deepest gratitude is to my wife, Katrin, who came along for the ride, and whose strength and love have sustained me through this endeavor and many others. *Efharisto, agapi mou.*

Lastly, I thank my wonderful sons, Elias Harry, who was born right around the time I learned I'd be getting a chance to write this book, and Alexander Loukas, who arrived just as I completed it. A more joyful distraction from my work, I could not imagine.

January 2015, Berlin

Index

Index

constitution of 1822, 160–61
corruption and King Otto, 35–37
crime level and drugs, 252–53
ethnos, defined/described, 35
EU, membership, 2, 6–9, 18, 70–71, 81–82, 84
EU, withdrawal/ejection from, 13–14, 17, 20, 90–91
Imia territory dispute, 69–73, 77, 81
kombolói, in Greek culture, 28, 29, 127, 155, 192, 202–3
Muslim presence/influence, 204–7
national anthem, 23
official language, 168
population exchange with Turkey, 169–70, 204–5
post-war communist insurgency, 244–45
Regime of the Colonels, 232, 245–46
revolution and birth of nation, 163–70
state visit by Heuss, 110
state visit by Merkel, 89–92
state visit by Schäuble, 88–89
U.S. aid and Cold War policy, 245
See also Hellenism
Greek Federation of Bank Employees Unions, 141
Greek Independence Day, 1–5
The Greece Lie (TV documentary), 62–63
Greek Orthodox Church. *See* Orthodox Church/traditions
Greek People's Liberation Army (ELAS), 85, 103–4
"Grexit," 17, 20
Grigorios V (Patriarch), 168
The Guardian (newspaper), 64, 66

H

Haidari, Safar, 255
haratsi (Ottoman era tax), 57
Hellas (poem, Shelley), 11
Hellenic Republic (Greece), 9. *See also* Greece
Hellenism, about concept of, 11–12, 160, 165–67, 187, 230, 261, 267, 276. *See also* Greece
Heraclitus (philosopher), 230
Hess, Rudolph, 232
Heuss, Theodor, 110, 111
Hitler, Adolf, 232

Hoelscher-Obermaier, Wolfgang, 93
Homer (epic poet), 189
Hondros, John Louis, 102
Howaldtswerke-Deutsche Werft (HDW), 77–78
Human Rights Watch, 190, 220, 254–55
Hürriyet (newspaper), 71–72
Hussien, Mohamad, 223–24
Hydra (island), tax evasion, 53–58
Hymn to Liberty (Solomos), 23

I

Imia territorial dispute, 69–73, 77, 81
immigration
  anti-immigration protest, 226–29
  closure of playground incident, 235–39
  fear of crime, 252–54
  Golden Dawn's use as political issue, 229–35
  Orthodox clerics' response to protest over, 239–47, 257–58
  rioting, 256–64, 267
  serious attacks on migrants, 254–56
  Syriza's stance on, 247–50
  television and media coverage, 250–52, 256
  See also asylum/asylum seekers; migrants, treatment
The Independent (newspaper), 217
International Financial Commission, 14–15
International Monetary Fund (IMF), 2–3, 5, 15, 18, 24, 158. *See also* "the Troika"
Ireland, 6, 9, 13
"The Island of the Blind." *See* Zakynthos
The Isles of Greece (Byron), 164
Italy, 67, 111, 195–96

J

Jama, Mukhtar, 264–65
Jews
  anti-Semitism, 48, 182–84, 203, 263
  betrayal during occupation, 185–88
  deportation during WWII, 104, 112–14, 173, 182, 185
  during Ottoman rule, 167–68, 172–74
  election to office, 176
  German reparations, 108
  Sephardic Jews, 163, 172–73
  Thessaloniki, arrival in, 172–73
  Zionism and creation of Israel, 246–47

Index

Index

Nazi occupation, 112
Orthodox Church influence, 181–82
Ottoman Empire, liberation from,
   35–36, 158–62
Ottoman liberation celebration, 158–62,
   175, 178, 184–87
protests/attack on German diplomat,
   93
Yad Lezicaron Synagogue, 186
Thucydides (Greek historian), 130
Torcaso Investment Ltd., 76, 79
Toronto *Globe and Mail*, 177
tourism, 18, 47–48, 55, 59, 172, 198
Tourkokratia (Ottoman period), 166
Tragas, Giorgos, 92
Transparency International, 26
Treaty on the Final Settlement with
   Respect to Germany, 115
Trelawny, Edward John, 11–12
Trikala (city), 150
"the Troika"
   control of tax evasion, 56, 64
   effect of bailouts on Greek economy and
     debt levels, 17–20
   first bailout, 2–16, 19, 39, 60, 77
   forecasts for Greek economy, 15
   public sector reform/layoffs, 121–25,
     134, 137–38
   public sector wage cuts, 148–54
   review of benefit programs, 44–48
   second bailout, 16–20, 24–25, 30
   See also European Central Bank;
     European Commission; International
     Monetary Fund
Truman Doctrine, 232, 245–46
Tsagkaropoulos, Akis, 37–38
Tsiakiris, Apostolos, 130–31
Tsipras, Alexis, 19–20, 58, 64, 87, 100, 116
Tsochatzopoulos, Apostolos ("Akis"), 69–76,
   78–84, 176
Tsoutsoura, Margarita, 62
Turkey
   animosity and ongoing rivalry, 169
   efforts to improve relations, 174–75
   Greek invasion of Anatolia, 169–70
   Imia territorial dispute, 69–72
   military expenditures, 5, 72–73
   population exchange with Greece,
     169–70, 204–5
   U.S. aid and Cold War policy, 245
Tychero (town), 189–92, 199

U

Ukrainian Revolution of 2014, 100
Ulbricht, Walter, 99–100
unemployment, 15, 18, 67, 94, 144, 149,
   179–80
United Democratic Left, 99
United Journalistic Organization for
   Supplementary Insurance Care
   (EDOEAP), 141
United Nations, 179
United Nations High Commissioner for
   Refugees (UNHCR), 196–97, 221
U.S. Central Intelligence Agency (CIA),
   94, 112
U.S. Marshall Plan, 111
U.S. State Department, 220

V

Vartzelis, Nikolaos, 43–46
Varvitsiotis, Miltiadis, 222–23
Vathis, Georgios, 238
Vaxevanis, Kostas, 65–66
Venizelos, Evangelos, 75
*The Voice of the Residents of Agios
   Panteleimonas* (newspaper), 247–48
Vozaitis, Panagiotis, 49–50

W

War of Independence, 1–5
weapons/defense spending, 72–84
welfare. *See* disability benefits
West Germany. *See* Germany (Federal
   Republic of Germany)
White Terror, 244–45
White Tower of Thessaloniki (*Lefkos
   Pyrgos*), 159, 178
World Jewish Congress, 113
World War I, 111, 169
World War II
   German invasion of Crete, 96
   German reparations, 111
   German reunification, 115
   Glezos as symbol of resistance, 95–99,
     106–10
   Greek deaths, 103
   Greek resistance movement, 103–5
   Italian invasion of Greece, 101–2
   Ligkiades massacre, 105–6
   Nazi arrival in Athens, 95
   Nazi atrocities, 98
   Nazi collaborators, 244–45